Dance Theatre in Ireland

Dance Theatre in Ireland

Revolutionary Moves

Aoife McGrath

© Aoife McGrath 2013

First published 2013 by
PALGRAVE MACMILLAN

Palgrave Macmillan in the UK is an imprint of Macmillan Publishers Limited, registered in England, company number 785998, of Houndmills, Basingstoke, Hampshire RG21 6XS.

Palgrave Macmillan in the US is a division of St Martin's Press LLC, 175 Fifth Avenue, New York, NY 10010.

Palgrave Macmillan is the global academic imprint of the above companies and has companies and representatives throughout the world.

Palgrave® and Macmillan® are registered trademarks in the United States, the United Kingdom, Europe and other countries.

ISBN 978–1–137–03547–9

This book is printed on paper suitable for recycling and made from fully managed and sustained forest sources. Logging, pulping and manufacturing processes are expected to conform to the environmental regulations of the country of origin.

A catalogue record for this book is available from the British Library.

A catalog record for this book is available from the Library of Congress.

10   9   8   7   6   5   4   3   2   1
22   21   20   19   18   17   16   15   14   13

Printed and bound in Great Britain by
CPI Antony Rowe, Chippenham and Eastbourne

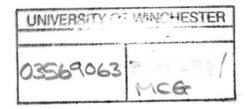

Contents

List of Figures

Acknowledgements

It is with great pleasure that I thank the many people who supported the writing of this book. The project started as a PhD thesis written while I was a postgraduate student at Trinity College Dublin (TCD) and I am indebted to my supervisor, Brian Singleton, who encouraged me to undertake this research and was a constant and generous source of advice, support, insight and inspiration throughout the entire process. It has truly been an honour to work with him. I want to thank my former teachers at the TCD School of Drama, especially Matthew Causey, Melissa Sihra, Eric Weitz, Steve Wilmer, and Aoife Monks (now at Birkbeck, University of London) who have each given me wonderful feedback at different stages of this project. I am also indebted to Ann Mulligan and Rhona Greene at the School of Drama for their support through all the highs and lows of my undergraduate, postgraduate and adjunct lecturer career at TCD. Thanks also to my students at TCD who helped shape my ideas about dance theatre in our workshops and seminars. Susan Leigh Foster and Gabriele Brandstetter co-supervised my research project on *Tanztheater* during a DAAD scholarship year at the Freie Universität Berlin and I am very grateful to have had their generous guidance and encouragement in the early stages of my studies. I also wish to thank the members of the International Federation of Theatre Research (IFTR) Choreography and Corporealities working group who provided valuable feedback on early versions of three chapters.

I am profoundly grateful to the dance theatre practitioners whose work inspired this book. Many of the practitioners that I write about have been extremely generous with their time, providing me with interviews and access to their personal archives. I would particularly like to thank Michael Keegan-Dolan and Marina Harten at Fabulous Beast Dance Theatre, David Bolger and Jenny Traynor at CoisCéim Dance Theatre, Colin Dunne, Sarah-Jane Scaife and Joan Davis. I would like to thank Paul Johnson at Dance Ireland for directing me to archive material at DanceHouse and thanks also to the staff at the Department of Manuscripts at the National Library of Ireland. I would like to thank my publisher Palgrave Macmillan for supporting this book and I would particularly like to thank Paula Kennedy, Benjamin Doyle and Frances Tye for their assistance during the editing and production process.

Thanks to all my friends and colleagues at TCD who listened to my woes and shared my small victories over far too many plates of chips in the Buttery, especially Emma Meehan, Marcus Tan and Nora Butler. Thanks to my colleagues at Queen's University Belfast for their support during the final leg of the process. Finally, and most importantly, thanks to Benjamin, Toby, Eimir, Sorca and Daragh for their unending patience, love and support.

Research for this project was supported in part by a Trinity College Dublin foundation scholarship and a Government of Ireland scholarship from the Irish Research Council for the Humanities and Social Sciences. All efforts have been made to secure rights for material used in this book. I gratefully thank photographers Kip Carroll, Pat Redmond, Ros Kavanagh, Johan Persson and T Charles Erickson for their kind permission to use their photographs. Earlier versions of sections of this book have appeared in the following publications: an early version of Chapter 5 was published as 'Choreographing the Unanticipated: Death, Hope and Verticality in Fabulous Beast Dance Theatre's *Giselle* and *The Rite of Spring*', in *Contemporary Theatre Review*, 21: 2 (2011), pp. 154–70. Earlier versions of portions of Chapter 6 were published as 'The Less You Bump the Faster You Go?: Staged Scenes of Dissensus in CoisCéim's *Dodgems*', in Rhona Trench (ed.), *Staging Thought: Essays on Irish Theatre Scholarship and Practice*, (Bern: Peter Lang, 2012), pp. 255–68. A section of Chapter 7 expands and rewrites a review essay commissioned by Dance Ireland, published as 'Home-grown Dance at The Fringe', *Dance Ireland News*, (Dublin: Dance Ireland, October Issue, 2010). If any material used here is not credited appropriately, please contact me through my publishers.

1
Introduction

Over the past two decades, dance theatre has become a vital site of innovation and transformation in the Irish performance landscape. In addition to being instrumental in a movement of aesthetic change in performance practices, dance theatre works have also played a pivotal role in reflecting and critiquing socio-political and cultural developments in Ireland. In 2003, Brian Singleton proposed that, 'the most exciting new playwrights in this country are choreographers who have come from dance theatre: David Bolger and Michael Keegan-Dolan. They are speaking about Ireland and writing about Ireland, using all the languages of the actor's body, rather than speaking from an authorial perspective'.[1] The pivotal shift of perspective from the 'authorial' to the corporeal recognised in the work of these choreographers is particularly remarkable given the overwhelmingly literary tradition of Irish theatre practice. It is a well-rehearsed lament that theatrical performance in Ireland habitually gave primacy to the written word over the performing body,[2] leading director Conall Morrison to describe the body in space and time as 'the great unexplored'.[3] This focus on the authority of the word routinely confined the body to a function of interpretation rather than creative articulation, and has contributed to the marginalisation of theatrical dance in Ireland. Resisting this positioning of dance has been an ongoing struggle for chronically underfunded and culturally undervalued choreographers and dancers in Ireland, and the battle for recognition of the cultural importance of theatre dance has a long history. Yet the flourishing of dance theatre over the past two decades, particularly since the emergence of companies such as Bolger's CoisCéim Dance Theatre and Keegan-Dolan's Fabulous Beast Dance Theatre in the mid-1990s, has marked an important turning point, in which groundbreaking works have achieved not only a greater visibility for dance, but have also provoked a rethinking of the perception of the body in Irish theatrical performance and Irish culture. Operating from the margins and materialising in a disciplinary interval, these companies do not adhere to any genre divides. Experimenting with the intertwining of the corporeal and the textual, they challenge the usual delineations and dichotomisation of genre in Ireland. Their interdisciplinary works inhabit the space between dance and theatre to tell stories through hybrid mixes of various dance and movement vocabularies in combination with text, music and other performance media. These stories explicitly comment on socio-political issues, altering perceptions of the communicative capabilities and socio-political agency of dancing bodies in a traditionally word-focussed theatre culture. Refusing to confine dance to a realm of the aesthetic divorced from the political, their choreographies critique Irish society, highlighting and questioning the invisibility of certain corporealities and challenging the hegemony of others.

The emergence of these new dance theatre practitioners coincided with Ireland's 'Celtic Tiger era'; a period (which I will discuss in further detail later) that resulted in profound economic, cultural and political change. In this study I am particularly interested in examining how certain dance theatre works tackle some of the most urgent and difficult socio-political and cultural questions that arose during this era, and in its immediate wake. It is important to note that this study does not conduct an essentialist interrogation into what is specifically 'Irish' about these works, but rather it will analyse how these boundary-defying dance theatre choreographies comment on and intersect with cultural and political issues in Ireland. As such, this study aims not only to examine a particular facet of Irish dance culture and to contribute to wider international discussions of dance theatre, but also to offer a study of Irish culture from a fresh perspective, through the lens of choreographies of the dancing body.

Susan Foster writes that '[d]ance is uniquely adept at configuring relations between body, self, and society through its choreographic decisions' and that in viewing choreography as a theorisation of bodies, 'choreographic conventions can be seen as particular stagings of the body's participation in the larger performance of the body politic'.[4] How bodies are organised in time and space in a performance can then be read in relation to how bodies are organised in society, producing a correlation between the dancing body and the body politic. In the dance theatre works discussed here, disruptions and reconfigurations of the usual positioning of bodies in societal structures allows for alternative views of society to achieve visibility. Following this notion of choreography as theory and extending its application to the social choreography of bodies in everyday life, I will interrogate the cultural context out of which these choreographies emerged and the resonance they have with specific events and specific bodies in Ireland.

This study does not attempt a comprehensive overview of all contemporary dance theatre practice in Ireland. Instead it provides detailed analyses of a selection of seven contemporary works: *Giselle* (2003), *The Bull* (2005) and *The Rite of Spring* (2009) by Fabulous Beast Dance Theatre; *Ballads* (1997) and *Dodgems* (2008) by CoisCéim Dance Theatre; *Does She Take Sugar?* (2007) by Jean Butler; and *Out of Time* (2008) by Colin Dunne. This selection should not imply that the works discussed are the only representatives of dance theatre in Ireland that merit critical attention; indeed there exists an ever increasing community of both established and emerging dance theatre choreographers working in Ireland whose practice provides an exciting body of work for future discussion.[5] However, for this project I have chosen to structure my investigation around specific socio-political and aesthetic issues. The organising principle in choosing which contemporary works to discuss is based on two defining characteristics: firstly, that the work resists disciplinary and genre limitations in an Irish context, expanding notions of what constitutes dance and theatre performance, and secondly, that it engages in explicit social commentary and critique, with choreographies of the dancing body that highlight the moulding of subjectivities and suggest alternative corporealities. Many of the works that are analysed use a combination of dance, spoken text and music intertwined in a narrative to create pieces that reinterpret stories of Ireland's past and present, and envision possible futures. Others, such as *Out of Time* by Dunne and *Does She Take Sugar?* by Butler, use similar modes of performance to communicate more personal narratives, which are nevertheless critically engaged with political and aesthetic issues of corporeality in Ireland. The remainder of this introductory chapter provides an outline of the cultural context out of which the contemporary dance theatre practitioners emerged, an introduction to CoisCéim and Fabulous Beast, a positioning of this project within dance scholarship in Ireland, and an explanation of the study's methodological underpinning.

Cultural context: the Celtic Tiger, *Riverdance* and other transformations

The following sketch of notable events in the last decade of the twentieth century and first decade of the twenty-first in Ireland positions and contextualises the dance theatre work discussed within the social, cultural, and economic backdrop of the 'Celtic Tiger-era' (*c*. 1990–2008). After decades of financial struggle resulting in high unemployment and emigration, Ireland's economy entered a period of unprecedented growth in the early 1990s. Unemployment figures shrank and Ireland became a popular destination for economic migrants for the first time in its history. The US investment group Morgan Stanley named the Irish economy the 'Celtic Tiger' in 1994, and the title is now used to describe a phase of economic growth in Ireland which began in the early 1990s, peaked in 1999, slowed in tandem with the global economic downturn in 2001, and after a brief resurgence on the back of the housing market, continued to decline until its pronounced 'death' in 2008 with the onset of global recession. The 1990s was also a decade of significant cultural and political change, and it began with a 'surprising shock to the body politic' with the election in 1990 of Ireland's first female president, Mary Robinson.[6] Robinson's election was a disruption to several longstanding traditions that had been upheld since the election of the first president, Douglas Hyde, in 1937. Sponsored by the Labour Party and supported by a 'new constituency' made up of socially active groups not aligned to any political parties, Robinson challenged the historical dominance of Fianna Fáil[7] candidates. Additionally, in the application of her determined feminism and skills developed while working as a constitutional lawyer, she began to transform the perception of the role of president from being purely ceremonial and symbolic, to being an active and inspirational force for social change. Prior to her election, she was integral in contesting several laws that had sought for many decades to control and suppress the actions of certain bodies in Irish society. Her activities included successful campaigns in challenging the ban on the importation and sale of contraception (1979, 1992)[8] and in securing the decriminalisation of homosexuality (1980, 1988, 1993).[9] The optimism resulting from Robinson's election to presidency coincided with another notable, although much less lofty, cultural event. In 1990 Ireland's international soccer team qualified for the World Cup for the first time and despite all odds (never actually winning a match outright), made it to the quarter-finals. As all eyes focussed on the success of the Irish team's campaign in Italy, Diarmaid Ferriter reported that Dublin streets 'came close to the atmosphere of Rio in carnival time'.[10] Interestingly, in contrast to the (relatively) unrestrained joy performed in the streets, the choreographic tactics of manager Jack Charlton that permitted these positive outpourings were criticised as resulting from 'negative' football; the Irish team played defensively, preventing their opponents from playing their 'own' (meaning more skilful) game. The defensive 'negative' choreography of Irish soccer at this time could be read as perpetuating a nationalistic tendency of defensively opposing dominant cultures. Yet at the same time, the wholehearted national embrace of a sport shunned by the GAA[11] for its Englishness, the employment of an English manager for the national squad, and the fact that the majority of the players on the team were born in England or Scotland was also, albeit paradoxically, an important step towards post-nationalism.

Another important cultural shift and significant change in the Irish social fabric was the undermining of the moral authority of the Catholic church in the wake of a series of clerical child abuse and sex controversies. From its inception, the ideology of the Irish state was closely intertwined with the teachings of the Catholic church and it was largely the church's influence in state matters that had sustained the rigid and repressive control of sexuality in Ireland to a 'strictly enforced sexual code'.[12] Although the power of the church was already on the wane in the early 1990s, the spate of scandals relating to abusive and paedophile priests that began to emerge after 1994, when Father Brendan Smyth was found guilty in Belfast of 17 charges of child sexual abuse, and later pleaded guilty to a further 74 counts in the Dublin courts in 1997, came as a shock to the nation. Arguably the most disturbing aspect of Smyth's case, and several of the cases that followed, was that many instances of child abuse might have been prevented if senior clergy had not tried to cover up the actions of perpetrators by silently moving them from one parish to the next. This deception caused the reputation of the church to suffer severe damage. Following these revelations, Terence Brown writes that, 'the moral policing in sexual matters the church had enforced in the early decades of independence had almost completely broken down', and Mary Kenny goes further, proposing that, 'the very concept of "Catholic Ireland" was by the end of the century, gone'.[13] These seismic pressures on the previously unshakeable Catholic-nationalist social order fuelled the growing movement towards secularisation. Joe Cleary argues, however, that a more significant consequence was 'a wholesale reconstruction of Irish middle-class subjectivity, now decreasingly defined in terms of participatory citizenship or of adherence to communal Church practices, and articulated [...] in terms of individual capacity to participate in various modes of consumer lifestyle'.[14] On the one hand oppressed communities and corporealities benefited from socially transformative legal actions and the relaxation of the church's stranglehold on sexuality, while simultaneously, consumer capitalism, with its disregard for those in society who cannot keep pace, started to come into its own.

In 1994, the same year as the arrival of the 'tiger', a new-found fiscal confidence and national pride seemed to be perfectly embodied in a seven-minute showcase of Irish culture broadcast to millions of television viewers around Europe. *Riverdance* was initially choreographed as the interval entertainment of the 1994 Eurovision song contest held in Dublin, which Ireland won for the third time in a row that year, and an unprecedented sixth time overall (Ireland would go on to win the competition for a seventh time in 1996).[15] The piece is credited with having modernised the competitive Irish step dance form (adding arm gestures to the normally stiffly-held, straight-backed, arms-by-the-sides upper body posture) and famously added a sexually charged dimension to a dance form that Flann O'Brien once described as 'emotionally cold, unromantic and always well-lighted'[16] (this was particularly evident in a duet for champion dancers Jean Butler and Michael Flatley in which Butler performed a stepped circle around Flatley with her arm trailing around his waist, while they gazed into each other's eyes). However, the most memorable moment of the piece was the exhilarating finale in which one long line of 25 perfectly synchronised Irish step dancers closed the performance in a thunderous chorus line. Following the hugely positive response to this original incarnation, producer Moya Doherty, director John McColgan and composer Bill Whelan put together a full-length commercial show, and since its premiere in Dublin's Point Theatre in 1995, *Riverdance* is estimated to have been seen live by 21 million people worldwide and to have grossed well over US$1 billion.[17] The phenomenon of *Riverdance* has been the cause of much debate, with some praising its perceived 'revitalisation' of Irish step dancing and creation of employment for Irish dancers, and others, such as Liam Fay, connecting it to an 'ongoing campaign to sell Ireland abroad and to ourselves as a bucolic idyll peopled with happy-clappy bodhrán rapping riverdancing rustics'.[18] In an examination of the attraction of the show for the Irish diaspora in the United States, Natasha Casey highlights the tensions in *Riverdance* between its ability to appeal to a consumer hungry for a connection with the past (albeit a mythic past) through an experience of what is perceived to be an authentic folk tradition, and the show's simultaneous desire to represent modern Irish culture. Referencing a *New York Times* article that appeared in 1996 under the headline, 'Ireland Without Clichés', Casey argues that *Riverdance* was promoted as embodying, 'a new respectable Irishness, neoteric and traditional, spiritual rather than religious, sanitized – devoid of both political signifiers and [...] stage leprechauns'.[19] Casey provides an insightful analysis of how the sanitised and commercialised Irishness at work in *Riverdance* is consumed, however I would further argue that a choreo-political[20] reading of certain elements of the show troubles an understanding of the piece as depoliticised. Producer Moya Doherty states that her intention in *Riverdance* was to show an Ireland that is, 'modern and in step'.[21] The step-dancing bodies in the piece are perhaps no longer overtly performing a dance of exclusionary nationalism, but their demonstration of synchronisation advertises their ability to be economically 'in step' with the global market. The chorus line scenes in the show can be read as spectacular displays of corporeal conformity and the subjugation of the body to an external force. In order to aid the illusion of perfect synchronisation, the steps in these chorus lines have been simplified and the tapping sounds of the dancers in the live performance are supplemented by a pre-recorded soundtrack, which is intended to help cover up any irregularities caused by dancers mis-stepping.[22] Reminiscent of the precision dances of the Tiller Girls,[23] a brand of chorus-line dance troupe that came to international prominence in the 1920s, the chorus line of dancers in *Riverdance* can be viewed as an example of a living commodity that is trapped in a site that allows for no indeterminacy, obediently embodying both the technology and ideological machinery of its creation and the product itself. In Siegfried Kracauer's essay on the Berlin Tiller Girls in *The Mass Ornament*, he compares the precise regulation of the dancing bodies in the chorus line to the bodies of workers on an assembly line dictated by the efficiency principles of Taylorism. For Kracauer, the machine-like movements of the Tiller Girls function as a 'surface manifestation' and 'sign' of the capitalist economic and social systems in which they exist.[24] Similarly, I would argue that the chorus line in *Riverdance*, using the technique of competitive step dance, can be read as an example of an aestheticisation and advertisement of a late capitalist Irish labour force that is young, dynamic, mobile and always striving to move upwards and forwards 'in step'. Perhaps then, following Kracauer's mode of analysis, it is not merely a coincidence that the current 'farewell tours' of the *Riverdance* troupes are synchronous with the recent global economic recession and the collapse of the Celtic Tiger economy that provided the underlying system for their origin. As Aoife Monks observes, the promotional material for *Riverdance* is overwhelmingly oriented towards discussion of its economic success rather than its aesthetic value and she proposes that the 'stories of quantities, percentages and money [that] circulate around the show [...] offer a site for aspiration and desire in Irish culture'.[25] This precedent set by *Riverdance* can also be found in the promotional material of subsequent Irish dance spectaculars, with the *Gaelforce* (1998) show, for example, advertising itself as 'the Ferrari of Irish dance'.[26] However, the prize for the most excessive bombast must go to Michael Flatley's description of his 2005 *Celtic Tiger* extravaganza, for which he announced, 'I've got the biggest TV screen in the world – 72 tons, [...] the best dance troupe on earth, a lighting show that rivals Pink Floyd, $3 million worth of costumes, the best sound effects and a musical score [...] that's like an Irish rock concert'.[27] Discussion of Flatley himself, who is also a world champion step dancer and the original male soloist of *Riverdance*, is similarly surrounded with numerical superlatives: he is the highest paid dancer in the world, earning US$50 million per annum and his legs are insured for US$40 million.[28] In this spectacularised format of Irish step dance, the most visible site of competition has arguably been relocated from the performance of dancing figures, to the performance of numerical figures.

Far away from the international commercial whirlwind of *Riverdance*, the beginning of the 1990s did not initially look at all optimistic for theatrical dance. In Ireland, the Arts Council (a government agency that funds and develops the arts) provides the vast majority of financial support for non-commercial theatre dance. Any discussion of the development of dance therefore necessitates a consideration of Arts Council policy. By 1989, following the recommendations of a report commissioned by the Arts Council and published in 1985 (Peter Brinson's *The Dancer and the Dance: Developing Theatre Dance in Ireland*), funding to three professional dance companies, including the Irish National Ballet and the Dublin Contemporary Dance Theatre (DCDT), the two leading representatives of their respective disciplines at the time, had been cut.[29] The 1980 Arts Council Report for expenditure in the arts in 1979 records that dance received a mere 14.3 per cent of the funding awarded to drama.[30] In 1989 the total funding for dance plummeted from £417,114 in 1988 to a paltry £214,000 (representing 2.9 per cent of the total annual budget) and the percentage in relation to the funding for drama (£3,013,000 – 40.8 per cent of the total budget) had dropped to 7.1 per cent.[31] Although some recent publications about the Arts Council decisions in 1989 suggest a *tabula rasa* situation of all dance funding being cut, in fact this was not the case.[32] The stranglehold placed on the Arts Council by their attempts to sufficiently support the expensive Irish National Ballet had resulted in almost all available dance funds being swallowed by the company to the detriment of the development of other dance forms. The cut of funding to DCDT, which had been favourably mentioned in the Brinson Report, was a severe blow to dance theatre at the time. However, the early years of the 1990s saw the founding of a profusion of new companies and the shift of emphasis in funding from a struggle to support a touring ballet company, to the nurturing of performance and choreographic talent in many smaller organisations and individuals. This effectively ended the dominance of ballet and the hierarchical funding structure that had existed, and promoted a more democratic model. In 1989, the same year as the Brinson cuts and the beginning of the Yeats Festival at the Abbey Theatre (1989–93), the New Music/New Dance Festival was founded. This festival functioned as an important platform for the emergence of several of the most successful dance companies operating today. In 1989 Robert Connor and Loretta Yurick, formerly of DCDT, regrouped to found their own company, Dance Theatre of Ireland (DTI). In 1991, two further former DCDT collaborators also founded companies: Paul Johnson founded MaNDaNCE and John Scott founded Irish Modern Dance Theatre (IMDT). David Bolger, who had been presenting work at the New Music/New Dance Festival, decided to found his own company, CoisCéim Dance Theatre, in 1995. In the same year, the annual Arts Council report offered a 'recognition of the fact that dance as an art form has suffered severe neglect in Ireland', and also noted the long-awaited first appointment of a dedicated dance officer, Gaye Tanham, albeit part-time.[33] After working as a freelance choreographer for dance, opera and theatre companies, Michael Keegan-Dolan founded the Fabulous Beast Dance Theatre in 1997. Up to this point there had been a major increase in funding for dance, and the proliferation of dance companies during this period is evidence that attitudes towards dance were slowly changing.

In a social context, marginalised corporealities were beginning to be liberalised in the 1990s. However, in tandem with these positive developments, the sudden increase in wealth of a nation that had been economically weak for most of its existence caused a questioning of social and moral values, and the demographic shift towards a multicultural, global society heightened the crucial importance of intercultural communication skills and the potential dangers of racism. The contemporary dance theatre works interrogated in this study are all explicitly commenting on both the positive and negative fallout from these rapid cultural shifts in Ireland. Evidence of a change in cultural consciousness can also be found in the work of playwrights from the period, and a retrospective look at the concurrent dance and theatre practice that was emerging in the 1990s reveals a fascinating parallel. At the same time that the dancing body was becoming increasingly visible in Ireland, and marginalised corporealities were beginning to achieve political agency, a collection of playwrights experimenting with the monologic form also came to prominence. Arguably traceable back to Brian Friel's *Faith Healer* (1979),[34] a monologue movement began to achieve critical force in the 1990s through the work of dramatists such as Conor McPherson, Eugene O'Brien and Enda Walsh. At first glance the works of the dance theatre companies and the monologue dramatists would seem to have nothing whatsoever in common with each other; on the one hand dance theatre practitioners created vibrant choreographies of dancing, singing, speaking bodies, brimful of movement, dialogue and dispute, and on the other hand, the monologue dramatists produced plays for still, lone bodies (or two/three bodies that did not interact) in dialogue with themselves, on typically empty stages. The dance theatre works challenged the dominance of the word with articulate, moving bodies, while, at times, the monologue playwrights seemed to want to enshrine a disembodied word. In his article, 'Am I Talking to Myself?', Brian Singleton suggests that the emergence of the monologue plays, 'points to an attempt to turn theatre into a purely literary medium', and that 'a trend of uncommunicability, isolation, and the unaware self emerges'.[35] Following Singleton's assessment and adding a view from a choreographic perspective, these seemingly divergent developments in drama and dance theatre could be seen to be operating at opposite poles of a corporeal continuum. The dislocated monologic corporeality presents precisely the entrapment and stasis of a theatre dominated by the disembodied playwright's word – it follows the literary hegemony through to its mono-logical conclusion. It could then be viewed, curiously, as a faithful representation of the corporeality created and maintained by the status quo in Ireland: a mind separated from its troublesome body. Raymond Williams, writing of the emergence of the soliloquy in English Renaissance drama, believes that a formalist analysis of the soliloquy as 'device' can concomitantly shed light on its sociological background. Applying this idea, the simultaneous emergence of waves of both the monologic and dance theatre forms could be understood, to quote Williams, as 'an articulation, by technical discovery, of changes in consciousness which are themselves forms of consciousness of change'.[36] Ironically then, in these two divergent technical approaches to reflecting the changing times, just as the literary dominance in Ireland was arguably reaching its performative apogee, it was simultaneously being shattered by the work of the dance theatre choreographers. Conor McPherson has since moved away from the monologic in his work, and in a review of his period writing in the form, he wonders if, in light of the 'momentous changes' of the Celtic Tiger years, '[i]t may be argued that Irish plays became intensely personal in a radical attempt to preserve and explore our sense of identity during such an unprecedented transformation of our society'.[37] The contemporary dance theatre examined in this study addresses the same cultural transformations, yet instead of retreating into solipsism, and a wish for stable identity in the comfort zone of the literary norm, it rattles the patriarchal 'iron cage' and shatters the hegemony of the word with a celebration of heterogeneous corporealities.

The visibility of theatre dance in the cultural landscape of Ireland improved significantly in the first decade of the twenty-first century. In 2003, dance was finally included as a named art form in the government's Arts Act.[38] Dance audiences markedly increased in numbers and the establishment of the hugely popular International Dance Festival in 2002 (re-named the Dublin Dance Festival in 2008) gave Irish theatre dance an international platform. DanceHouse, a dedicated state-of-the-art facility for dance in Dublin, opened its doors in January 2007, marking a further important milestone for dance development in Ireland. This facility provides a much-needed focal point for performers, choreographers and dance teachers working in Ireland and, crucially, it also makes available that rare commodity: suitable studio space for dance rehearsal purposes.[39] DanceHouse also houses a small library and in November 2011, a national dance archive was opened at the Glucksmann Library of the University of Limerick. These developments mark an increasing awareness in Ireland of the cultural importance of dance. Additionally, Irish theatre dance is establishing an international presence, and the works of Bolger, Keegan-Dolan, Butler and Dunne (and many other choreographers) have toured widely to critical acclaim, contributing to a new perception of Irish dance abroad. Importantly, because the work of the choreographers discussed in this study is located between the disciplines of dance and theatre, it is also attracting audiences who would not traditionally go to see dance; this phenomenon extends the influence of dance on the Irish performance landscape, and addresses the limiting dichotomisation of genres.

Introducing CoisCéim

CoisCéim (which means 'footstep' in Irish) was founded in 1995 by Dublin-based dancer and choreographer David Bolger (b.1968). In 1993 the New Music/New Dance Festival (1989–94) at the Project Arts Centre in Dublin had provided the platform for Bolger's first choreography, *Silent Scream* – a piece about the life of Charlie Chaplin. After successfully persuading the Old Museum Arts Centre in Belfast to programme his work in 1995, Bolger realised he would need to found a company to present it. CoisCéim Dance Theatre duly came into existence and premiered its first production, *Dances With Intent*, as part of the 1995 Belfast Dancetime Festival. Billed as 'an action packed cocktail of humour, compassion and acrobatics which displays the diversity of CoisCéim',[40] this work brought together three pieces choreographed by Bolger – *Taps with Sax, Hon Nin Myo*, and *Temporary Arrangements* – and went on to tour the 1995 Galway Arts Festival (at An Taibhdhearc) and the 1995 Dublin Theatre Festival (at the Samuel Beckett Theatre). These short pieces highlighted Bolger's talent for humorous social observation, and *Irish Times* dance critic Carolyn Swift praised the work's 'wit' and 'laughter inducing' effect.[41]

The qualities of wit and humour became a trademark for subsequent CoisCéim productions, as did Bolger's love of mixing different movement styles, using elements from acrobatic physical theatre and tap or jazz, in addition to more strictly modern or balletic techniques. Although subsequent works began to address socio-political themes – for example *Reel Luck* (1995) charted the transformation of Ireland, '[f]rom the land of De Valera's vision and moving statues to Eurovision and peace in the North'[42] – social commentary was presented in a predominantly lighthearted manner. A shift occurred in Bolger's practice when he began working on *Ballads* (1997), a piece about the nineteenth-century Great Irish Famine. He felt that the 'slapstick element of humour', that had become a cornerstone of his practice was inappropriate for 'a story of such huge catastrophe and loss', and after two years researching the piece, he explains, 'I started to feel that I didn't want to do the slapstick stuff anymore, that there was something else driving me'.[43] Humour has remained an essential element of Bolger's practice, yet over the years it has been increasingly employed in the service of storytelling works that incorporate social commentary. When asked if he considered himself a 'choreographer with a social conscience', Bolger replied, 'I think every choreographer must have a point of view, or an opinion'.[44] Whatever the format, style or subject matter, a common thread running through all CoisCéim productions is Bolger's interest in telling 'human stories', and the company's manifesto expresses a desire to, 'demonstrate and articulate stories and emotions that are relevant to the landscapes in which we live'.[45]

To date, CoisCéim have premiered 23 original works, and productions have embraced a variety of formats, including works for proscenium arch venues, site-specific pieces (for example *Chamber Made* (2004), which toured to hotel rooms, and *Swept* (2003), which re-imagined the foyer space of the Peacock Theatre in Dublin), dance for camera (for example the multi-award-winning *Hit and Run* (2002),[46] a dark, gangland encounter set in a derelict industrial building, or *Swimming with my Mother* (2010), in which Bolger and his mother, Madge Bolger, swim a tender duet in their local swimming pool), and large-scale events such as the opening ceremony of the Special Olympics in Dublin for 75,000 participants (2003).[47] Subject matter has ranged from contemporary reworkings of well-known ballets such as *The Rite of Spring* (2002), *Nutcracker* (2005), and *Faun* (2010) (a homage to Nijinsky's *L'Après-midi d'un faune*), to works inspired by music genres (such as *Toupées and Snare Drums* (1998),[48] a work set in a 1966 dancehall in the show-band era, and *Back In Town* (1997), inspired by the music of Dublin rock band, Thin Lizzy), to more explicit pieces of socio-political commentary such as *Dodgems* (2008), which was set on a full-size bumper car track and dealt with issues surrounding citizenship and immigration.[49] Bolger has also played an important role in the physicalisation of Irish theatre, having choreographed works such as *Tarry Flynn* (1997), Conall Morrison's physical adaptation of Patrick Kavanagh's novel at the Abbey Theatre in Dublin, and the acclaimed *Synge Cycle* (2005), directed by Garry Hynes for the Druid Theatre Company.[50] Bolger also choreographed the famous dance scene for the film version of Brian Friel's *Dancing at Lughnasa* (1998), starring Meryl Streep and directed by Pat O'Connor.

The Irish Arts Council have supported CoisCéim from 1995 to the present, and the company is one of six so-called 'regularly funded' dance organisations in Ireland.[51] CoisCéim have toured their work to a number of international festivals[52] and have also been awarded several prizes, including the *Irish Times* 'choreographer of the year' and 'dance show of the year' awards (1996, 1997), the 'sexiest show' and 'best production' awards at the Dublin Fringe Festival (for *Chamber Made* (2005) and *Knots* (2006) respectively), and two Fringe First awards at the Edinburgh Fringe Festival (also for *Chamber Made* and *Knots*). In 2007, Bolger and choreographer Cindy Cummings became the first two dance practitioners to be elected to *Aosdána*, a peer-nominated group of artists who are considered to have made an outstanding contribution to the arts in Ireland.[53]

Introducing Fabulous Beast

Dancer and choreographer Michael Keegan-Dolan (b.1969) founded Fabulous Beast Dance Theatre in 1997. Keegan-Dolan started to choreograph during his time as a student at the Central School of Ballet in London (early works for Ballet Central, the school's graduate company, include *Kiss Kiss*, and *What Fools These Mortals Be*), and after graduating he founded his first company, Cartoon Dance Theatre. Following a showing of his choreography as part of an evening of short works at The Place in London he was offered a place on the Gulbenkian international course for choreographers and composers, where he was mentored by Robert Cohan, former artistic director of London Contemporary Dance Theatre. During this time he got a job dancing in a production of the musical, *Carousel*, choreographed by Kenneth MacMillan and directed by Nick Hytner for the National Theatre in 1992.[54] When MacMillan unexpectedly died during rehearsals, a shocked Keegan-Dolan was asked (with fellow dancer Simon Rice)[55] to finish choreographing the final number of the show. In recognition of his choreographic talent, his former Central Ballet School teacher, Christopher Gable, then offered him a job as assistant choreographer at Northern Ballet Theatre; however, feeling that he was not ready for such a position, Keegan-Dolan turned him down. Instead he worked as a dancer for physical theatre company The Kosh, Second Stride Dance Company, and Pilobolus Dance Theatre and in 1996 he choreographed his first opera: *Ariodante* at the English National Opera.[56] Peter Hall then hired him as movement director for his production of the *Oedipus* plays at the theatre of Epidaurus in Greece, but this was a difficult experience for Keegan-Dolan and he was considering a career change when he received a phone call from Mary Brady at the Institute of Choreography and Dance in Cork asking him to choreograph a piece at Cork's Firkin Crane centre.[57] This commission led to Keegan-Dolan's founding of Fabulous Beast Dance Theatre and the creation of the company's first work, *Sunday Lunch*, which premiered at the Firkin Crane and was revised for the Dublin Fringe Festival in 1998. Setting the satirical and often violent tone of future productions, and demonstrating Keegan-Dolan's skill for choreographing acutely observed social interaction, this work was an exploration of, 'the dysfunctional Irish family, preparing for (and surviving) a Sunday lunch'.[58] His next work, *Good People* (1998), included scenes of childbirth and defecation, and involved, 'the contents of a latrine bucket' being thrown at the audience, and 'the transformation of a moonscape into a swimming pool'.[59] Fabulous Beast was then awarded its first Arts Council funding to create *Fragile* (1999), which premiered at the Tallaght Civic Theatre as part of the Dublin Fringe Festival. Inspired by a quote from the painting, *Human Frailty*, by Renaissance artist Salvator Rosa – 'Conception is sinful; Birth a Punishment; Life, Hard Labour; Death Inevitable' – the work was billed as a 'head-on collision between Jean-Paul Sartre and Hieronymous Bosch',[60] and experimented with a use of powerful visual images that was to become a signature feature of later works; some of the most memorable such images from *Fragile* included a large, blue, Guinness-drinking 'Buddha', dancing corpses in bathtubs of flour, and struggling bodies in a giant water tank. This piece, and the later work, *The Christmas Show* (2001), used narrative in quite an abstract fashion.[61] However, in *The Flowerbed* (2000), Keegan-Dolan created his first reworking of a well-known story, *Romeo and Juliet*, transposing the Capulet/Montague rivalry onto a pair of clashing suburban families warring over a strip of grass between their houses.

The reworking of narrative was continued in *Giselle* (2003), the first work in Keegan-Dolan's *Midlands Trilogy*, and the piece that established him as a choreographer of international renown.[62] Transferring the original setting of the romantic ballet to the fictional midlands village of Ballyfeeney, an asthmatic and down-trodden Giselle falls in love with a bisexual line dance teacher from Bratislava, and in the famous final image of the piece, she defies the traditional ending of the story to jump joyfully on a trampoline. *Giselle* marked several significant shifts in Keegan-Dolan's working methods. Importantly, it was the first work in which he based his movement approach on his yoga practice. Keegan-Dolan never felt at home in any of the dance disciplines that he trained or performed in ('I really don't feel I'm part of any tradition')[63] and his search for a form that he could be comfortable with led him to yoga teacher, John Evans, who introduced him to shadow yoga and Batto-do, a modern form of traditional Japanese swordsmanship. In turning to this practice, Keegan-Dolan was reacting against his feeling that in contemporary culture, 'dancers are perceived as less than prostitutes is some ways – as silly people who jump around and have no voices'; the practice of Batto-do, in which movements are accompanied by powerful vocalisations, helped him to, 'reclaim some [...] energy and power', and also led him to think about, 'the position of an artist in society, a dancer in society'.[64]

Perhaps unsurprisingly, this production also marked the introduction of the spoken voice into Keegan-Dolan's practice. Seeing no difference between acting and dancing, Keegan-Dolan states, 'an actor or dancer with an intelligent body and a stupid mind is no better or no worse than an actor or dancer with an intelligent mind and a stupid body. Both are only half formed'.[65] Further describing his approach to the dancing/acting body, he observes, '[i]t's about a body fully inhabited. The brain, the mouth, the legs, the hand, the eyes all work together in some sort of beautiful harmony. [...] I try to tell stories through using dance, acting and imagery'.[66] During the audition process for *Giselle*, Keegan-Dolan invited dancers to take a week-long yoga workshop with himself and Evans, choosing to work with dancers that were open to this method. The ensemble that he built for this piece included a core of eight dancers that also worked with him on the next two pieces of the *Midlands Trilogy. Giselle* was also the first work to be set in the Irish midlands in the counties of Longford, Westmeath and Roscommon, which is an area of personal importance to Keegan-Dolan.[67] Known for its flat and boggy landscape, Keegan-Dolan explains that he connects this area with 'images of "heaviness"'.[68] The unchanging 'heaviness' of this landscape is used as both a grounding device in a rapidly changing globalised Irish culture ('I'm terrified of the cappuccinos and the four-wheel drives and the blonde hairdos')[69] and a comparative base for Keegan-Dolan's corporeal re-visioning of stories and histories. The bog was brought onto the stage in Fabulous Beast's next work, *The Bull* (2005), in the form of several tonnes of peat moss. This second part of the *Midlands Trilogy* was a reworking of the ancient Irish epic, *An Táin Bó Cúailnge*, transposed to Celtic Tiger Ireland. The show's blend of cultural critique, acerbic, foul-mouthed humour, and unrelenting cartoon-like violence sharply divided both audiences and critics.[70] The final work of the trilogy, *James Son of James* (2008), explored the role of heroism in society, showing the betrayal of a messiah-like figure (who teaches yoga) by a jealous, selfish, and fearful community. After premiering at the Dublin Theatre Festival in 2008, the production went on to tour in the UK, supported by the Dance Touring Partnership and Culture Ireland.[71] In 2009 Keegan-Dolan undertook the largest Fabulous Beast project to date, staging a version of Stravinsky's *The Rite of Spring* with the orchestra of the English National Opera at the Coliseum in London.[72] The same year also saw a work-in-progress showing of a further storytelling piece, *Helen and Hell*, featuring actress Olwen Fouéré, dancer Rachel Poirier, double bass and singing saw player Martin Brundsen and musician/actor Liam Ó'Maonlaí. Fabulous Beast's latest work, *Rian* (2011), has a multinational ensemble which includes dancers with cultural roots in Ghana, Finland, Nigeria, India, Greece, England, the Ukraine and Indonesia. This work is another collaboration with Ó'Maonlaí that celebrates, 'the meeting of musician and dancer', and is based on Ó'Maonlaí's album of Irish language songs, *Rian* (2005).[73]

The Irish Arts Council has supported Fabulous Beast since 1999 and in 2007 the company was invited to become an artistic associate of the Barbican Centre in London. The Barbican had co-produced *Giselle* and *The Bull* in partnership with the Dublin Theatre Festival, and this further level of endorsement in the company gave them 'an artistic home away from home',[74] and provided them with a large and well-established audience base in London.[75] Keegan-Dolan and the company have won several prestigious awards for their work: *Giselle* won the *Irish Times* Judges Special Award in 2004 and was also nominated for an Olivier Award in London in 2006; *The Flowerbed* was nominated for a Critic's Circle Dance Award in the UK in the category of Best Modern Choreography in 2006; in 2007 *The Bull* was also nominated for the Critic's Circle award and won it; in 2010 *The Rite of Spring* was also nominated for an Olivier Award; and in 2012 the company was nominated for a Judges' Special Award at the Irish Times Theatre Awards for their latest production, *Rian.*

Location of this study within the field

Despite the exciting developments over the past few decades, there is a dearth of published critical writing about contemporary dance in Ireland. Whereas traditional Irish dance and social dance has enjoyed a surge in critical interest (for example publications by Brendan Breathnach, Helen Brennan, Catherine Foley, Barbara O'Connor and Frank Hall), and an increasingly visible academic presence due to the strong leaning towards traditional Irish dance at research centres in Limerick and Tralee, contemporary dance and dance theatre remains an, as yet, relatively neglected field.[76] However, there are several publications that provide collections of interviews with choreographers working in Ireland. Although they are predominantly edited collections of primary materials and oral histories that do not critically interrogate or contextualise the choreographers' work, they have provided valuable resource material for this project. Of these books, Deirdre Mulrooney's *Irish Moves* (2006) provides a broad historical overview of dance and physical theatre in Ireland, mostly through interviews with practitioners. Three books focussing on contemporary dance in Ireland – *Dancing on the Edge of Europe: Irish Choreographers in Conversation* (2003) edited by Diana Theodores and two volumes of *Choreographic Encounters* edited by Mary Brady (2003, 2004) – are also primarily collections of interviews with and essays by dance practitioners about their own work. Anthropologist Helena Wulff's book *Dancing at the Crossroads* (2007) conducts an ethnographic and cultural analysis of mainly traditional Irish dance, but also of some dance theatre, focussing on questions of 'Irishness', Irish national identity and cultural memory.[77] Vida Midgelow briefly discusses Fabulous Beast's reworking of *Giselle* in the introduction to her book, *Reworking the Ballet* (2007), and Lisa Fitzpatrick discusses the trope of the midlands in the work of Fabulous Beast and playwright Marina Carr in her essay, 'Bogland Parodies: the Midlands Setting in Marina Carr and Fabulous Beast Dance Theatre' (2008).[78] An issue of the *Irish Theatre Magazine* (Volume 3, Issue 12, Summer 2002) dedicated to dance includes an article by choreographer and Dance Ireland chief executive Paul Johnson, tracing the relationship between Arts Council policy and the development of dance in Ireland up to 2002. This issue also includes an article by Seona MacRéamoinn, which gives an overview of the dance scene at the time of the inaugural International Dance Festival (2002). Although some newer publications on Irish theatre and culture have highlighted the recent developments in Irish dance theatre as worthy of critical notice (e.g. Bernadette Sweeney, *Performing the Body in Irish Theatre*, 2008), most discussions either make no mention of dance[79] or do not extend their investigations beyond *Riverdance*.[80] This book aims to go towards filling this gap, contributing to dance studies through its investigation of dance theatre, and due to its interdisciplinary approach, also contributing to theatre studies and cultural studies. The following section considers some of the most important theoretical threads that underpin and weave through my interpretative and analytical discussions throughout this book.

Thinking the dancing body

Why are investigations of the dancing body particularly useful in conducting a political and cultural reading of a society? Elizabeth Grosz proposes that 'a history of bodies is yet to be written, but it would involve looking at the mutual relations between bodily inscription and lived experience'.[81] It would seem that an interrogation of the dancing body could help in providing just such a history, as differing from many other cultural productions, dance requires the physical body to enact its own representation. The inherent 'doublings' of the performing dancing body lends it the unique ability to simultaneously present a somatic identity as well as a cultural one. As dance scholar Ann Cooper Albright proposes

> [i]n a historical moment when the 'body' is considered to be a direct purveyor of identity [...] [and] artists and politicians are struggling to understand the cultural differences between bodies, dance can provide a critical example of the dialectical relationship between cultures and the bodies that inhabit them.[82]

Dance can make visible how bodies are ordered and symbolically coded in society, but it can also simultaneously foreground our embodied understandings of the world. In understanding this idea, it is useful to consider the *Körper/Leib* distinction. Unlike English, the German language has two different terms for the body: *Körper*, which refers to the instrumental, structural and objectified body, and *Leib*, which refers to the living, experiential, subjective body. Arguing against scholarship that addresses only one of these aspects of the body, sociologist Bryan S. Turner proposes instead that the 'double nature of human beings' must be considered, so that 'the weakness of the Cartesian legacy [...] which has almost exclusively treated the human body as *Körper*, rather than both simultaneously *Körper* and *Leib*' can be overcome.[83] This then allows for the expression of 'the ambiguity of human embodiment as both personal and impersonal, objective and subjective, social and natural'.[84]

The dancing body is at once the body that is seen to be dancing and the body that is doing the dancing, the perceived body and the experienced body (for both performer and spectator). The 'ambiguity' of this simultaneous subjectivity and objectivity of the body's corpo-reality and the inadequacy of the Cartesian mind/body dichotomy is also a question fundamental to the philosophy of phenomenologist Maurice Merleau-Ponty. Criticising the way in which transcendental forms of 'intellectual' and 'analytic' thought place the subject outside of the world in order to make sense of it, he argues that our perception of the world is created through our bodily experience. Challenging the primacy of mind over body, Merleau-Ponty believes that, '[t]he perceiving mind is an incarnated mind.'[85] He maintains that the formation of consciousness, the 'self', can only be comprehended through the lived body. Mind and body can never be separated, but rather they are intertwined with each other and with the world. Viewed this way,

> [...] the body is no longer merely *an object in the world*, under the purview of a separated spirit. It is on the side of the subject; it is our *point of view of the world*, the place where the spirit takes on a certain physical and historical situation.
> [Merleau-Ponty's own emphasis][86]

Proposing an inter-relatedness of body and world, Merleau-Ponty strove to uncover and re-establish the 'roots of the mind in its body and in its world.'[87] As Taylor Carman explains, Merleau-Ponty's notion of the 'chiasm' refigures our perception of the relation of body and world so that, 'they are not two distinct things, but sinews of a common flesh, threads in the same fabric, related to one another not as situation and reaction [...], but as a single woven texture, like the overlapping and interlocking lizards and birds in an Escher drawing.'[88] Mind, body and world are not identical, but they are inextricably linked in the experiencing of the world and the subjective understanding of 'being-in-the-world'; the perception of the world is always an embodied perception. The body, situated in space and time, is then necessarily implicated in all thought and language. This enables a conceiving of thought (perception) and a conceiving of movement (sense) beyond the separating binary of mind and body, allowing for a thinking body and a bodily thinking.

Merleau-Ponty's phenomenology has been criticised by feminists, such as Judith Butler, who argue that his readings do not take gender or sexual specificity into account; although he speaks generally of all bodies, Butler argues that his viewpoint is always skewed as he is writing from his own experience as a male body.[89] While acknowledging the dangers implicit in an essentialist view that reads the world from a subjective standpoint, and while also agreeing with Iris Marion Young that there can be no, ' "pure" embodied experience prior to ideology',[90] it is nevertheless possible to view Merleau-Ponty's thought as promoting an understanding of perception that is not confined to purely one category of experience in its difference to another. Grosz recognises that, 'experience cannot be taken as an unproblematic given, a position through which one can judge knowledges, for experience is of course implicated in and produced by various knowledges and social practices', yet she also argues for the importance of Merleau-Ponty's 'understanding of the constructed, synthetic nature of experience, its simultaneously active and passive functioning, its role in both the inscription and subversion of sociopolitical values [...]'.[91] Turning to dance scholarship, the writings of dance phenomenologists such as Maxine Sheets-Johnstone, who employ a purely phenomenological approach to the study of dance works, present difficulties. Sheets-Johnstone proposes that

> [t]o approach dance as a phenomenal presence is to presuppose nothing in advance of the immediate experience of dance. Because nothing is taken for granted, dance is looked upon as a totality whose structures are intrinsic to it.[92]

To suggest that some 'essence' of a dance piece can be experienced outside of any cultural, political and historical influence is problematic. The dance, the dancers and the spectator are all inextricably linked to their socio-cultural backgrounds. While acknowledging the importance of a kinaesthetic and embodied perception of dance, and drawing on Merleau-Ponty's thought in approaching an understanding of the intertwining of mind, body and world, it is necessary also to be aware of the dangers implicit in viewing dance as a 'pure zone'. Philipa Rothfield calls for an awareness of the limitations of a purely phenomenological approach, yet also advocates the recognition of the kinaesthetic experience of dance, stating that

> experience is not a pure zone whose analysis can reveal a set of structures whose totality expresses the phenomenological essence of dance. But it is an important aspect of the practice of dancing and its perception. The experiential aspect of dance, which we might call its perception, is an embodied corporeal act, one which is embedded in the conditions of its articulation.[93]

In discussing the emergence of the dancing body in a society dominated by the word, such as Ireland, Merleau-Ponty's notion of the incarnated mind is very useful in providing a starting point from which to argue the importance and relevance of an analytical *and* kinaesthetic corporeal reading of society. This then allows for what Thomas Csordas calls 'somatic modes of attention' which combine both a phenomenological reading and a discursive reading.[94] In dance analysis, this offers the possibility of both a close reading of the experience of a dance movement in a performance (and the movement of bodies in everyday practices) and a theoretical reading of their choreography.

Positioning this study within the discourse of dance scholarship

Until the 1980s dance scholarship was made up largely, as Jane Desmond summarises, of 'historical narratives, aesthetic valuations, or auteur studies of great dancers and choreographers'.[95] Due to its perceived ephemeral nature, dance, aligned always with the feminine and the 'other',[96] was considered incapable of intellectual or critical expression.[97] Analyses of the dancing body, in line with more general scholarship relating to the body, focussed on it primarily as 'natural' and as a site for the projection and display of signs. However, a shift in thought occurred with Michel Foucault's studies of how the body is regulated and inscribed by cultural power relations and mechanisms. Foucault proposes that there already exists a kind of 'history of the body', but that its purpose was solely to interrogate the body's demographic, pathological, biological and physiological attributes, the 'science of its functioning', with no consideration as to how the body operates in political fields.[98] In his seminal work *Discipline and Punish: the Birth of the Prison* (1975), Foucault extends the knowledge of the body to examine how state apparatuses, and other institutions of power, dominate it in order to create a productive subject, and how power relations 'invest it, mark it, train it, torture it, force it to carry out tasks, to perform ceremonies, to emit signs'.[99] Applying Foucault's theory to the dancing body would then imply that the signs it emits can only ever be those that are already conditioned/choreographed by the dominant cultural forces at work on and through it. Although Foucault's genealogical writings shed light on the control and inscription of bodies, his theories posit a body that is, 'passive raw data manipulated and utilized by various systems of social and self-constitution, an object more or less at the mercy of non-intentional or self-directed, conscious production'.[100] However, an epistemological rupture occurred in dance studies when scholars began to apply poststructuralist theory to the 'reading' of choreography and the dancing body.[101] This began the trend of recent dance scholarship, within which this project situates itself, that proposes that the dancing body is not only a palimpsest of cultural inscriptions, but also capable of generating meaning of its own creation. Susan Foster, acknowledging the important work of theorists such as Foucault in bringing the body to the fore in academic discourse, argues that his delineation of the 'hegemonic peregrinations of power' inadequately addresses the possibility of an individual body's agency.[102] Foster responds to this entrapment of the body in a position of inarticulacy with her notion of 'corporeality', 'a consideration of bodily reality',[103] that brings the materiality of the body in motion into focus, recognising its ability not only to signify, but also to make history. Viewing dance as a particularly creative instance of 'meaning-filled physicality',[104] Foster goes further, suggesting that, '[d]ance, perhaps more than any other body-centred endeavor, cultivates a body that initiates as well as responds'.[105] Dance then becomes a creative physical practice that can both register and realise cultural change. Calling for an understanding of how the body has the ability to generate meaning, she proposes that

> [t]he possibility of a body that is written upon but that also writes [...] asks scholars to approach the body's involvement in any activity with an assumption of potential agency to participate in or resist whatever forms of cultural production are underway. It also endows body-centred endeavors with an integrity as practices that establish their own lexicons of meaning, their own syntagmatic and paradigmatic axes of signification, their own capacity to reflect critically on themselves and on related practices. Dancemaking [...] becomes a form of theorizing.[106]

Importantly, Foster argues that gesture has no 'fixed' meaning and that the movements made by bodies need to be read in the cultural and historical context in which they occur. For this project I am especially interested in how Foster's opening up of dance studies to include a consideration of the body's involvement in 'any activity' allows for a theoretical examination of the agency of the body and its potential for resistance to hegemonic power structures both within and outside of dance performance. This not only enables a critical reading of the choreography of everyday movements and situations, but also makes possible an examination of how dancing bodies are choreographed in, and reflect, specific political and socio-cultural contexts. Foster's idea of viewing dance as a form of theorising is an important underlying thread that runs through all the analytical readings of this book.

In attempting to reach through the dance performances discussed in this project to analyse their link with social and political situations in everyday life, Randy Martin's inquiries into the relationship between the movement in dance, 'social movement' and political mobilisation has proved a useful example of one way to approach the task. In *Critical Moves: Dance Studies in Theory and Politics* (1998)

Martin, following Foster's insistence on the dancing body's agency and choreography's potential for cultural resistance, views dance as:

> the reflexive mobilization of the body – that is, as a social process that foregrounds the very means through which bodies gather. Through dance, the means and ends of mobilization are joined together and made available to performers and their publics. Dance, so conceived does not name a fixed expression but a problem, a predicament, that bodies find themselves in the midst of, whose momentary solutions we call dancing.[107]

As the works interrogated in this study all directly comment on societal 'problems', Martin's notion that the corporeal tackling of these problems in a dance work can connect with the problems encountered by bodies beyond the performance, lends weight to the idea that dance can motion toward change. He also, importantly, includes an analysis of spectatorship in the 'gathering' of bodies that constitutes a dance performance, acknowledging the importance of the work of the audience. In addition to these ideas, I have found Martin's notion of 'overreading' to be an important influence in my project of interrogating the aesthetic and political links of certain works to their social context. According to Martin, overreading a dance performance breaks down the 'stable demarcation' of a formalist reading that separates the interiority from the exteriority of a piece and views any discussion of the context of a work as an interference to its 'veracity'. Instead, overreading 'rests on the assumption that the subtext displayed in dance accounts for more than that particular aesthetic activity' and enables a 'read[ing] through and past the dance to the point where it meets its own exterior or context'.[108] Although Martin's aim in *Critical Moves* is to apply 'methodological insights' gained from his practice and study of dance to a new understanding of political theory, the insights that he reflects back onto dance through his theoretical readings create a platform for thinking through the relationship between dance and politics. Politics, he says, 'goes nowhere without movement'[109] and he argues that a 'disjuncture between political ideas and social mobilization' has led to a situation of stasis in the imagining of how progressive politics can effect social change and 'mobiliz[e] against the fixity of what is dominant in the social order'.[110] Yet, although Martin sees dance, grounded as it is in movement, as being the perfect intermediary in imagining how motion could inhabit the gap between political thought and social action, he concedes that dance's influence beyond its own sphere will always be limited. However, bearing in mind dance's marginalised positioning in Ireland within its own sphere of theatrical performance, the question of the potential influence of dance takes on a specifically localised focus. In Ireland, contemporary dance theatre must first achieve visibility in the very system within which it operates. The dominant order of theatrical performance in Ireland upholds a reverence for the written word to the exclusion of the corporeal; a literary bias that could be interpreted as perpetuating an ennervating stasis. Due to their marginalised positioning in this textual order, contemporary choreographers are always already operating from a resistive location, and so their emergence within the sphere of theatrical performance carries with it an important potential for influence and change.

The tactics of the choreographer in Ireland

Choreographers in Ireland have, by necessity, always had to be skilled tacticians, constantly finding new ways to move the dancing body towards visibility in an unwelcoming terrain. The choreographers discussed in this book are particularly interesting in that they are operating beyond disciplinary boundaries in an in-between space between dance and theatre. This positioning stems from a disregard for the limitations of the normative, that develops from a desire to use whatever means necessary in order to best tell their corporeal stories. In approaching an examination of how these choreographers are resisting the dominant cultural order and creating their own antidisciplinary practice, Michel de Certeau's cultural study *The Practice of Everyday Life* (1984) provides a helpful framework.[111] De Certeau is interested in how individuals, going through their everyday activities such as reading, walking or cooking, have the agency to choose not to follow the rules of cultural behaviour norms. Describing these considered and thoughtful 'antidisciplinary' acts, he explains that, '[t]hese "ways of operating" constitute the innumerable practices by means of which users reappropriate the space organized by techniques of sociocultural production'.[112] His scheme for interrogating these deviant 'ways of operating' is based on his differentiation between 'strategies' and 'tactics'. Strategies are the overarching structures of power relationships that occur when an organisation (e.g. scientific, military, political) adopts what de Certeau calls a 'Cartesian attitude' in order to stake out its own place in the world, which is distinguishable from the place of its other.[113] They are the panoptic power structures that dominate the social order and attempt to regulate the actions of individuals. A tactic, on the other hand, is the means by which the supposedly dominated 'weak' disrupt these strategies by operating in the terrain regulated by the strategy, but simultaneously creating a space for the other; it is 'a calculated action determined by the absence of a proper locus' that has 'no delimitation of an exteriority'.[114] The tactic is the agency that playfully and knowingly defies the deterministic structure of society. This notion of a tactical disruption of the dominant by bodies operating from the margins, the space of the other which allows for their autonomy, has great resonance with the position of the choreographer in Ireland. Not adhering to the cultural dominance of the written word, the choreographer uses tactical corporeal manoeuvres to resist the body's invisibility. However, like de Certeau's concept of the tactic, the dancing body in Ireland is always moving in 'a terrain imposed on it and organized by the law of a foreign power'.[115] The foreign power is the written word, which has been dislocated from the corporeal to dominate the landscape of theatrical performance in Ireland.

Dead flesh and other colonial concerns

In order to further understand why these tactics are necessary, the 'strategical' context from which they emerged must be outlined. Two questions come into view: how did the disembodied written word achieve pre-eminence? And why were theatrical dancing bodies marginalised? In thinking of dancing bodies moving on a terrain governed by the laws of a foreign power, while also considering the critical anxiety caused by the work of choreographers who create pieces for performing bodies that dance *and* speak, this argument leads us to a consideration of Ireland's colonial past. Declan Kiberd proposes that the English, in their project of colonisation, helped invent a notion of Ireland. He writes, 'through many centuries, Ireland was pressed into service as a foil to set off English virtues, as a laboratory in which to conduct experiments, and as a fantasy-land in which to meet fairies and monsters.'[116] Looking through a corporeal lens, one of the effects that this shaping of Ireland by its dominant 'other' produced, was the positioning of the Irish as the feminine foil to English masculinity. The dualism created by the forging of an oppositional Irish identity by the coloniser created a need for those involved in the nationalist cause to stress masculine qualities. To combat the charge of a backward Irish ineffectuality and irrationality opposed to a progressive, rational English logic, a demonstration of a mastery of the coloniser's language was necessary.[117] The nationalist imagining of an Irish Renaissance that would contribute to the ideology of a free state was significantly fuelled by the work of writers such as Yeats, in a revivalist literary movement that gained visibility with the founding of the Irish Literary Society in 1882. The political project of the Society was, of course, not the first intersection of the political and the literary in Ireland, as the legislative sanctions of the English against Irish storytellers and poets in the sixteenth century demonstrate.[118] However, as Kiberd points out, it was the first movement since the overthrow of the Gaelic Order in 1601 that made 'Ireland once again interesting to the Irish', achieving 'nothing less than a renovation of Irish consciousness and a new understanding of politics, economics, philosophy, sport, language and culture in its widest sense'.[119] This project of renovation was also extended to the corporeal and although its efforts to prove false the masculine/feminine, strong/weak, rational/irrational dichotomies were, in many ways, concentrated in the demonstration of literary superiority, this did not mean that the body was ignored. In an attempt to redress the indignity of a feminine identity – for to be feminine at the end of the nineteenth century was to be the negative to a masculine positive –[120] nationalists founded the Gaelic Athletic Association in 1884, with the intention of 'purg[ing] themselves of their degrading femininity by a disciplined programme of physical-contact sports'.[121] This disciplining of an 'Irish' body is also evident in the attention paid by the Gaelic League to traditional Irish dancing. Established in 1893, the League's primary interest was in a revival of the Irish language. However, the organisation quickly became a powerful influence in the movement towards defining a 'native' Irish dance form that was free from 'alien' influences. Helen Brennan proposes that the arguments about what constituted Irish dance and what did not were, 'in essence, a cultural civil war with dance as the arena of combat'.[122] The intention of the nationalists, as described by a letter to the Gaelic League's newspaper *An Claidheamh Soluis* ('The Sword of Light') in 1906, was to be rid of 'baneful, suggestive foreign dances such as the polka, the waltz, the Welsh Dance, the Cat Walk, the Cake Walk and all foreign monstrosities'.[123] Only the League's own brand of step dancing and *céilí* dancing was considered 'safe' and so the Irish dancing body was regulated and restricted in its co-optation by the nationalist cause. Not only was *céilí* dancing, with its strict geometrical patterns and minimal body contact between partners, promoted as the most appropriate social dance form, but all other forms of social dance were denounced as 'dubious' and linked with images of fiery evildoing on the 'hobs of hell' or depraved immorality in the 'fleshpots of Egypt'.[124] Theatre dance was also highly problematic. In Western society, theatre dance has been aligned and intertwined with the feminine since the Baroque period,[125] and as Ramsay Burt argues, representations of masculinity in dance over the past century and a half, 'have threatened [...] to disrupt and destabilize masculine identity'.[126] Needless to say, dance was not the only area of cultural expression that was subject to this kind of censorship. Gearóid Ó'hAllmhuiráin also lists, 'women's fashions and immodest dress [...] evil literature, theatrical performances [and] cinema exhibitions', as offering potential sites of, 'shameful abuses in Irish social life', that were denounced alongside 'indecent dancing'.[127] Unsurprisingly, debates around the standardising rule that in competitive step dancing the arms must be held immobile at the side of the body are also prevalent at this time; the corporeal was being straightjacketed.[128] Sociologist Barbara O'Connor links the promotion of *céilí* dance by the Gaelic League to the desire for a dance form that would reflect the body politic's need for both racial and sexual purity in their invention of a sovereign national identity.[129] The GAA also imposed a ban on its members' partaking in 'foreign' sports, and the 1901 convention called for

> the young men of Ireland not to identify themselves with rugby or association football or any form of imported sport which is likely to injuriously affect the national pastimes which the GAA provides for self-respected Irishmen who have no desire to ape foreign manners or customs.[130]

This moulding of an exclusionary 'Irish' body by nationalist organi-sations shows that the body was viewed as a potentially problematic and subversive site that, through practices deemed to be ideologically unsound, might pollute the nationalist purity of an individual's mind and soul.

Discussing the nationalism of writers such as Yeats, Edward Said points out that the articulation of an 'expression of Irish iden-tity as it attaches to the land, to its Celtic origins, to a growing body of nationalist experiences and leaders [...] and to a specifically national literature' is a process of ' "simultaneous abstraction and reification" '.[131] Both of these expressive aspects of national identity were to have negative repercussions for theatrical dance in Ireland. Speaking of the importance placed on the word by colonised soci-eties, Kiberd explains that '[a] writer in a free state works with the easy assurance that literature is but one of the social institutions to project the values which the nation admires [...]. A writer in a colony knows that these values can be fully embodied only in the written word'.[132] Due to the inescapable reality of the physical body's colonised state, a de-colonised identity could only be imag-ined through the dematerialised word. Outside of the word-focussed rehabilitation and re-figuring of an 'Irish' identity, the body, a sep-arate entity to the mind, had to be disciplined, regulated and kept under control.

In *The Tremulous Private Body* (1995), Francis Barker, discussing the emergence of the modern subject in seventeenth-century literature, examines the individual's struggle for autonomy against an absolutist state. His interrogation of the emergence of a 'discoursing subject which is sceptical of its body and guilty of its sexuality [and] which is committed to writing',[133] has resonance with the emergence of postcolonial subjects in Ireland from a corporeal perspective. Barker proposes that modernity creates two bodies; one that is seen as 'dead flesh', the mere container and 'extraneous shell' of consciousness, and the second, which is 'out there' in the world and becomes 'the object of the disciplinary interventions which will thenceforward sanitise it, train it, and prepare it for labour'.[134] In colonial Ireland, with its necessary emphasis on the literary to repel 'alleged unreliabil-ity, emotional instability and mental disequilibrium',[135] an articulate body with a perceived threatening corporeal agency would seem to have been quashed and relegated to a state of 'dead flesh'. At the same time, it was of importance that the body 'out there' performing the national identity was not viewed as feminine, and if the body happened to be the one acceptable and sanctioned type of dancing body, that all sexual associations were nullified. In the attempts of these cultural organisations to liberate Ireland from a colonising power, the body was re-colonised by the nationalist campaign; this could be read as a neo-colonial project, in the sense of it being a continuation of past colonial practices that had dominated Irish bodies.[136]

The control of the Irish dancing body extended well beyond the establishment of the Free State in 1922 and became a legislative matter with the notorious Public Dance Halls Act of 1935, which sought to regulate social dancing by confining dance meetings to licensed premises and imposing a government tax on admission tickets. If a public dance was to be held, a licence for the premises had to be obtained from the district court; only people considered to be 'reputable' were granted licences, and only under controlled conditions. An example of the oppressive combination of state and church authority in Ireland, this bill was introduced following pressure on the government from church leaders who sought to counteract the functioning of private house dances as sites that allowed for what they termed 'occasions of sin' and the practice of morally 'dubious' foreign dances.[137] Social dance is not the same as theatrical dance, yet hopefully this interrogation of these formative ideas, laws and practices at the beginning of the twentieth century can contribute towards an understanding of the focus on the literary and the marginalisation of the theatrical dancing body in the context of Irish performance culture.

Reanimating the dead flesh

In choosing to inhabit an in-between space between dance and theatre, where articulate bodies can generate meaning and practice social commentary, the choreographers interrogated here are resisting the positioning of the body in 'the place of silence exterior to language', and 'extraneou[s] to the constitutive centre where the male voice speaks'.[138] Considering their use of dancing bodies that also speak, the 'norm' of the marginalisation and straightjacketing of the dancing body in an Irish context means that their work is bridging a divide between the body relegated to a state of 'dead flesh' on the one hand, and the speaking subject with agency on the other. The dancing body can then embody and articulate the repressed corporeality, the feminine, the 'other', which was denied a voice, while simultaneously critiquing the division between body and word. In a discussion of 'spatial stories', de Certeau examines the significance of the bridge in the work of Hieronymus Bosch and proposes that in its function as a transgression of a limit, the bridge represents

> a departure, an attack on the state, the ambition of a conquering power, or the flight of an exile; in any case, the 'betrayal' of an order. But at the same time as it offers the possibility of a bewildering exteriority, it allows or causes the re-emergence beyond the frontiers of the alien element that was controlled in the interior, and gives objectivity (that is expression and re-presentation) to the alterity which was hidden inside the limits, so that in recrossing the bridge and coming back within the enclosure the traveler henceforth finds there the exteriority that he had first sought by going outside and then fled by returning.[139]

In the context of Irish theatre practice, the 'alien element' is the articulate, expressive body that has been repressed and hidden, and the 'enclosure' is the patriarchal order of nationalism and the written word. Read this way, de Certeau's bridge highlights the construction of a subjectivity that tries to alienate its own corporeal foundation by positioning it as other, but which, through stepping outside of the structure which maintains the controlling of the body, is confronted with the re-emergence of that which was repressed. In its need for a monolithic 'Irish' identity, the nationalist revival may have rendered articulations of alternative corporealities politically invisible, however, in the emergence of an articulate body within antidisciplinary dance theatre works, these alternative modes of subjectivity (e.g. the feminine, the foreign) can be 're-presented'. Alterities that were strictly controlled and exiled to a position outside of discourse, can then emerge to question and trouble the hegemonic order. Indeed, as the second chapter of this book will show, there have been several historical instances in theatrical dance and theatre performance, prior to the contemporary dance theatre works discussed here, in which articulate dancing bodies have sought to resist the dominance of the literary and reanimate the 'dead flesh' of the Irish body.

Joseph Roach proposes that, 'through the magical sway of legal fictions [...], laws transmit effigies – constructed figures that provide templates of sanctioned behavior – across generations.'[140] On the one hand, this wonderful image of a body shaped by law moving unchanged through time resonates with the notion of a petrified corporeality in Ireland. Yet looking to the old Latin origins of the word – *effingere* (to fashion artistically) – Roach's effigy takes on a sculptural form that retains a plasticity which allows for a possible remoulding. Benedict Anderson suggests that a nation is an 'imagined community' in which members may never have met each other, yet 'in the minds of each lives the image of their communion'.[141] The works of the practitioners discussed in this book each make visible the imagined foundations of communities in Ireland. The picture that emerges is often an unflattering reflection of the more oppressive, violent and corrupted aspects of contemporary society. However, the emergence of these choreographers in Ireland owes itself to a positive imagining. As David Bolger explains, to bring his dance theatre company into existence in 1995 was, 'extraordinary, taking a leap, and saying, "This is what we believe in, let's try it"'.[142] The 'legal fictions' of the nationalist project may have tried to silence certain corporealities, but that does not mean that all bodies in Ireland conformed to the mould. As de Certeau might argue, the fact that these rules existed in Irish society suggests that there were always deviant bodies resisting them, imagining and putting into practice alternative corporealities and communities. The emergence of the dance companies and choreographers discussed in this book is proof.

The following six chapters of this study are divided into two sections. The first section, comprising Chapters Two and Three, contextualises the work of current dance theatre choreographers in Ireland within both an historical and contemporary framework of national and international developments in dance theatre. Chapter Two considers the work of three major figures in the development of Irish dance theatre pre-1990: William Butler Yeats in his collaborations with Michio Ito and Ninette de Valois, Erina Brady and her Irish School of Dance Art, and Joan Davis and the Dublin Contemporary Dance Theatre. In Chapter Three I consider the affinities of Irish dance theatre practice with German *Tanztheater* and international choreographers of political dance theatre who consider their works 'acts of citizenship'. This chapter also conducts an investigation into the genre questions and critical anxiety raised by works that deviate from established notions of what dance 'is' in an Irish context, and includes a reading of the important re-imaginings of the traditional Irish dancing body in the recent choreographies of ex-*Riverdance* soloists Jean Butler and Colin Dunne. The second section of the book provides detailed readings of five seminal dance theatre works by CoisCéim and Fabulous Beast. In Chapter Four, I discuss how CoisCéim's *Ballads* (1997) and Fabulous Beast's *The Bull* (2005) challenge the sanitisation and erasure of bodily realities in constitutive stories, myths and memories. Chapter Five conducts a reading of gender and sexuality in Fabulous Beast's *Giselle* (2003) and *The Rite of Spring* (2009), examining how the choreography of unanticipated endings in these works resists the oppression of certain femininities and masculinities in Ireland. Chapter Six discusses how a dissensual choreography of space in CoisCéim's *Dodgems* (2008) highlights the inequalities of citizenship laws and the 'social blindness' that arises through depoliticising projects of social consensus. Finally, Chapter Seven summarises thematic connections between all of the works discussed and also introduces the latest generation of dance theatre choreographers.

2
Danced Precedents from Yeats to Davis

On 2 April 1916, three weeks before Pádraig Pearse's proclamation of the Irish Republic on the steps of the GPO in Dublin, which would signal the beginning of the Easter Rising, a dress rehearsal performance of a dance play by Yeats, *At the Hawk's Well*, was held for a select, invited audience in the London drawing room of Lady Emerald Cunard.[1] On the surface, the aristocratic setting for this drawing room staging, which made it necessary for the performers to carefully negotiate a Louis XV table, would seem to place the two events as being as ideologically removed from each other as can be imagined. Yet the authors of both the uprising and the dance play shared a common goal: Irish independence. Yeats (1865–1939), co-founder of the Irish Literary Society, the Gaelic League and the Abbey Theatre, the national theatre of Ireland, was committed throughout his life to decolonisation. A resistive poet who looked to ancient Irish myths for inspiration in his imagining of a de-anglicised Irish culture, he constantly searched for new forms of artistic expression to communicate 'the idea of a nation'.[2] Declan Kiberd writes that Yeats, 'began in his teens writing poetry of octogenarian senility, yet ended his days creating passionate celebrations of the human body'.[3] In constructing himself as a national artist, Kiberd argues that for Yeats, a decolonisation of the body was 'almost' as important as the decolonisation of native culture, and that Yeats viewed the 'thinking of the body' as being a 'democratic equality of matter and mind'.[4]

The aim of this chapter is to locate contemporary developments in dance theatre within a historical framework, both in Ireland and internationally. It will focus specifically on choreographies, such as

Yeats' dance play, that resisted the dichotomisation of genres into the strictly verbal and the strictly physical, or as Susan Foster eloquently puts it, '[jumbled] the familiar hierarchies which deprive speech of its sensuality and movement of its mindfulness'.[5] An attempt to construct a narrative of such instances in Ireland has proved problematic. André Lepecki notes, that a 'who begat who' account of dance history has been, 'rightly discarded as unbearably Oedipal in its obsessive persistence'.[6] Luckily such a study would have immediately been thwarted, as it seems that any amount of 'obsessive persistence' would have been of little avail in bringing it to fruition, due to several reasons. Firstly, because of the marginalised positioning of dance in comparison with literary theatre, documentation of choreographers' work was severely neglected until very recently. Secondly, it would seem that although innovative choreographic experimentations with genre did occur in Ireland, it is often the case that there is no direct evidence of how this work was commented on, or used as inspiration for future developments by other practitioners. Cultural critic Seamus Kelly, writing in the *Irish Times,* reflects on his experience of this phenomenon in 1948: '[f]rom time to time Dublin awakens to a consciousness of the dance – that is, the dance as an art form, rather than as an entertainment – and for a while we have a spate of ballet shows, dance dramas and choreographic festivals. Then [...] the whole thing peters out again'.[7] Perhaps the marginalised position of theatre dance prevented choreographic developments from ever properly taking root. Or perhaps it is simply the case that, due to lack of documentation, what seem to be periods of inactivity and stagnation are merely gaps in the narrative, which continued scholarship in the field will uncover and fill in. Inevitably, due to its progression forwards through time, the account that follows would seem to posit a linear narrative that charts a progressive development of dance theatre in Ireland from the early twentieth century to the early 1990s. Yet it is important to note that any neat and tidy account of this kind is problematic as, in certain instances, later practitioners seem to have been wholly unaware of earlier experimentations. Rather than viewing the development of dance theatre in Ireland diachronically, it is necessary then to take a synchronic approach, and so I have chosen to focus on those who I have identified to be the three major figures in the development of Irish dance theatre pre-1990: William Butler Yeats in his collaborations with Michio Ito and Ninette de Valois, Erina Brady and her Irish School of Dance Art, and Joan Davis and the Dublin Contemporary Dance Theatre. This chapter proceeds, then, with an open acknowledgement that the skeleton of this narrative is probably still missing some bones that remain to be unearthed through continued research.

Yeats, Ito and de Valois: searching for forms

Poet and dramatist William Butler Yeats was not only keenly aware of the expressive ability of the dancing body, but his dance plays were also an important predecessor of contemporary dance theatre developments in Ireland. There are of course many performative disciplines in Ireland, both imported and indigenous, that use a mixture of spoken language, movement/dance and music, such as traditional mumming, pantomime, musical theatre or operetta. Yet although there are instances in which dance and text are combined in these genres (for instance, in a musical when performers execute choreographed ensemble movement while singing a song text), choreographed dance is primarily used in isolated 'numbers', and an attempted sustained synthesis of movement and text that extends throughout the entire performance is not an aesthetic objective; different disciplines are placed side by side rather than there being an intertwining dialogue between them. The first notable instance of an attempt to achieve this synthesis in Ireland can be found in Yeats' dance plays. My interest here is focussed solely on Yeats' experiments with dancing bodies in performance and the first section of this chapter will attempt to chart the impact of the dancers and choreographers Michio Ito and Ninette de Valois on the development of Yeats' use of the dancing body in his dance play idiom.

Yeats is, of course, internationally renowned as a wordsmith and it is often argued that although the image of the dancer is a central theme in his work, he was in fact no great fan of dance performance. His idea to have the Abbey actors rehearse in barrels in order to rid their performance of extraneous gesture is often cited as proof of his fear that movement could get in the way of an appreciation of his text.[8] Yet it could also be argued that his desire for an elimination of superfluous gesture in fact demonstrates a keen awareness of the potent ability of the body to communicate, and perhaps his mischievous suggestion of putting castors on the bottom of the barrels so that he could 'shove them about with a pole when the action required it' could be seen to show a rather crude, but discernable acknowledgement of the necessity of the choreography of bodies in space.[9] As Mary Fleischer suggests, Yeats' early efforts to reform the dominant realistic mode of theatre at the beginning of the twentieth century were influenced in part by a reaction against what she describes as, 'the excesses of nineteenth century acting styles, of romantic histrionics on the one hand and a surfeit of realistic detail on the other'.[10] Searching for a way to lend materiality to poetic imagery through the medium of theatre, Yeats found inspiration in the experimentations of visual art movements such as those of the Pre-Raphaelites, who explored the relationship between word and image.[11] Edward Gordon Craig's innovations in set and lighting design and the use of masks, music and movement in theatre were also to prove highly influential.[12] From the point of view of the development of Yeats' movement aesthetic, a stage direction describing the movement of the Old Man in *At the Hawk's Well* points to evidence of Craig's influence: '[h]is movements, like those of the other persons of the play, suggest a marionette'.[13] A response to Craig's well-known call for the actor to be a new kind of puppet – an 'Über-marionette' – so that there would no longer be, 'a living figure to confuse us into connecting actuality and art [...]' can be seen at work in the dance plays.[14] In his famous text written in 1907 and published in 1911, Craig explains that

> [t]he über-marionette will not compete with life – rather it will go beyond it. Its ideal will not be the flesh and blood but rather the body in trance – it will aim to clothe itself with a death-like beauty while exhaling a living spirit.[15]

To build his theory of actor-as-puppet, Craig looked to certain forms of non-Western theatre for the antidote to naturalism in the Western tradition, which, he argued, promoted a 'debased stage-realism'. Yeats, as will be discussed later, also found inspiration for his renovation of theatre in a non-Western form.

A further major influence on the work of Yeats was the late nineteenth-century French Symbolist movement, in particular its followers' desire for a unity of art forms, or *Gesamtkunstwerk*, as represented by the work of Wagner, and their fascination with the image of the dancer as embodied by solo dance artists such as Loïe Fuller.[16]

An admirer of Stéphane Mallarmé, Yeats was aware of his writings on the image of the dancer as the embodiment of the confluence of form and meaning, hovering on the border between art and nature; the *'incorporation visuelle de l'idee'*.[17] It is important to note that Mallarmé, rather problematically, did not consider the dancer as an articulate agent capable of producing thought of her own through dance. She remained oblivious to the meaning created by her dancing, the 'illiterate ballerina, flutteringly engaged in her profession'; meaning was attributed by the literate (read 'male') viewer.[18] Another important influence on Yeats' view of dance, and one of the most influential cultural events of the early twentieth century, was the arrival in Europe of Sergei Diaghilev's Ballets Russes. Diaghilev, a Russian impresario, strove to create a new form of ballet performance that would combine three artistic disciplines: music, visual art and choreography. The dazzling role-call of artists that he gathered to collaborate on the Ballets Russes productions which toured Europe in the early years of the twentieth century includes the painters Picasso, Matisse, Bakst and Benois, composers Stravinsky, Debussy, Prokofiev and Ravel and dancers (some of whom also choreographed) Fokine, Nijinsky, Nijinska, Karsavina and Pavlova.[19] Yeats probably attended one of the first London performances of 1911, but it is certain that he saw a production in 1913 (three years before the first performance of *At the Hawk's Well*) which he describes in a letter to Lady Gregory as being '[t]he one beautiful thing I have seen on the stage of recent years'.[20]

Perhaps the most commonly cited influence on the dance plays is Yeats' fascination with Japanese Noh theatre. Although probably aware of the art form for some years previously, Yeats was introduced to a collection of Noh play texts by Ezra Pound, who, in 1913, was in the process of making 'poetic translations' of a collection of plays researched in Japan by Ernest Fenellosa.[21] Yeats was struck by the potential that the structure of Noh plays, in his understanding of them, presented for the dramatic synthesis of music, poetry and dance and the possibility of an expression of images and ideas 'beyond the limits' of language. In his introductory essay, 'Certain Noble Plays of Japan', Yeats writes specifically about the dance in Noh:

> I have lately studied certain of these dances, with Japanese players, and I notice that their ideal of beauty [...] makes them pause at moments of muscular tension. The interest is not in the human

form but in the rhythm to which it moves, and the triumph of
their art is to express the rhythm in its intensity. [...][22]

It is perhaps not surprising, that in his reading of this dance, Yeats
elevates the importance of the expression of rhythm over the shaping of the human form; rhythm being also a primary concern for a
poet. Rhythm was also to become an important point of connection
between Yeats and a choreographer who would be the inspiration
for the staging of his dance plays. The choreographer Michio Ito
(1892–1961) was one of the 'Japanese players' mentioned by Yeats.
His collaboration with Ito on the play *At the Hawk's Well* was Yeats'
first adaptation of the Noh genre in his dramatic work and the first
of his *Four Plays for Dancers* (published 1921).[23]

Richard Taylor has established that Yeats used Fenellosa's version of
the Zeami Noh play *Yoro* as the base for *At the Hawk's Well*, although
he substantially altered the original scenario.[24] Written for three
actors and three musicians, *At the Hawk's Well* is set at the site of an
ancient well on a mountainside. Cúchulainn, who has heard that the
waters of the well can lend whoever drinks them immortality, arrives
at the site to find two figures: an old man who has been waiting for
the waters to rise for fifty years, and the Guardian of the Well (played
by Ito) – a mysterious hawk-like woman shrouded in a black cape.
The old man advises Cúchulainn to leave and not to waste his life
as he himself has done (every time the waters arrive the old man is
sleeping), but Cúchulainn stays, and when the Guardian of the Well
is possessed by a hawk spirit and begins a hypnotising and seductive dance, he follows her away from the well and into the mountain
rocks. Hidden in the rocks, the hawk-woman summons Cúchulainn's
adversary, the warrior queen Aoife, and so he must leave the well
to go and fight Aoife's army. French illustrator, musician and mask-
maker Edmund Dulac designed the costumes, make-up and masks
for the work, and also composed the score for drum, gong, flute,
and zither or harp. The minimalist set consisted only of a patterned
screen as a backdrop and a blue cloth on the ground representing the
well. The musicians, who opened and closed the piece with a 'fold-
ing of the cloth' ceremony,[25] and the Guardian of the Well, all wore
face paint resembling masks, and the old man and young man wore
full masks. A striking visual element was the Hawk costume worn by
Ito: 'his arms extended into the wing-sleeves with sticks a là Loie

Fuller, [giving] him an expansive wing span; the black, gold and crème feather patterned headdress, and face and eye make-up, gave the impression of a fierce gaze and predatory beak'.[26] Ito not only choreographed his own movement, but also devised movement for the old and young man and for the musicians. Helen Caldwell, a later dance pupil of Ito's who saw him teach the Hawk dance to Lester Horton (also Ito's student) some years later in the US, describes it as,

> a modified Noh dance – tense, continuous movement with subtle variations on its monotony, inducting a trancelike state in both personages and audience.[27]

In comparison with the theatrical realism prevalent at the time, this esoteric mix of Japanese Noh, ancient Irish myth, Egyptian art and the myriad other influences found in the play must have seemed quite strange for the audience, yet the accounts that survive from the performances in 1916 are very favourable. Winston Churchill's secretary, Edward Marsh, attended the first performance at Lady Cunard's, as did T. S. Eliot. Marsh reports that he got 'quite worked up and impressed', whereas the performance caused Eliot to discard his image of Yeats as 'a minor survivor of the '90s [1890s]', and to view him 'rather as a more eminent contemporary'.[28] Yeats himself was 'pleased', writing, 'I believe I have at last found a dramatic form that suits me',[29] suggesting also that he had, 'invented a form of drama, distinguished, indirect, and symbolic, and having no need of mob or Press to pay its way – an aristocratic form.'[30] Ito's influence on the evolution of this play, and on the 'invention' and development of Yeats' dance play aesthetic in general, cannot be overestimated. Curtis Bradford's study of Yeats' five manuscript drafts and two typescript versions of *At the Hawk's Well* show that over the course of the rehearsal period, Yeats cut several songs and speeches as he became aware of the capacity for communication in Ito's dancing.[31] Ito, who was performing and living in London at the time, was initially recruited by Pound in 1915 to help him understand Fenellosa's texts. There is a degree of mystery surrounding the details of Ito's training in traditional Japanese theatre forms. It is generally believed that he may have had some informal Kabuki training (his biographer Helen Caldwell describes this as 'early training'), however it is certain Ito had no formal education in the classical Noh style.[32] He allegedly become interested in modern dance after seeing Nijinsky and Isadora Duncan perform in Paris where he was studying singing, subsequently leaving Paris to study at the Dalcroze Institute in Hellerau, near Dresden. Émile Jaques-Dalcroze, a professor of music at the music conservatory in Geneva before the founding of the institute, had devised a system of teaching music based on rhythmic principles, which incorporated the body of the student. Following the social trend of his generation's fascination with the concept of rhythm, which was 'discovered [to be a] life-determining principle, the foundation of all being' ('*entdeckte [...] als lebensbestimmendes Prinzip, als Grundlage allen Seins*'),[33] Jaques-Dalcroze wanted to find a way to develop his students' rhythmic sense, which he felt was being stifled by the traditional concentration on technique and theory. A more harmonious integration of rhythm, he believed, would restore the balance between body, mind and soul that had been disrupted by modern industrial living. Concentrating then on the relationship between musical and bodily rhythms, he developed a series of physical exercises, known as 'Rhythmischen Gymnastik' (rhythmic gymnastics) whose aim was to translate every component of a musical score into a corresponding physical movement. Over time this system became so complex that it could be used to create a physicalisation of entire orchestral scores.

Ito's first performances in London were of the Dalcrozian dance compositions he had choreographed in Hellerau, and he called the products of his subsequent choreographic experimentations 'dance-poems'. He found himself, however, having to cater for Western society's desire for Japonism: '[b]ecause I was billed as "The Japanese Dancer," I had to create a "Japanese" atmosphere'.[34] Recruited for being Japanese by Pound and Yeats, Ito was in fact more interested in exploring the meeting of the orient and the occident in his work, stating: '[i]n my dancing it is my desire to bring together the East and the West. My dancing is not Japanese. It is not anything – only myself.'[35] Whatever ambitions Ito had for himself, he seems to have been doomed to a perpetual state of 'otherness' both in Europe, and later in the US, where he went to pursue his career after his collaboration with Yeats. Although he is often categorised under the supposedly racially ambiguous title of 'international artist', his Japanese racial identity led to his imprisonment in an internment camp (originally called a 'concentration camp' by President Roosevelt) in New Mexico

after the bombing of Pearl Harbor during World War II.[36] The orien-
talist gaze that Ito was often subjected to is demonstrated clearly in
the preface of a 1927 review of his dancing that, however objection-
able to current sensibilities, was intended at the time to be positive:
'I sing a song of Mr. Ito, Who dances on his little feet, O, He's Japanese
and very neat, O, He's small and swift like a mosquito'.[37]

It is easy to speculate that Yeats was probably also guilty of essen-
tialising Ito, and indeed a reading of the final scene of Cúchulainn
being bewitched and sexually aroused by a male dancer playing a
supernatural hawk woman which he then chases up a mountain,
is further complicated by the fact that Ito's oriental identity would
have positioned him as feminine in a western patriarchal hegemony.
However, there is little doubt that Yeats had a genuine admiration
for Ito's choreographic skills and found in him a collaborator who
shared a desire for a synthesis of forms and cultures based on a rhythmic structure. Ito's choreography and performance of the dances in
At the Hawk's Well would seem to have embodied Yeats' notions for
his dance play perfectly, and he writes of Ito's craft:

> [I saw him] as the tragic image that has stirred my imagination
> [...]. [H]e was able, as he rose from the floor, where he had been sit-
> ting cross-legged or as he threw out an arm, to recede from us into
> some more powerful life. Because that separation was achieved
> by human means alone, he receded, but to inhabit as it were the
> deeps of the mind.[38]

This description is a good illustration of the accord to be found in
Yeats' thought with the Symbolist belief that the image of the dancer
can gesture towards the transcendent through the 'human means'
of the body, which acts, as Mallarmé proposed, in a metaphorical
capacity.[39] In his use of elements of Noh for the creation of his dance
play idiom, Yeats departs from the Zen Buddhist ideals of 'restraint,
austerity and economy of expression' and the striving toward *yûgen*
(suggestive beauty) that are central to traditional Noh performance.[40]
His use of dance in the climactic scene of his work also differs greatly
from the *kuse mai* (sung-dance) that closes a Noh play, in that instead
of it signifying the 'culmination and celebration of peace attained'
after the climax of the plot, or the 'final manifestation of truth in a
world of illusion', the dances at the end of Yeats' plays are physical

demonstrations of emotional turbulence or conflict that continue the narrative rather than representing a coda to the action.[41] The climax of *At the Hawk's Well* occurred when Ito, who had until this moment remained a motionless, cloaked figure guarding the well, 'suddenly threw off a black cloak to reveal the glittering costume of a hawk and begin the mesmerizing dance that fires Cuchulain's [sic] passion even as it leads him from his quest.'[42] In the drawing-room performances of the play, Yeats placed the audience in close proximity to the actors and Ito's dancing body. Murray draws attention to the fact that '[t]he main point about [the dance plays] is that they are dream plays', which places their action 'at one remove from the audience [...] in some space beyond the real.'[43] Added, then, to this tension between the nearness of Ito's body embodying the Hawk Woman of the well and the gesturing towards another plane of consciousness/the unknown, is the fact that the hawk symbolised death and the supernatural for Yeats.[44] Ito's dancing body, lending flesh to Yeats' words while symbolising the supernatural, was at once earthbound and transcendent, resonating with Alain Badiou's notion that dance can function as 'the permanent showing of an event in its flight, caught in the undecided equivalence between its being and its nothingness'.[45]

Although Yeats had written five dance plays by 1919, his collaboration with Ito on *At the Hawk's Well* was the only one to be performed. These initial stagings, taking place in aristocratic London circles and utilising non-proscenium minimalist settings, were at some remove from what was happening at Dublin's Abbey Theatre at the time. During the Abbey's infancy, Yeats' initial experiments with using movement in a play in his production of *Deirdre* had not met with a favourable reception. Inspired by Oscar Wilde's *Salomé*, which Yeats had seen in London the previous year, the dance elements were judged to be too sensual, and Lady Gregory pronounced the play to be a degradation of the stage.[46] Yeats had left Dublin in 1913 'in some disgust' due to the Abbey's need to rely on more commercial, realist productions following patron Annie Horniman's withdrawal of funding in 1910.[47] Twenty years after *Deirdre*, and ten years after his work with Ito, Yeats finally set about finding an alternative venue in Dublin that would be more appropriate for his experimental style. With his dance plays in mind, he was instrumental in establishing the new Peacock Theatre, adjacent to the Abbey, in 1926. This smaller theatre provided the intimate setting that Yeats wanted for his dance plays, but he was still in need of a dancer/choreographer to replace Ito, who had departed for New York in 1916. The person he found to fill this creative role was Ninette de Valois (1898–2001).

De Valois came into contact with Yeats when he saw her performing her own choreography to a poem by Gordon Bottomley at Terence Gray's Festival Theatre in Cambridge in 1927, where she was working as choreographic director. Impressed with her work, Yeats saw in her the possibility to revive his dance plays, which had not been performed since Ito's departure. 'Ninette de Valois', who went on to found the Royal Ballet in England, was the stage name of the Irish dancer and choreographer Edris Stannus. Born in 1898 in Wicklow, she studied ballet in London with Enrico Cecchetti and danced with the Ballets Russes from 1923–5. Although classically trained, de Valois was greatly influenced by the more modern ballet and demi-caractére choreographers that she came into contact with during her time with the Ballets Russes, such as Michel Fokine, Leonide Massine and Bronislava Nijinska. In a *Dancing Times* interview from 1926, de Valois gives her opinion that, 'the true aim of modern ballet is a serious practical effort to extend the authentic methods of the classical ballet. [...] It is to forward and expand the art of dancing in harmony with the other arts of the theatre'.[48] De Valois had a wealth of experience in diverse 'arts of the theatre'. This included not only work as a solo dance artist, but also choreographing and performing in operas, pantomimes, and revues.

After hearing favourable reports of de Valois' choreography for a production of his own play *An Baile's Strand* at the Cambridge Festival Theatre in 1927, Yeats hoped to recruit de Valois as a movement director for the Abbey, and when he met with her in Cambridge in the same year, he asked her to come to Dublin. Accepting Yeats' invitation, de Valois engaged teachers to set up the Abbey School of Ballet, which was active from 1927 to 1933, and visited Ireland every three months to supervise the teaching at the school and to collaborate with Yeats on the revival of the dance plays.[49] De Valois describes Yeats' intention behind this move as wanting to ensure that, 'the poetic drama of Ireland would live again and take its rightful place in the Nation's own Theatre, and the oblivion imposed on it by the popularity of peasant drama would become a thing of the past'.[50] Although these lofty ambitions to combat the 'popular' were doomed to failure (Yeats himself called his experimentations an 'unpopular theatre'), their first collaboration in 1929 on Yeats' adaptation of his dance play *The Only Jealousy of Emer*, which he renamed *Fighting the Waves*, succeeded in calling attention to an alternative mode of theatre both in Ireland and internationally. Because de Valois refused to speak on stage, Yeats restructured the play so that the speeches of Fand (the character played by de Valois) were turned into dances.[51] This represented a significant further shift in Yeats' work towards a more equal relationship between words and movement. The production also featured masks by the Dutch sculptor Hildo Krop (1884–1970) and a musical score composed by George Antheil (1900–59), who described himself as the 'bad boy of music'[52] and was fascinated by the 'energy and movement of technology', using machine sounds and amplifiers in his work.[53] At home in many genres, Antheil wrote music for film and opera, composed for dancers Mary Wigman and Martha Graham and also worked on an operatic version of *Ulysses* with Joyce. The collaborative team for this production represented an exciting cross-disciplinary meeting of leading avant-garde artists in dance, music, drama and sculpture. Interest in the work extended well beyond Ireland and an article in the New York Times that appeared after the show's premiere in Dublin on 13 August 1929 claimed, 'Yeats, Dutch masks, Russian dancing and American music will constitute a combination without parallel on the Abbey stage'.[54] The production also toured to the Lyric Theatre in Hammersmith the following year when de Valois included it in a triple bill performed by her London dance school, The Academy of Choreographic Art. As with the earlier *At the Hawk's Well*, the innovatory nature of *Fighting the Waves* was acknowledged by many, and Yeats himself, in a rather self-congratulatory mood, writes

> [it] has been my greatest success on the stage since Kathleen ni Houlihan [...] the masks by the Dutchman Krop magnificent and Antheil's music. Everyone here is as convinced as I am that I have discovered a new form by this combination of dance, speech and music.[55]

Yeats was not the only theatre practitioner at the time that was experimenting with a merging of disciplines. Examples of other collaborations between poets/playwrights and dancers/choreographers can also be found in the work of Gabriele D'Annunzio with Ida Rubenstein, or Paul Claudel with Jean Börlin. The newness of a form that combines dance, speech and music can be contested. However it can be argued that Yeats' innovations, made possible by his collaborations with choreographers Ito and de Valois, were indeed 'new' in the degree of integration of the different art disciplines that was achieved. *Fighting the Waves* was met with quite a mixed reception at its premiere in Dublin, with not everyone as enamoured of this new form of theatre as Yeats himself. Dubliner Joseph Holloway, a committed theatre-goer who wrote extensively about his theatre visits in his journals, expresses some bewilderment after seeing the performance of *Fighting the Waves* at the Abbey on Thursday, 13 August 1929:

> I met F. J. McCormick and Eileen Crowe as I came out of the Abbey at 11 o'clock after the ballet *Fighting the Waves* and Mac said to me 'I see you have survived it. Oh, what noise!' [...] It was a pity to waste such talent on such strange materials. In the balcony, people started to leave shortly after the ballet started [...].[56]

The critic for the *Irish Independent* comments on the 'decorative' quality of the dance, and although his review is more tempered, his concluding thoughts are more damaging, as he suggests explicitly that Yeats fails to successfully combine the different disciplines in his dance play:

> The dance of Cuchulain fighting the waves which serves as a prologue and Fand's concluding dance of despair were delightfully decorative and Miss Ninette de Valois and her pupils interpreted them perfectly; but I confess it seemed to me that they were rather pieces of ornament tacked on to the play than that they heightened its emotion or expressed some deeper significance than it is possible to convey in words.[57]

Whether or not the dances seemed 'tacked on' in execution, this criticism is useful in that it highlights the difference between Yeats' experimentations with the intermingling of movement and text from the perspective of a playwright, a shaper of words, and the efforts of contemporary dance theatre practitioners to combine dance and spoken text from the perspective of the choreographer, a shaper of movement. For Yeats, the dancing body was used as a tool within a play to signify the transcendent, the ephemeral, the extra-linguistic; de Valois and her chorus of Abbey Ballet dancers never spoke on stage. It could be argued that Yeats' adaptation of Noh is a diluted, lesser copy of the original, or worse, that in its distortion of the Japanese form, it is guilty of a colonial appropriation of the exotic 'other', both in the form of the already doubly translated texts from Pound and the corporeal form of Ito (including its later developments by de Valois). Yet Yeats did not intend to simply reproduce a version of Noh and it would seem that when the plays were later performed in Dublin, the links to the earlier Japonism influence were being severed. Chris Morash proposes that dating from *Fighting the Waves*, 'Yeats' private search for a form began to coalesce in a type of theatre which can only be described as Yeatsian'.[58] Writing about a performance of the piece in 1930, an *Irish Times* reviewer supports this notion, suggesting that the work was, 'neither poetry, drama, ballet, nor music [yet] being something of all four, is good theatre'.[59] De Valois performed *At the Hawk's Well* for a revival at the Abbey in 1933 and it is interesting to see how she is at pains to distance the dance play from its original Japanese and Egyptian influences in her re-choreographing of the piece. Although visually the production must have looked very similar using the original designs by Edmund Dulac (de Valois even wore Ito's Hawk costume), de Valois is careful to point out that in her search for the 'style and spirit behind it', there was 'no question of pseudo-Oriental productions. It never entered into W.B.'s head at all, or Lennox Robinson's [the then director of the Abbey], and certainly not into mine'.[60] This distancing might indicate that Japonism and the 'pseudo-Oriental' was considered passé in Dublin by 1927, or that de Valois simply felt the need to distance her new choreography from Ito's original work. However, it could also be read as an intimation of a desire to stress a more unambiguously 'Irish' national identity for the transfer from a comparatively liberal and experimental London, to an increasingly conservative Dublin. Alternatively, it might also signify a development within Yeats' own style further away from Noh as an original source of inspiration.

In searching for a way to expand the expressive possibilities of poetry and dramatic text, Yeats experimented with dance in a way that was new for Irish theatre. Yeats was not a choreographer and had no practical interest in the creation of dance, leaving this to the choreographers he chose to collaborate with. Yet, although it could be argued that Yeats' dance plays always originated in the written word and that the primary concern in his use of dance was an exploration of its power to enhance the performance of his text, his experimentations with movement certainly resisted the genre boundaries of dance and theatre performance practice in Ireland. Yeats was well aware of his reliance on choreographers to make his dance plays viable for the stage, writing in the preface to his *Four Plays for Dancers*, that if he attempted to 'arrange and supervise performances, the dancing will give me most trouble, for I know but vaguely what I want'.[61] Both Ito and de Valois were innovators in their own right, and without their input the dance plays would not have been developed for performance. Although Yeats was attempting a dialogue between poetry, movement and music, the separate disciplines always remained distinguishable as distinct entities, as shown in Yeats' own description of *Fighting the Waves*: 'The play begins with a dance which represents Cuchulain fighting the waves, then after some singing by the chorus comes the play'.[62] Yet despite this, Yeats' work is undoubtedly an important predecessor to current interdisciplinary developments. The dance plays, if viewed as an early form of dance theatre, are linked through their choreographers with developments in Europe (Dalcroze and the Ballets Russes) and England (Gray). At a time in Irish history when the postcolonial need for racial, sexual and religious 'purity' of identity was creating strict definitions of permissible bodies, Yeats' dance plays were a wonderful site of exciting experimentation and resistance to the status quo. It is perhaps not surprising that his theatrical innovations did not take root in Ireland as he might have wished, yet his dance plays do have a substantial legacy, both in Ireland and internationally. Samuel Beckett, another playwright deeply interested in the body, declared that he would, 'give the whole of Shaw for a sup of the Hawk's Well',[63] and Yeats is also cited as an influence for playwrights such as Harold Pinter and Edward Bond.[64] Although it was to take many years after Yeats' death before the dance plays were performed again at the Abbey in Dublin, they did continue to be produced internationally. Perhaps the most interesting development is the important role that *At the Hawk's Well* has played in Noh theatre in Japan. Noh scholar Mario Yokomichi's first adaptation of the dance play, *Taka no Izumi* (Hawk's Well), was the first Irish play to be staged in the

Noh form in Japan, and was directed by the Noh actor Umewaka Minoruin in 1949. Yokomichi went on to create a second adaptation, *Takahime* (Hawk Princess), in 1967, which was directed by Noh actor Hisao Kanze. *Takahime* is still regularly performed, and a recent production at the Tokyo Summer Festival in 2005 featured Noh master, Hideo Kanze (1927–2007), as the Old Man. An interesting example of adaptations that occurred during the 1970s are choreographer Jean Erdman's versions of the dance plays for her New York-based company, Theatre of the Open Eye, for which she added to the number of dancers in the original plays and also had new music composed by Teiji Ito, Michio Ito's nephew.[65] The Lyric Theatre in Belfast also began staging the dance plays in the 1970s and *At the Hawk's Well* was finally performed again at the Abbey in 1978, in a double bill with *The Only Jealousy of Emer*, directed by Hideo Kanze and featuring Fiona MacAnna as the Guardian of the Well, Desmond Cave as the Young Man, Michael O'Briain as the Old Man and choreography by Iain Montague. Another significant revival of the dance plays occurred during the Yeats International Theatre Festival, which ran at the Abbey from 1989 to 1993. Produced by James Flannery, this festival staged 15 Yeats plays, including some of the dance plays, and the revival of *A Full Moon in March* in 1991 witnessed a further shift towards the dissolution of the boundaries between disciplines that Yeats' work pointed towards but never quite achieved during his lifetime. This play originally required two performers to play the role of the Queen: an actor who spoke the play-text and a veiled dancer who switched with the actor to perform the danced scenes. For the revival production, the danced and spoken elements of the Queen's role were combined into one by the performer and choreographer Sarah-Jane Scaife, the then movement director at the Abbey. Scaife's straddling of the traditional actor/dancer disciplinary divide in this work was an important precursor of the contemporary developments in dance theatre focussed on in the following chapters of this book.[66]

Erina Brady: 'a mysterious woman to be sure'[67]

As argued in the introductory chapter, the postcolonial project of reinventing an exclusive 'Irish' identity resulted in a promotion of literary expression at the expense of corporeal expression in the arts, and the strict control of the body in society in general. Yeats' dance plays were an exciting development in performance in Ireland, yet perhaps due to their 'strangeness' for an Irish audience and the existing socio-political climate of the time, or perhaps more simply due to the fact that they were not often performed, their influence on future avant-garde performance was arguably greater in an international context (prior to the revivals at the Yeats Festival) than in Ireland itself. In surveying the developments in dance theatre in Ireland after Yeats, it is at first glance tempting to make a leap of about half a century forwards in time to the founding of the Dublin Contemporary Dance Theatre in 1979 by Joan Davis and Karen Callaghan. Certainly, this is the first instance of an Irish company that describes itself as a 'dance theatre' company. However, if an attempt is being made to chart the efforts of those theatre and dance practitioners in Ireland who were concerned with extending the limits of the genre that they were operating within beyond those laid down by convention, an account of a different shape emerges. Larraine Nicholas has observed that the lack of a comprehensive survey of early modern dance in Britain has resulted in a 'gap in the records which could be interpreted as "nothing going on" '.[68] This is also the case in Ireland, where, until very recently, it was thought that there were no early modern dance practitioners. A significant contribution towards filling this gap was made by Jacqueline Robinson (1922–2000), a Second World War refugee (her father was Jewish) whose family left Paris for Dublin in 1941. The author of *Modern Dance in France* (1997), an extensive survey of French dance developments from 1920–70, she donated a manuscript copy of her unpublished text *Modern Dance in Dublin in the 1940s (yes, there was …)* (1999) to the Association of Professional Dance in Ireland shortly before her death in 2000.[69] Just 24 pages in length and including some tantalising photocopies of photographs from Robinson's private collection, this brief but fascinating text provides an account of dancer, teacher and choreographer Erina Brady's (1891–1961) activities in Dublin from 1939 up until Robinson's return to Paris in the late 1940s.

   Born in the German town Bad Homburg vor der Höhe to a Cavan man and a German woman of Irish descent who settled in Switzerland, the particulars of Brady's movements and dance experience before her arrival in Dublin in 1938 are rather hazy and Robinson must resort to making ample use of such words as 'likely', 'perhaps' and 'seems' in her description of Brady's dance training.

A more definite account is given in an article that appeared in the *Independent* in 1941 promoting Brady's first dance recital in Dublin.[70] However, citing this article, Robinson cautions that, 'one can not totally rely on the odd press cutting'.[71] It is presumed that Brady studied classical ballet in Paris with Madame de Consoli, prior to training with Émile Jaques-Dalcroze in Geneva. From there she is believed to have moved to Frankfurt to study, and possibly perform, with Rudolf von Laban (1879–1958) before travelling to Dresden to study, teach for, and again possibly perform, with Mary Wigman (1886–1958).[72] Robinson calls her a 'mysterious woman to be sure', yet if her piecing together of Brady's movements prior to her arrival in Ireland are accurate, Brady was in direct contact with several of the most significant and influential European modern dance practitioners and innovators of her time.[73] Robinson speculates that Brady, possibly in an attempt to escape the increasing tensions in national socialist Germany, arrived in Dublin in 1938. What can be stated with certainty, however, is that Brady opened the Irish School of Dance Art at 39 Harcourt Street, Dublin, in January 1939 (coincidentally the year of Yeats' death) and left Ireland to return to Switzerland in 1951.[74]

Arriving just four years after the passing of the censorial Dance Halls Act, Brady's school can be viewed as a site of danced revolution. Whereas Germany and the US had witnessed cultural movements promoting the expression of the 'natural' body, which had, in turn, influenced early modern choreographers, in Ireland there had been no such movement.[75] In fact there had been a cultural shift in quite the opposite direction, and the Catholic clergy in particular seemed determined to re-enforce a puritanical concept of a 'proper' body based on Victorian principles that were being challenged elsewhere. Although the 1930s saw some important modernising changes happening in Ireland – for example electrification[76] and the establishment of groups such as the National Council of Women, which campaigned for women's rights – Melissa Sihra writes that, 'life was extremely restrictive for the majority of the population, and for women in particular'.[77] Significantly shaped by the social views of the Catholic Church, the first constitution of the Irish Republic (*Bunreacht na hÉireann*) was published in 1937, and in response, women's rights campaigner Hanna Sheehy-Skeffington proposed that it had its foundation in, 'a fascist model, in which women would be relegated to permanent inferiority, their avocations and choice of

callings limited because of an implied invalidism as the weaker sex'.[78]
Legislation such as the Censorship of Publications Act of 1929, that
allowed the state to ban any literature containing information about
contraception, or the 1932 marriage ban, which forced women in
public service and teaching jobs to leave employment on marriage,
can be seen to have established a different class of citizenship for men
and women. It was into this unequal and repressive cultural climate,
in which the 'prevailing image of Irish women [was] as wives and
mothers, an ideal fostered by both church and state',[79] that the 'very
strong [...], very unusual, and very bright' Erina Brady arrived.[80]

Brady's school was to become host to a multitude of activities
including dance classes for children, adults, actors, and aspiring
choreographers, professional dancers and teachers. There were also
music lessons (taught by Robinson), music recitals, lectures in dance
history[81] and regular dance performances. The school comprised of
one large, light-filled studio, and anticipating the 'loft living' of 1970s
New York dance artists by many years, Brady slept in an alcove of
the studio, living and working in her dance space and collapsing
the boundary between her private and public existence. This was an
unorthodox mode of living for a woman in Ireland at the time and
Brady's philosophy of dance was also a new departure for the Dublin
dance scene. Brady gave her first public performance in Ireland in
December 1941 and the title of an article in the *Irish Times* advertising
this recital, 'Barefoot Dancer at the Mansion House', gives an inkling
as to the unconventionality of Brady's style for an Irish audience.[82]
Dancing barefoot was not in itself something new – some of Ninette
de Valois' pieces for the Abbey Stage involved barefoot dancing –
however the style of Brady's dance certainly was. The moniker 'barefoot dancer' was most famously used for the Californian dancer,
choreographer and teacher, Isadora Duncan (1877–1927). Brady cites
Duncan in both the *Independent* and the *Irish Times* articles as being
the 'originator' of her style of dance and Robinson writes that Brady
decided to become a dancer after seeing Duncan perform. Brady
accompanied her solo recitals, which she toured around several
towns in Ireland, with a talk promoting her form of dance and in her
1942 talk in Waterford, she again named Duncan as a central figure
of influence: '[i]n a short talk on Dance as an Art Form, Miss Brady
began by explaining the importance of Dance in the life of primitive
man. She traced the evolution of Dance to the present day, naming

Isadora Duncan as one of the outstanding exponents in recent years of "contemporary dance".[83]

Duncan was one of a group of American female soloists that included Loïe Fuller (1862–1928) and Ruth St. Denis (1879–1968), whose performances contributed to a redefinition of dance at the turn of the twentieth century. Duncan, perhaps the most well known of these dancers, developed a style that was alternately labelled 'natural dancing', 'aesthetic dancing' or 'classic dancing'.[84] Performing alone on a bare stage to musical accompaniment, and dressed in long flowing robes inspired by her studies of ancient Greek art, Duncan sought in her dances to counter the limitations of movement imposed on the female body by conventional dance training, such as ballet training, and the restrictions of Victorian culture on the female body in general. In her essay 'I See America Dancing' (1927), Duncan is at pains to distance her practice from ballet and jazz dance, which she found to be respectively too 'servile' or too 'sensual', citing instead the jigs learned from her pioneer Irish grandmother as a dance origin of her movement vocabulary.[85] Rejecting ballet's codified virtuosity, her dances were made up of 'simple' steps such as hopping, skipping, leaping and running and she borrowed elements from the physical culture movement of her time, which included rhythmical gymnastics and artistic statue-posing. She also rejected the narratives of pictorial theatrical dance, attempting instead a 'free' expression of the soul through the body. In imbuing her dances with theological and philosophical values, Duncan campaigned against Western society's view at the time of dance as a morally and culturally unacceptable pursuit for 'respectable' women, and the general perception of dance as a low art form.[86] In connecting her modern experimentations with the culturally legitimate dances of Greek classicism on the one hand, and the kinaesthetic responses of the upper-class ladies who recognised her movements from their amateur statue-posing and gymnastic pursuits on the other,[87] Duncan achieved a reframing of dance as a 'high' art form. She was also concerned with the nationalist project of developing an 'American' theatrical dance form distinct from contemporary European and African imports and her writings on this matter, particularly in relation to jazz dance, which she believed to have its roots in the 'convulsion[s] of the South African negro', have distinctly racist overtones for a contemporary reader.[88] A parallel could be drawn here with the ambitions of Yeats and the Irish Literary Theatre to forge a 'Celtic and Irish' tradition, where (supposedly) none had existed before. For example, Christopher Morash writes of the Irish Literary Theatre's founders' erasure of an existing tradition and fabrication '*ad ovum*' of a 'new' tradition in order to give themselves the necessary 'empty space' in which to create new idioms.[89]

Erina Brady mentions Duncan both in the promotional material for her performances and for her school, and certainly several parallels can be drawn between them. June Fryer, another of Brady's pupils, speaks of Brady's being, like Duncan, 'very much against classical ballet' and, of course, they were both female dance soloists who performed barefoot.[90] However, although there are arguably traces of, or responses to, Duncan's ethos and style to be found in every modern dance practitioner of her time and beyond, Brady's claim that Duncan is the originator of her practice in the sense of there being any direct correspondence between Brady's and Duncan's choreographic styles, is unconvincing. Robinson makes the point that Brady probably used Duncan's name as a point of reference as it would have been much better known in Ireland at the time in comparison with that of Laban or Wigman. Even though she never performed in Ireland, Duncan's name would have been known due to her international celebrity, which stemmed from, but extended well beyond, the 'dance' world. Although there was no Irish equivalent of the likes of Margaret Morrison in England, who was part of a British movement of 'Hellenic' dancing following on in the Duncanesque mode,[91] Robinson suggests that there was 'a trace of the influence of Isadora Duncan' to be found at the time in Ireland in the form of 'Greek dancing'.[92] However, studying the photographic evidence of Brady's work suggests, as Robinson confirms in her account, that the strongest and most pervasive influences on Brady's work were the teachings and choreographic style of Mary Wigman (1886–1973).

Wigman began her dance training in 1910 at the (relatively) late age of 23 when she left her home in Hannover to enrol herself in Émile Jaques-Dalcroze's new educational institute in Hellarau – the same institute in which Michio Ito would study. As Susan Manning points out, the Dalcrozian system gave Wigman a structured method of formal movement analysis and a way to approach improvisation in which, 'movement became not only a "subjective" response to music but also an "objective" visualisation of musical qualities'.[93] Wigman became an apprentice to Laban in 1913 and began creating solos in the style of *Ausdruckstanz* or *Absoluttanz*, expressionist dance that, 'realizes the modernist ideal of an art that refers solely to its own medium and condition'.[94] Her work quickly gained a large following in Germany and as Melissa Benson and Susan Manning explain,

> [h]er dances embodied the spirit of expressionism, its pervasive angst, and escape into ecstasy. For Wigman, the soloist's projection of the spontaneous self no longer sufficed. She required a form that transcended the individual, a requirement fulfilled by her use of masks, and by her all-female group. [...] Her solos were neither auto-biographical nor overtly feminine, as were Isadora Duncan's; rather, she projected an image of gender that escaped and confounded the conventional distinctions between masculinity and femininity.[95]

Although Brady seems to have relied on the fame and relative respectability of Duncan's name to promote herself and her school, Robinson writes that when talking about her practice to her pupils in the Harcourt Street studio, it was Wigman's name to which, 'she referred so often'.[96] In her Dublin debut at the Mansion House on 9 December 1941, Brady performed 12 short dances choreographed by herself and accompanied by Robinson on the piano, followed by a talk by May Carey about Contemporary Dance Art. The dances seem to have been examples of *Ausdruckstanz* in the style of Wigman; 'The Prisoner' was 'tragic' and set to Fauré, 'The Storm Queen' was 'daemonic' and set to Beethoven, and 'In the Moonlight' was 'delicately lyrical' and set to Prokofiev.[97] The works provoked a very favourable response from the critics, with the wholly positive reviews being quite rapturous and the negative ones still acknowledging Brady's skill as a dancer. The *Evening Mail* recognised the performance to be, 'a milestone in the history of dancing Ireland,'[98] and Liam O'Laoghaire in the *Independent* writes, '[h]er first dance revealed a sureness of purpose with a finished technique that led one to believe that she is possibly the finest dancer that has appeared here in years. Her sense of the stage is remarkable, her feeling for music is sensitive [...] One's impression [...] that of a flawless artistry.'[99] The *Irish Times* reviewer, although he critiques what he perceives as the 'monotony' and 'dullness' that result from Brady's, 'favour[ing] the free bare-foot technique, which combines simplicity with a certain lack of variety [...] which one feels to be just a little too easy', nevertheless professes her to be, 'an excellent dancer, possessing a perfect sense of rhythm, a feeling for music most uncommon, she can express more with her arms than the average dancer can express with her whole body'.[100] After this successful debut, Brady was invited to perform in Cork, Kilkenny and Waterford and also began to choreograph for theatre productions.

In 1944 the Lyric Theatre Company staged a production at the Abbey that included two plays by Austin Clarke (*The Plot is Ready* and *The Viscount of Blarney*) and a piece choreographed by Brady based on Samuel Ferguson's poem *The Fairy Thorn* (1834). A personal letter from Brady to Clarke in 1944 discussing this production gives an insight into the difficulty that Brady was experiencing in getting recognition for her work. The letter opens with Brady reminding Clarke why she had suggested they should collaborate on the production: 'I did so not with an idea of personal gain, but out of my sincere and warm appreciation for the excellence of your work'.[101] She then gets down to business, wryly assuring Clarke that she is certain, 'it was not in your intention that my name should be passed over with dark silence with regard to the *Fairy Thorn*, both in the advance notices and in your curtain speech'.[102] Further on she also wishes that 'it had appeared on the programme that my small group were pupils of my school'.[103] The 'dark silence' that Brady experienced here was to become a source of great frustration, ultimately leading to her departure from Dublin. However, in the following year she began work on what was perhaps her largest project in Ireland: the *Tuberculosis Ballet*. In 1945 the Irish Red Cross Society held a 'Tuberculosis Exhibition' to raise awareness of the disease, and commissioned Brady to choreograph a 'propaganda ballet against tuberculosis'; the *TB Ballet* was opened by then Taoiseach Éamon de Valera at the Peacock Theatre on 28 May 1945 and ran for three weeks.[104] Brady's 'choric dance fantasy' was a dance theatre piece that combined movement with 'choric speech' (including sonnets by Rainer Maria Rilke), and which also featured a score of Mozart, Strauss, and 'a mechanical "machine rhythm"'.[105] The synopsis of the show explains that the masses have been warned of the 'Great Destroyer, Tuberculosis', but choose not to listen.[106] Into their 'modern city life' comes 'The Harbinger of

Disease', which they also ignore by, 'bringing themselves into night life and yet more excitement'.[107] When they contract tuberculosis, their final error occurs when, '[i]nstead of fighting the disease, they become resigned to what they believe to be inevitable'; luckily, however, '[h]elp comes in the form of Hope, Rest, Air and Sunlight, restoring them to Health'.[108] Although the moralistic tone of this work might seem comically didactic in a modern context, and the connection between 'excitement' and a bacterial disease might seem a little dubious, the TB issue was a source of great concern at the time, and there was a genuine need of re-education regarding people's perception of it. An infectious and often fatal disease, tuberculosis is caused by mycobacteria that usually attack the lungs, but can also attack other sites in the body. The disease was associated with a large degree of social stigma in Ireland, as it was long thought to be caused by 'unclean' behaviour. While mortality rates due to TB were in decline at the end of the nineteenth century in countries such as England and Wales, they increased in Ireland, peaking in 1904, when TB was the cause of 16 per cent of all deaths (13,000).[109] Due to the social stigma, many people chose not to report their illness to the TB services set up to care for victims, suffering and dying 'quietly and privately beyond the gaze of officialdom'.[110] Although the mortality rate had dropped to 1.25 per 1000 by 1945, Diarmaid Ferriter writes that, 'much shame was still attached to the condition, with friends of victims often not writing to the sanatorium, but to nearby addresses instead'.[111] An Irish Red Cross Society advertisement in the *Irish Times* publishing the donations raised to support their 'man sized task' of combating tuberculosis in 1946, lists the '[p]roceeds of Ballet per Miss Erina Brady, Peacock Theatre' as having raised nineteen pounds, four shillings and sixpence.[112] Robinson makes no mention of the funds raised by the work, but it can perhaps be concluded that it was very well attended, as she does write that the *TB Ballet* provided an opportunity, 'for Erina's work and Modern Dance to be appreciated by a vast public'.[113] Brady followed this success with another work (billed as a 'dance-drama') at the Peacock the following year: *The Voyage of Maeldune*, which was based on Tennyson's poem, featured narration by George Green and Patrick Nolan, a group of six dancers, and a score including pieces by Chopin, Mussorgsky, Holst, Debussy, Paderewsky and Dukas.[114] Any tensions between Brady and Austin Clarke would seem to have been resolved (at least professionally) by June 1946 when she collaborated with him again on a Lyric Theatre production at the Abbey for which she choreographed a 'tragic poem for players' by Thomas Sturge Moore, titled *Niobe*.

Despite these apparent successes, Brady seems to have become increasingly disappointed in the development of her dance practice in Ireland. In 1948, towards the end of her time in Dublin, Brady founded the 'Dublin Dance Theatre Club', appointing District Justice Kenneth Reddin as President. In an article about the club in the *Sunday Independent* she cites the reason for its founding being the difficulty she was having in securing a stage for her 'modern ballet' performances.[115] The club, located at her Harcourt Street studio, was to provide a venue for, 'the presentation, by local and visiting artists, of Dance Performances, Musical Recitals and Lectures'.[116] An *Irish Times* review by Seamus Kelly, which is rather dismissive in tone, gives a picture of what it was like to attend the first performance at the club in June:

> [a] gold curtain divided the room into stage and auditorium. In the latter, three tiers of raised benches, the sort of thing you would see at a country circus, supported an audience of about 25 people. Other decorations included a huge mass of flowers, clustering around a stove, and a modernistic painting of a lot of pale legs, running away from something.[117]

Kelly, possibly wishing that his own legs could run away, did not enjoy the close proximity to the dancers' bodies that this intimate setting afforded. He declined from discussing the content of the performance 'to the accompaniment of radio gramophone records', except to comment on the unsuitability of viewing dance at such 'close range'.[118] This reaction of incomprehension and dislike to a raw 'bumps and all' encounter with dancing bodies is hardly surprising considering the rather prudish cultural climate of the time, and was probably nothing new for Brady. Nevertheless, this review of her new venture must have been disheartening. Robinson writes that the last years that Brady spent in Ireland were, 'a real struggle both financially, and to obtain the recognition she hoped for – for herself no doubt, but [also] for dance as she conceived it, to which she devoted herself, with no compromise'.[119] Brady's own words, written in 1947, leave no doubt as to her disappointment: 'I simply must get myself out of Dublin or I shall simply die of it [...] Dublin has hurt me so badly [...] By now I have learned to hate Ireland'.[120] By 1952 she had returned to live in Switzerland, where she died in a hospital in Vevey in 1961. Brady's direct influence on the dance scene in Ireland is difficult to establish. Although Robinson left Dublin to continue her dance career in France, Brady's other professional student, June Fryer, did go on to work briefly as a choreographer at Carolyn Swift and Alan Simpson's Pike Theatre, where she created dances for Swift to perform at the theatre's revue evenings, of which the first, *The Follies of Herbert Lane*, premiered in 1953.[121] Brady was well connected to many artists working in other disciplines in Dublin who often came to events held at her Harcourt Street flat, and it can be speculated that her work may have influenced them, or at least encouraged an appreciation of dance in these circles. Robinson reports that those who regularly attended performances and lectures included artist Basil Rakoczi and other members of the White Stag Group, abstract painters Mainie Jellett and May Guinness, film director Liam O'Laoghaire and poet John Betjeman. During their time studying with Brady, and as part of their teacher training, both Robinson and June Fryer taught children's modern dance classes in various schools in and outside of Dublin.[122] However, the classes do not seem to have taken root, and both mention the difficulties that they encountered due to the school authorities' notions of decency. Fryer remembers that in Kilkenny the nuns would not allow her students to dance barefoot[123] and Robinson writes about an incident during a teaching job in a Brigidine Convent where she was summoned to the office of the Mother Superior to be told, 'Miss Robinson I hear that you lifted your skirt, revealing your legs, which furthermore, were in a wide stance. [...] No question of your doing that here.'[124] Second position pliés, the culprits of the 'wide stance', were banned, and Robinson was told that she should teach the class in her coat and skirt. After the first term of classes the local bishop (unnamed) decided that there would be, 'no more dancing classes of that type at the Convent'.[125] It would seem that after Brady left, there was, 'no more dance of that type' performed in Dublin. Summing up the rather bleak end to the Brady era, Fryer suggests, 'Erina's work was very modern. When she left Dublin there was nothing. Just this big gap.'[126]

Dublin Contemporary Dance Theatre

After Erina Brady's departure in the early 1950s, the developing Irish dance theatre seems to have departed with her. Yet, even if there were no home-grown dance theatre performances of note taking place, the end of the travel restrictions caused by the Second World War, known in Ireland as the 'Emergency', re-opened Ireland as a destination for visiting companies. During the decade described by dance and theatre critic Carolyn Swift as the 'halcyon 1950s', the Olympia Theatre, Gaiety Theatre and Theatre Royal in Dublin presented seasons of dance that included productions by dance theatre and classical companies such as the Sadler's Wells Theatre Ballet, the Royal Ballet, American Ballet Theatre, Le Ballet Theatre de Paris de Maurice Bejart, Ballets Jooss, Ram Gopal's Indian Dancers, Japanese Kabuki Dancers, Keita Fodeba's African Dancers, Ximinez-Vargas, Jose Greco and Pilar Lopez's Spanish Dance companies, the Royal Danish Ballet and Ballet Rambert.[127] Swift argues that exposure to the work of these international artists created an appreciation for dance and an Irish dance audience educated in current dance trends that, however, by the time of her writing in 1981 had dwindled in tandem with the decline in visits by international companies, due to the difficult economic climate. Theatre dance in Ireland during the 1950s, 60s and 70s was dominated by classical ballet. Joan Denise Moriarty reigned over the Irish ballet scene for over forty years, and her various dance companies included the Cork Ballet Company (1947–93), the Irish Theatre Ballet (1959–64) and the Irish Ballet Company (1973–83), the latter of which became the short-lived Irish National Ballet (1983–9). This balletic hegemony of the dance scene was reflected in Arts Council funding: as late as 1977, ballet was the only funded dance genre in Ireland and of the total £113,369 awarded to dance, Moriarty's Irish Ballet Company received £110,000, her Cork City Ballet received £1000 and the Dublin Ballet Club received £569.[128] This is parallel to similar developments in Germany, where ballet also dominated during the first two decades after World War II. However, the movement away from the strict hierarchical structure and perceived artistic constraints of ballet, towards the democratisation of dance that gained momentum in the US in the 1960s with the postmodern Judson Dance Theatre choreographers (e.g. Yvonne Rainer, Steve Paxton), or in Germany in the 1970s with the work of *Tanztheater* choreographers (e.g. Pina Bausch, Reinhild Hoffman, Susanne Linke, Johann Kresnik), does not seem to have reached theatre dance performance in Ireland until the early 1980s with the arrival of Dublin Contemporary Dance Theatre (DCDT). With Brady long forgotten, Joan Davis and DCDT were hailed as the pioneers of modern dance in Ireland.[129]

In 1963, a visiting company at the Dublin Theatre Festival inspired Dubliner Davis (b.1945) to join her first modern dance class. The company was the Jean Erdman Theatre of Dance, and the production, *The Coach with the Six Insides* was a multi-award-winning off-Broadway show that had premiered in New York in the Village South Theatre in 1962. Erdman (b.1916) had danced with Martha Graham's first company, but like Merce Cunningham, left to found her own company that broke away from the Graham model. *The Coach with the Six Insides*, alternatively described as a 'dance drama' or a 'musical drama', was a dance theatre version of Joyce's *Finnegan's Wake*; a combination of 'dance, mime and Joycean stream of consciousness'.[130] Creating an intriguing link with Irish dance theatre history, the original music for the piece was composed by Michio Ito's nephew, Teiji Ito, who, as mentioned earlier, was later to work with Erdman on her versions of Yeats' dance plays. *The Coach with the Six Insides* charts the 'life cycle' of Joyce's mother character ALP (Anna Livia Plurabelle), and an *Irish Times* review of the version that toured to Dublin described the piece as a 'prismatic presentation which distils every nuance of beauty and horror from the spoken word, the body's agility, and the equivocal musical score'.[131] Having attended tap dancing classes as a child at the Evelyn Burchill School of Dancing in Harcourt Street, this work was Joan Davis' first experience of contemporary dance, inspiring her to begin attending the Graham technique classes of Terez Nelson in Dublin at the relatively late age of 29. Nelson had trained with Graham in the US before founding the Terez Nelson Dance Group at her Monkstown studio in 1973, and Davis took part in the Dance Group's first performance at St Mark's Hall, Pearse Street, in 1975. In 1976 Davis founded the Dublin Contemporary Dance Studio in Harold's Cross, teaching the contemporary dance techniques she studied on her biweekly weekend trips to the open classes at the London School of Contemporary Dance, and later engaging dancers she met there to come and teach in Dublin. In 1979 Davis founded the Dublin Contemporary Dance

Theatre with Karen Callaghan (who departed for New York after the first year), and in the same year, the company presented its first work at the Project Arts Theatre in Dublin.[132] Finola Cronin, who worked with Davis on an early work set to the music of Eric Satie at the Project, before going on to dance with Pina Bausch in Wuppertal, believes that all developments in contemporary dance in Ireland can be traced back to the experiments of DCDT.[133] Over the course of its 10-year existence, the company had various members; however the core group for most of the performances was made up of Davis, Robert Connor and Loretta Yurick, who became Co-Artistic Directors with Davis.

DCDT functioned as a repertory company, performing original works choreographed by both company members and visiting guest choreographers, predominantly from the US. In a company manifesto written in 1986,[134] Davis describes the company style as being founded in contemporary dance (rather than ballet or jazz) and that the different contemporary techniques used in the company's works reflect the different training backgrounds and ages of the dancers who perform in them. When choosing what style to use in particular works, both the choreographic needs of the company and the 'Irish temperament' were considered. It is not the company's temperament that is implied here, as a large number of dancers working with DCDT were not Irish (for example half of the core group, Connor and Yurick, are American, and early collaborators Ruth Way and Judy Cole are English), but rather the temperament of their audience. DCDT always strove to create works that were accessible and relevant to a wide audience base. The company were also acutely aware that contemporary dance was 'new' in Ireland, acknowledging the need to build an audience base for the art form. The emphasis placed by DCDT on their educative role seems to have informed many of the artistic choices made, including their choice of guest choreographers, who were chosen both for their ability to expand Irish audiences' horizons and their ability to contribute to the artistic development of the company.

Due to their all-encompassing ethos of inclusion, the eclectic works of DCDT ranged in genre from postmodern pieces in the pedestrian style of Judson Dance Theatre, to productions that had a more narrative-based approach, to works incorporating explicit sociopolitical critique. An example of the use of aleatoric methods in the style of Merce Cunningham is to be found in works like Ruth Way's *Passing Time* (1980), which included an audience-directed 'improv' in which, as Carolyn Swift explains, 'a delighted audience is allowed to devise patterns and dynamics by calling out numbered sequences to dancers identified by colours'.[135] *Word Works* (1985) was a series of short, humorous pieces devised around everyday phrases: *Eireann Go Breá* included movement inspired by responses to the word 'Ireland' such as 'lovely between showers' and 'rosary beads and large families', whereas *Telecom Erring* involved a frustrated Connor trying to get a public telephone (played by Davis, Mary Nunan and Yurick) to function.[136] Several pieces explored the meeting of movement and text by Irish writers such as Nunan's solo work *Search* (1983), in which she attempted, 'a synthesis of mind and body',[137] using spoken text from Samuel Beckett's prose poem *Company* (1979). Similarly, guest choreographer Jerry Pearson's *Lunar Parables* (1986) used spoken text from Yeats poems and sought to investigate Yeats' interest in the 'power of symbols [...] using words, music and slides which link ancient celtic designs with lunar and galactic images of outer space'.[138] Featuring actor Niall Tóibín, the score for the work included music by De Danaan, Clannad, Stockton's Wing, the Bothy Band and Derek Bell. Using a more direct storytelling approach, *Ishmael* (1979), choreographed by Davis for three dancers and featuring live drumming by Sean Devitt and recorded music by the Dollar Brand Quartet, was a dance theatre piece about a barren woman who makes her servant bear her husband's child. Direct socio-political critique was to be found in works such as Sara and Jerry Pearson's *Acid Rain* (1982), set to music by Meredith Monk, which saw the company 'wilting from pollution, while the self-deception of mankind refuses to recognise how terminal is the menace from above',[139] and *Anna Livia* (1981), choreographed by Davis, which delivered an 'exploration of personal response in movement and words to the squabbles and confusions of Dublin politics, conveyed by [a] soundtrack of press cuttings and radio news'.[140] Although the vast majority of DCDT productions consisted of a bill of short works performed by the core company members, they also produced full-length works such as *Bloomsday: Impressions of James Joyce's Ulysses* (1988). Choreographed by Jerry Pearson, *Bloomsday* was produced for the Dublin Theatre Festival at the Lombard Street Studio and brought together a mixed cast of dancers, singers and actors who all performed in each other's disciplines. Focussing on the 'themes of love [and] Molly Bloom's big brass bed',[141] the piece enjoyed a very positive response from the critics, and Mary MacGoris, commenting on *Ulysses'* reputation as being a difficult read, suggests that this physical re-imagining of the literary masterpiece is, '[p]ossibly the most painless Joyce of the century', as it, 'joyously fleshes the bones of *Ulysses* while relieving them of some of the larding of self-regarding loquacity'.[142]

The Arts Council awarded the company its first grant of £1000 in 1979 and, apart from the cuts of 1982, which saw funding withdrawn from many small dance and theatre companies including DCDT, their grants increased annually. However, following an award of £81,200 in 1988,[143] the company's funding was cut completely in the major Arts Council revision of dance funding in 1989, forcing its closure. The decision came as a shock to the company, particularly due to the fact that Peter Brinson had commended the work of DCDT in his 1985 Arts Council report, *The Dancer and The Dance*, suggesting that qualitative issues[144] could be resolved through better funding, and recommending that DCDT should be supported, 'if Ireland is to have a modern dance company'.[145] The loss of DCDT was an undeniable blow for the dance community. However, former members went on to play highly influential roles in the Irish dance landscape and the subsequent founding of companies such as Dance Theatre of Ireland (founded by Robert Connor and Loretta Yurick, 1989), Irish Modern Dance Theatre (John Scott, 1991), Daghda (Mary Nunan, 1988) and MaNDaNCE (Paul Johnson, 1991) kept alive the creative momentum and growing dance audience built up by DCDT over the years.

Parallel to the work of DCDT, further significant developments in dance and physical theatre were taking root in the 1980s. The Grapevine Arts Centre (1973–89), later renamed the City Arts Centre (1989–2002), was established by three Dublin teenagers in the early 1970s as a 'support and production network' for contemporary arts.[146] Initially operating the organisation out of their bedrooms in the northside Dublin suburbs of Artane and Cabra, Jackie Ahern, Anto Fay and Sandy Fitzgerald set up their first public base at 53 Mary Street in 1974. The location of the centre moved several times during the decade, finally ending up at its current Moss Street location on Dublin's City Quay. The Grapevine Centre was to become a crucible for experimental dance and theatre performance in Dublin throughout the 1980s. One of the choreographers who regularly taught and performed at the centre was t'ai chi teacher Kalichi, who, after working in children's theatre with Tom McGinty (also known by his street artist name, The Diceman), established his Liberation Dance Workshop at the centre in 1979 (−85). This workshop was used as an experimental base and recruitment site for Kalichi's 'dance plays', and he explains that the dancers used in his pieces were not formally trained, but had 'a commitment to explore new ideas about how dance could connect to dreams, moods, music, issues of power, male/female dynamics and a changing political landscape'.[147] Kalichi cites his main influences for these works as being, 'the spirit of Isadora Duncan' and the dance plays of Yeats. He was (and continues to be) particularly interested in exploring Yeats' legacy, believing there to be, 'a wealth of possibilities in re-imagining Yeats' notions of "dance plays" and its potential for an "Irish" form of dance theatre'.[148] In 1981 Kalichi's *Raven's Yellow Eye* was performed in the studio base-ment of the Grapevine's 50 North Great George's Street location. The movement for the piece was based on Kalichi's t'ai chi vocabulary and the performance included poems by Dane Zajc (*All the Birds*) and Marge Piercy (*Rape Poem*), masks by Jackie Aherne, and a soundscape that included traditional music from Japan and Java, the Rolling Stones, and (intriguingly) 'Dublin street rhymes'.[149] Swift describes it as, 'an ambitious project, seeking to ally music, movement, poetry, philosophy and sound in a series of episodes [...]'.[150] Swift was not convinced that this eclectic mix was successful as a performance, but generously adds that Kalichi has, 'succeeded in filling the free time of a number of people in exploring ideas and movement for their own benefit and that of audiences'.[151] Her review of the 1982 piece, *Refugee in the Empire*, is not so forgiving however, and the overuse of repetition in Kalichi's lengthy solo caused her to regret that the, 'nuclear countdown did not lead to his destruction'.[152] Raymond Keane, who practiced 'alternative hair cutting' in his Hairwork Stu-dio at the Grapevine centre ('with a whole philosophical approach to hair and social consciousness'),[153] performed in Kalichi's final Liberation Dance Workshop piece, *Foreign Territory*, in 1984. Keane later went on to found Barabbas The Company, which specialises in theatre of the clown, mime and physical theatre, with Veron-ica Coburn and Mikel Murfi in 1993. In 1980, Vincent O'Neill, a graduate of Marcel Marceau's International Mime School in Paris, founded Ireland's first mime company, the Oscar Mime Company. O'Neill's training in mime was to become an essential ingredient for a staged version of Patrick Kavanagh's poem, *The Great Hunger*, at Dublin's Peacock Theatre in 1983. The production was a devised collaboration between playwright Tom Mac Intyre, director Patrick Mason, and actors Tom Hickey, Bríd Ní Neachtain, Vincent O'Neill, Conal Kearney (also a graduate of Marceau's mime school), Fiona MacAnna and Martina Stanley. Bernadette Sweeney writes that Mac Intyre, who was influenced by his encounter with dance theatre in New York in the 1970s, and had previously written and produced a piece for US-based Calk Hook Dance Theatre in 1979, was interested in, 'combin[ing] language with the immediacy of movement, an appreciation of the physical presence of the actor and the implied "language" of image'.[154] *The Great Hunger* is often cited as a watershed event in the Irish theatre landscape, representing a radical departure in style from what was going on at the time. However, as has been shown here, it must also be noted that there had been several works by dance theatre choreographers produced prior to *The Great Hunger* that were also experimenting with the entwining of the physical and the textual in the interpretations of poems and other texts. Sarah-Jane Scaife and Olwen Fouéré are further examples of highly influential performers who were both engaged with projects that mixed genres and explored physicality in this period. Scaife trained in New York (1983–7) where she studied modern dance with the Eric Hawkins Dance Company, Polish physical theatre with Stephan Niedzialkowski, and Japanese Butoh with Maureen Odo. On her return to Dublin she felt it was time for Irish practitioners to, 'put [their] bodies on the line' in searching for ways to use physicality.[155] She appeared in Mac Intyre's *Snow White* in 1988 (as did Fouéré) and became the movement director at the Abbey theatre in 1989 (–93). During this time she worked as a performer, puppeteer and choreographer for the Yeats International Theatre Festival, also directing a series of five one-act plays by Samuel Beckett in 1990. Fouéré founded the Operating Theatre Company with composer Roger Doyle in 1981 (–2008), which sought to integrate music as an 'equal partner' in devised (often physical) theatre. Of particular interest to this project is Fouéré's work with Fabulous Beast Dance Theatre on their productions *The Bull* (2005), *The Rite of Spring* (2009) and *Helen and Hell* (2010).

In this chapter I have attempted to trace the activities of some of the most notable resistive practitioners working in the space between dance and theatre in Ireland up until the 1990s. The overview of Irish dance theatre practice that emerges posits the argument that the 'new' dance theatre of contemporary companies such as CoisCéim Dance Theatre and Fabulous Beast Dance Theatre is in fact building on the precedent set by Yeats at the beginning of the twentieth century and continued by a network of dancers, choreographers and physical theatre practitioners through to the present day. Within the performance landscape, echoes of Yeats' modernist experiments in merging movement and text can be traced through Brady's work at her Harcourt Street studio and at the Abbey and Peacock theatres in the 1940s, to the Grapevine Arts Centre experiments of the 1970s and early 1980s, to the eclectic works of the Dublin Contemporary Dance Theatre and the incorporation of French mime techniques by physical theatre companies/practitioners, and on to the work of the contemporary companies and practitioners in the 1990s and beyond. Within the theatre landscape this experimental approach to the physical can be found in the work of writers such as Beckett and MacIntyre. In addition to Barabbas The Company and Operating Theatre, further physical theatre companies that emerged in the 1990s include Blue Raincoat Theatre Company (1991), whose founder Niall Henry studied mime in Paris with Maximilian Decroux, and The Corn Exchange Theatre Company (1995), whose director Annie Ryan makes use of various corporeal techniques such as *commedia dell'arte*, Lecoq, and Ann Bogart's Viewpoints method.

With the exception of *The Great Hunger* and a few other notable productions, the earlier challenges to the primacy of literary theatre in the 1980s were perhaps not as accomplished and 'sure-footed' as those of the 1990s and beyond and, perhaps inevitably, they were not always well received or understood by the public. An example of a well-meaning, but rather lost, critic can be found in a 1982 *Cork Examiner* review of a DCDT show:

> [a]lthough contemporary dance is unfamiliar to Irish audiences, its potential is limitless. But to the untrained and inexperienced eye it initially appears to lack form or pattern. The dancers' techniques seem very basic, indeed almost primitive, but there is no doubting their skills. It just takes a bit of getting used to, but the result is very

interesting. [The audience], like me, appeared to need to discuss and analyse this unusual dance experience before finally deciding whether they liked it or not.[156]

In a 2006 interview Davis remarks that she continues to encounter, 'very fixed and limited views' of what dance is; however she also notes that dance is, 'still down at the bottom, but it's a hundred times better than it ever was'.[157] Although dance theatre and physical theatre forms can be seen to have achieved a certain level of critical mass in the 1990s, the genre-defying nature of some dance theatre works in the first decade of the twenty-first century have continued to push against established notions of 'what dance is' in Ireland. The following chapter will examine how choreographers such as Keegan-Dolan, Bolger, Dunne and Butler continue to resist these notions by contextualising their practice within both the contemporary dance landscape in Ireland, and international dance theatre practice from the *Tanztheater* of Kurt Jooss to the present.

3

Genre Debates: the Dance and the Bathwater

Following the discussion of the historical development of dance theatre in Chapter 2, this chapter locates the practice of contemporary dance theatre choreographers within the context of both the current Irish dance landscape and international dance theatre practice. As shown in the previous chapter, although there are several examples of interdisciplinary choreographies to be found in Ireland prior to the work of companies in the 1990s and beyond, the earlier practitioners found it difficult to achieve any substantial level of support or understanding for their work. Although they themselves were connected to international developments, Yeats, Brady and Davis were situated in geographic isolation from their European and US peers, and were all considered to be operating as lone pioneers in Ireland, struggling to forge a niche for their dance theatre practice in a largely unwelcoming cultural terrain. In contrast with this, the wave of dance companies founded in Ireland in the early 1990s began to establish a critical mass in the area of contemporary dance, and so when CoisCéim and Fabulous Beast emerged in the mid-90s, they joined a small, yet vibrant, contemporary dance scene. Yet the work of these two companies, positioned as it is between dance and theatre, differed in content and aesthetic from the practice of other dance companies. In order to understand how the work of Fabulous Beast and CoisCéim goes against current trends in contemporary dance, the first part of this chapter is structured around an investigation of the genre questions raised by their work. The cultural anxiety created by dance works that deviate from established norms will be addressed, and the historical division of contemporary dance in Ireland into the categories of 'pure dance' and 'dance with text' will also be discussed. The final part of the chapter will examine how genre-questioning choreographies can playfully re-imagine the very techniques that shape the bodies that dance them. To do this I will discuss the work of Jean Butler and Colin Dunne, two choreographers trained in the competitive Irish step dance technique who have created dance theatre pieces that attempt to re-imagine the 'Irish' step-dancing body.

'Jumping up and down, usually to music, but not always'

As this study argues that the work of choreographers such as Bolger and Keegan-Dolan contributes to a movement of aesthetic change in Irish performance and socio-political change in Irish culture, it is necessary to situate their works in context with other contemporary dance practice in Ireland. An interrogation of dance's ontology is not the aim of this study; however, in attempting to understand how these choreographers are working outside genre norms and current dance trends, it will be helpful to take a brief look at how the question 'what is dance' has been debated recently in an Irish context. This question, rather surprisingly, became a legal issue for the inaugural International Dance Festival of Ireland in 2002 (now the Dublin Dance Festival) when a performance of French choreographer Jérôme Bel's eponymous piece, *Jérôme Bel*, prompted audience member Raymond Whitehead to sue the festival on the grounds of obscenity and false advertisement. Bel's work, recognised as a seminal work of conceptual postmodern dance,[1] famously, or perhaps infamously, includes a scene where naked performers manipulate their genitals, and another in which two performers, again naked, urinate on the stage floor. Mr Whitehead objected to the nudity and the performance of lewd acts, but more importantly, he argued that *Jérôme Bel* was advertised as 'dance', but that in his opinion it was not. In a letter to the *Irish Times*, Whitehead described the necessary components required for a performance to be defined as a 'dance' performance as being, 'people moving rhythmically, jumping up and down, usually to music but not always' and that while doing this the dancers should convey emotion.[2] Luckily for the Festival, and more generally for the question of art censorship in Ireland, Whitehead lost his case.

It is easy to dismiss Whitehead's definition as either ridiculously over-generalised and reductive or simply not very well-informed, yet his description nevertheless raises several fascinating issues that are helpful in addressing the genre questions presented by the label 'dance theatre' in association with the works discussed here. Although completely different to Bel's brand of analytical, conceptual dance, some of the dance theatre examined in this book also creates ontological anxiety regarding 'dance' in an Irish context, and the placement of certain works under the term. Ironically, Whitehead's list of the components that are needed for a work to be defined as 'dance' are indeed all present in the pieces that will be analysed; there are people, they often move rhythmically, they sometimes execute jumping movements, this frequently occurs to musical accompaniment – but not always – and, relatively unusually for contemporary dance, the choreographies are expressive. Where they depart from this definition is in their addition of a multitude of further components into the mix: narrative is used and stories are told; scripts are incorporated and dancing bodies speak; pedestrian movement is used that does not always look like 'dance' movement; movement vocabularies from 'high art' dance forms are used alongside vernacular and folk forms; song is used and sometimes dancers play musical instruments; 'non-dancers' move alongside trained dancers; occasionally, technology creates digital bodies that dancers move 'with', and so on. Different combinations of elements from this expanded list of components would seem to constitute nothing especially out of the ordinary for contemporary dance theatre performance. However, looking to a recent example in Ireland, Keegan-Dolan's work *James Son of James* (2007) for Fabulous Beast provoked a debate that, while very different in its particulars, gave rise to another round of genre questioning. During a post-show discussion of *James Son of James* at the Samuel Beckett Theatre in October 2007, Keegan-Dolan was asked which genre he believed his company's work belongs to: Dance? Physical theatre? Theatre? Dance theatre? Obviously used to being asked this question, he answered that he refuses to label his work as belonging to any particular genre, and that his work is reviewed in Ireland by confused theatre critics, in England by confused dance critics and that he himself considers it to be 'indefinable'. In a rather damning review of the piece for the *Irish Times*, theatre critic Peter Crawley's main complaint was that it, '[relies] heavily on a dialogue drained of nuance and a less-than-subtle scenario', and that 'it largely neglects the transcendent powers of movement and thickens the suspicion that the company has thrown the dance out with the bathwater'.[3] The mixture of the use of dance and theatrical tools to tell a story results, for Crawley, in a 'fitful [...] and a garbled message' and the positive remarks he makes relate to the sections that he could define as 'pure dance' scenes; duets which were 'sometimes exquisite, sometimes ribald [and sometimes] sexually-charged'.[4] Similarly, the *Irish Times* dance critic, Michael Seaver, notes that in *James Son of James*, Keegan-Dolan, 'seems to have jettisoned movement for text and, in this production, song',[5] and Helen Meany, writing for *The Guardian*, is unconvinced by the 'unfocused mix of genres and disciplines' in the work and wishes for more of the piece to be devoted to pure dance, complaining that the 'magnificent dancers' were 'underused'.[6] Qualitative judgements aside, it might be fair to presume that the show did not fit the critics' expectations from an analytical perspective of either a theatre piece, or a dance piece. Dancing bodies that speak in order to tell a story are somehow shattering the traditional image of the ephemeral (because mute) dancing body in Ireland, and *James Son of James* cannot be pinned down as belonging to an identifiable positioning in the continuum of existing theatrical practices in Ireland. Keegan-Dolan is not alone in meeting with these reactions to his work. Colin Dunne has also encountered puzzlement as a result of the frequent breaking of genre rules in his choreography. Dunne explains that his recent solo work, *Out of Time* (2008), was an experiment that tried to fuse four different elements together in an exploration of his relationship with traditional Irish step dance: a practical and theoretical study of contemporary dance, archival footage of step dancers in the West of Ireland, experimental sound technology, and a new found 'theatricality' discovered in his work with Keegan-Dolan.[7] During a post-show discussion in Limerick, an audience member expressed a wish that there had been more 'proper dancing' in the piece.[8] The picture that starts to emerge from these criticisms is that, in being dance theatre works, these choreographies are necessarily departing radically from a notion of 'pure dance', yet intriguingly, they also seem to be pushing beyond an established notion of dance theatre in an Irish context.

Dance and text

In her forward to a collection of interviews with choreographers working in Ireland in 2003, Diana Theodores identified two main branches of contemporary theatrical dance practice in Ireland that divides the scene into choreographers who were 'grappling with words and language in relation to dance' and choreographers who shunned text and narrative with a 'much voiced aspiration for "pure dance"'.[9] Although there are inherent problems in dividing contemporary dance practice in Ireland so neatly into two opposing camps, it would seem that the choreographers discussed in this book would have to be placed into the 'words' branch. Nevertheless, it is important to note that these choreographers have produced works (often earlier works than those interrogated here) that have more in common with Theodores' 'pure dance' category. It could be suggested that within Theodores' grouping of the choreographers who are working with words, a further distinction can be made which divides the group into those who are working in a more clearly recognisable 'postmodern' mode (Dance Theatre of Ireland, Irish Modern Dance Theatre), and those who use narrative to tell stories (CoisCéim and Fabulous Beast). Giving an overview of the dance scene in 2002, Seona MacRéamoinn also sets up a dichotomy between 'theatre dance' and 'pure' dance companies. Interestingly, however, she also expresses the opinion that those companies working with narrative and with 'text and technology' are somehow at an inferior stage of development. She notes an 'evidence of a retreat from dance as drama, and some advance to the more abstract ground of dance as pure movement', and 'senses [...] that there is a question of confidence in exposing physical movement, unadorned and free-standing, and an anxiety about whether such movement can sustain itself with enough impact in its fundamental relationships with music, light and space'.[10] Apart from the contradiction of an 'unadorned and free-standing' pure dance that has a 'fundamental' relationship with music, this description bears a strong resemblance to Sally Banes' now disputed Greenbergian description of the 'modernist' aesthetic of postmodern dance.[11] As Ramsay Burt proposes, 'Banes [...] believed that formally pure, abstract dance was more sophisticated than the representational types of dance'.[12] MacRéamoinn goes on to hope that the exposure to international work at the inaugural International Dance Festival will 'help focus the mind and steel the nerve' of choreographers in Ireland in the 'challenge of grappling with pure movement'.[13] Five years later, in her introduction to Dance Ireland's 2007 publication *A Guide to Independent Choreographers and Dance Companies*, MacRéamoinn notes that choreographers in Ireland have moved away from the 'narrative strain' of dance-making, and that, 'there has been a shift away from fully representational work [...] towards innovation and the more experimental techniques and collaborative processes'.[14] The use of narrative and storytelling, in opposition to the 'advancement' of a pure dance teleology, interestingly positions dance theatre choreographers as being at odds with the official narrative of dance development in Ireland.

MacRéamoinn is not alone in voicing an opinion that choreographies using narrative and mixed media demand a lesser level of creative inventiveness and courage, or are somehow rooted in an outdated mode of practice, which must be left behind in pursuit of a more 'advanced' purity. It is echoed later on in this discussion, in Keegan-Dolan's fear that his use of narrative and a hybrid mix of dance and performance styles would be viewed as 'really naff' in a contemporary dance climate sceptical of dance that speaks directly of social and political issues.[15] It is also reminiscent, as mentioned above, of the wider debate surrounding definitions of postmodern dance, and the difficulty that the anachronistic expressionism in the work of Pina Bausch poses to those who view pure dance, and the pursuit of a formalist aesthetic, as being more 'truly' postmodern. As Burt suggests, this makes Bausch the 'bogey figure' for many dance scholars.[16] This overview goes towards establishing a sense of how the works of Keegan-Dolan and Bolger are regarded by some as similarly 'bogey' within current performance trends in Ireland.

Questions of genealogy

Attempting to position these Irish dance theatre works within an international context raises some interesting genealogical questions. To date, the only publication that I am aware of that attempts this is anthropologist Helena Wulff's study of dance in Ireland, *Dancing at the Crossroads* (2007), which includes a chapter on Irish dance theatre and ballet, titled 'Storytelling Dance', that refers to some of the early work of both Bolger and Keegan-Dolan. Wulff describes Irish dance theatre as 'a type of contemporary or modern stage dance with Russian roots'.[17] She proposes that the

> Ballets Russes [...] represents a turning point in the history of ballet: its choreography and the way some of it was executed were early signs of a break with ballet. In conjunction with the modernist movement in the arts, this would develop into modern dance, now often referred to as contemporary dance, and later dance theatre, first in the United States, and moving from there to Germany.[18]

This description is clearly only intended to provide a very broad outline, yet its brief account of the genealogical development of dance theatre raises some questions that need to be addressed. Certainly the experiments of the Ballets Russes in creating a total art form that combined music, visual art and movement were highly influential in the development of theatre dance (and in many other cultural fields), and Nijinsky's *L'Aprés-midi d'un faune* (1912) is often considered the first modernist ballet.[19] Yet Lynn Garafola points out that the most direct and important influence of the Ballets Russes on theatre dance was in fact in the area of the *danse d'école* as developed by the choreographers Michel Fokine and George Balanchine.[20] In the context of dance theatre, the influence of previous developments in early modern dance can just as easily be claimed as the 'turning point'. Before the 'early signs of a break with ballet' displayed in Ballets Russes productions, an early modern dance tradition was well underway in the choreographies and theories of practitioners such as Émile Jaques-Dalcroze, Rudolf von Laban, Loïe Fuller, Isadora Duncan and Ruth St. Denis, who were all working outside the ballet tradition. Dee Reynolds, for example, argues that, '[c]inematic art, multimedia, abstract performance, interactivity, contemporary dance: at the end of the nineteenth century, Loïe Fuller had already invented everything'.[21] Furthermore, the idea that modern dance is an American creation that 'moved' from the US to Germany has been challenged by dance scholars since the late 1970s.[22] Indeed within an Irish context, early modern dance developments in Germany can be seen to have had an important influence on the evolution of dance theatre in Ireland, and any account of the international development of dance theatre must include a consideration of the beginnings of *Tanztheater*, the German form of dance theatre.

Tanztheater: socially engaged dance theatre

In 1910 Émile Jaques-Dalcroze founded his institute in Hellerau, near Dresden, where he would develop his 'eurhythmics' method of teaching music, and a new performance style that attempted to corporealise musical scores. In 1912, collaborating with theatre innovator and stage and lighting designer Adolphe Appia, and the painter Alexander von Salzmann, he presented a performance of Gluck's *Orpheus and Eurydice*. Considered to be 'seminal to the history of western theatre',[23] and heralded by artists and critics as representing a 'sign of a new union of the arts',[24] the production experimented with the merging of movement, space, light and sound. A revival the following year was attended by 5000 people, among whom were such familiar names as George Bernard Shaw, Harvey Granville Barker, Max Reinhardt, Sergei Diaghilev, Vaslav Nijinsky, Anna Pavlova, Konstantin Stanislavski, Paul Claudel, Rudolf von Laban, Hugo von Hofmannsthal and Sergei Rachmaninov.[25] The influence of Jaques-Dalcroze's training method on the development of modern dance was immense, and his pupils included Mary Wigman, teacher of Erina Brady, Michio Ito, who worked with Yeats on his dance plays, and Myriam Ramberg (a former colleague of Ninette de Valois), who changed her name when she joined the Ballets Russes to Marie Rambert, helped Nijinsky with interpreting Stravinsky's score and creating the choreography for *Le Sacre du Printemps*, and later founded England's first modern dance company.[26] Another important influence on the development of dance theatre was the German choreographer and dance theoretician Rudolf von Laban who established a school in Munich concurrently with Jaques-Dalcroze's Hellerau Institute. Wigman also studied with Laban, as did Kurt Jooss, who is viewed as the father of *Tanztheater* (dance theatre). The term *Tanztheater* was actually coined by Laban to describe his theoretical development of *Ausdruckstanz* (dance of expression). Laban believed that the creation of an interdisciplinary total-art form would help combat the alienation caused by industrialisation, promoting 'a sense of community among members of a fragmented society'.[27] However it is Jooss' work that is usually credited with the genesis of

the form that later choreographers, such as his former pupil Pina
Bausch, would develop into *Tanztheater* as it is known in its various
incarnations today. In her monograph on Jooss, Patricia Stöckemann
proposes that

> [a]ls eine der ersten hat Jooss gesellschaftspolitische Themen und
> Typen aus allen sozialen Schichten auf die Tanzbühne gebracht
> [...] Abstraktionen haben ihn weniger interessiert als konkrete
> Inhalte und Aussagen. Sein Choreographien waren Erzählungen
> über den Menschen, in Form von Märchen oder aus dem Leben
> gegriffenen Geschichten. Macht, Tod, Liebe, Zerstörung, Krieg und
> die Verführbarkeit des Menschen sind wiederkehrende Motive in
> seinem choreographischen Werk.[28]

> [Jooss was one of the first to bring socio-political themes and char-
> acters from all social strata onto the dance stage [...] He was less
> interested in abstractions and more interested in concrete sub-
> ject matter and statements. His choreographies were stories about
> people in the form of myths or stories captured from life. Power,
> death, love, destruction, war and the seducibility of humans are
> recurring themes in his choreographic works.]

His seminal work, *Der grüne Tisch* (*The Green Table* (1932)), was a
powerful critique of war, and when put under pressure by Hitler's
government to fire his Jewish dancers, he chose instead to leave
Germany. While in exile in Dartington, England, Jooss and his partner Sigurd Leeder set up a dance school, where Laban also taught for
a period. During a second touring season of the English provinces
in 1939, Jooss and his company, Ballets Jooss Dance Theatre, brought
The Green Table to Dublin for the first time,[29] where he also gave a lecture on his practice.[30] Jooss was often confronted with the problem
of categorising his work and saw himself as operating between two
traditions: Laban's modern innovations on the one hand, and on
the other, Jean-Georges Noverre's eighteenth-century ballet reform,
which called for dance to convey meaning as opposed to dance for
dance's sake or as a display of virtuosity.[31] Echoing Noverre, George
Bernard Shaw, after being horribly bored at a ballet performance with
'an intolerable deal of drill' in 1893, pleads with the ballet-master,
dancer and manager to, '[m]ove us; act for us; make our favourite

stories real to us; weave your grace and skill into the fabric of our life'.[32] Jooss' political dance theatre could be seen as an early attempt to harness the emotive power of *Ausdruckstanz* to comment on the 'real' and show the 'fabric of life' with all its injustices and horrors intact. Jooss' visits to Ireland were remembered, and his influence on current dance theatre practice celebrated, in CoisCéim's season of dance events in 2006 titled *Threads*, which sought to 'threa[d] the influence of German expressionism through European dance theatre and the many vibrant dance connections between Ireland and Germany'.[33]

The work of Pina Bausch (1940–2009), arguably the most influential and internationally renowned *Tanztheater* practitioner, is noted by many Irish dance practitioners as having been inspirational in the development of their own dance theatre aesthetic; Keegan-Dolan, for example, cites a production of Bausch's *Rite of Spring*, which he saw performed in the Netherlands with a live orchestra in his twenties, as being a 'formative experience and something I'll never forget'.[34] Pina Bausch graduated from Jooss' Folkwang School in 1959, and after training in the Graham and Limon techniques at the Juilliard School in New York, danced for a season with the Metropolitan Dance Theatre under the artistic direction of Anthony Tudor.[35] In 1962 she returned at Jooss' request to become a principle dancer in his company and then later took over the direction of the Folkwang School. In 1973 she was appointed as choreographer and artistic director of the Wuppertal Tanztheater, where she continued to work, in between extensive periods of international research and touring, until her death in 2009. Building on Jooss' innovations as a catalyst for both dance and theatre practice, and pushing his experimentations further, Bausch's works also caused critics and scholars to question previous notions of genre divides.[36] David Price suggests that, '[w]hat distinguishes Bausch [...] is her development of an art form based upon a binary opposition that does not reproduce an either/or dichotomy; instead, Bausch's productions are both dance and theater'.[37] Though not the first choreographer to do so, Bausch famously extended the expressive ability of the dancing body through a liberation of the dancer's voice.[38] As Kay Kirchner points out, the dancing body then becomes 'a multi-expressive form that includes thought and speech just as much as movement. [...] Bausch has recognized that "what speaks there" isn't a separate, abstract great "spirit" but our body itself, an organic whole to whom the categorical division in soul-body-spirit is inimical'.[39] This idea of an expressive voice speaking the corporeal has great resonance with Keegan-Dolan's call for performers to develop dance and vocal techniques to an equal degree. In his critique of theatre and dance practice that separates the body from the mind and vice versa he writes, '[m]any actors are just talking heads and many dancers are not even headless bodies, as many have had the sense and power of their own natural physicality taken from them by the pursuit of an external manifestation of perfection. They have neither body nor voice'.[40] Also notable in this statement is Keegan-Dolan's clear rejection of dance as a display of technique or pure abstract form, which brings to mind Bausch's famous dictum, 'I am not so much interested in how people move as in what moves them'.[41] Bolger also expresses his interest in heterogeneous physicalities and an interest in how different people move, explaining that in rehearsal with non-dancers he tells them: '[...] I'm interested in the way you move, I'm not going to try and teach you a different way of moving. I will work with the way you move to sculpt and choreograph that'.[42] Further parallels between Bausch's practice and the work of Keegan-Dolan and Bolger can be found in their use of whatever media they find appropriate to create a piece. Royd Climenhaga writes that in Bausch's work, 'the overriding metaphor for each piece finds expression by which ever means are necessary, whether they be movement based, imagistic, or dramatic, and by employing whatever forms and techniques are available'.[43] As in Bausch's work, dancers also sing and act in Keegan-Dolan's and Bolger's pieces, calling for, as Gabrielle Cody terms it, a 'multilingual spectatorship [with] an alternate willingness to see and hear'.[44] The subject of multilingualism in the more traditional sense also highlights a further correspondence – all three companies are made up of performers from a variety of national, racial and ethnic backgrounds, and all three choreographers use a collaborative approach in the creation of their pieces, defeating any attempt to describe their work as expressing any essential 'Germanness' or 'Irishness'. Another point of correspondence can be found in a comparison of visual aesthetics. Several Fabulous Beast and CoisCéim productions have an affinity (albeit on a much smaller and financially constrained scale) with the Wuppertal Tanztheater's striking and visceral use of *mise en scène*. Both of the Irish choreographers have extensive experience choreographing for theatre and opera and their comfort in creating movement for vast stages has inevitably influenced their approaches to space.[45] The stage designs for Keegan-Dolan's pieces often create evocative environmental landscapes using materials such as grass, wood and water. *The Bull*, for example, covered the stage in peat moss, as did Bausch's *Frühlingsopfer* (*Le Sacre du Printemps*) (1975), and the stage is covered in grass for both Keegan-Dolan's *The Flowerbed* and Bausch's *1980* (1980). Although differing from Bausch's penchant for natural materials, Bolger's recent staging of a production on a fully functioning dodgems track had all the large-scale playfulness and inventiveness of a Bauschian design. Anette Guse proposes that Bausch 'has transformed dance craft into a unique form of visually strong performance art',[46] and Keegan-Dolan's work has also been viewed in this light, although he counters that this is not a conscious choice.[47] One further point of correspondence worth noting is Gabrielle Cody's intriguing connection between Bausch's work and the performance technique of the German dancer and cabaret artist Valeska Gert. Opposing her dances from the more abstract choreographies of Wigman or Bronislava Nijinska in the 1920s, Gert states, 'I don't want to dance these vague movements that have nothing to do with me or my time', and that instead she wishes 'to dance the people and the variegated mixture of gestures and movements of their daily life'.[48] Norbert Servos reads Bausch's work as being comparable to a form of Brechtian epic theatre,[49] and Susan Manning and Melissa Benson tell of a meeting between Brecht and Gert, 'whose theory of the social function of dance in many ways paralleled his theory of theatre. Once she asked Brecht to define epic theatre. He replied, "What you do".'[50] Gert made use of parodic, stereotyped gesture in her choreographies, which were sharply observed political critiques of 1920s and 1930s German society. Manning and Benson explain that she drew her movement inspiration from popular entertainment forms such as the Charleston, the circus, sports and clown and that 'Gert called the dancer a transition between the old theater and the new and believed that new forms could arise only from the breakdown of old forms'.[51] As Cody argues, the cabaret techniques of Gert certainly have a strong resemblance to the scenes in Bausch's *Tanztheater* in which the dancers speak directly to the audience often to tell them a joke or story. These moments of intimacy, or 'unmatrixed performance',[52] also occur regularly in the work of Keegan-Dolan and Bolger. In Keegan-Dolan's *The Bull*, for example, one of the male dancers, seating himself at a piano and donning a dress for the occasion, plays and sings Josephine Baker's *J'ai deux amours* for the audience, taking a bow and receiving applause when he finishes. In Bolger's *Dodgems*, African-American tap-dancer Jason E. Bernard, dressed in a female competitive Irish dancing costume complete with a blonde ringletted wig, gives the audience a mini-lecture on the Tipperary origins of the Burqa ('de Burke-a'), intermitted with bursts of Irish jigging for the audience's approval.

Although there are many affinities to be found between them, the experience of watching a Bausch performance is nevertheless quite different to watching the dance theatre of Bolger and Keegan-Dolan. Bausch does not intend to communicate clear, direct meanings in her pieces and says of her creative process: 'I can only make something very open. I'm not pointing out a view. There are conflicts between people, but they can be looked at from each side, from different angles'.[53] Norbert Servos writes of the difficulties that are encountered if a unified 'meaning' is sought in her work, and explains that

> [e]in Grund für die Irritation liegt im Prinzip der Montage, das sich zum beherrschenden Stilprinzip des Tanztheaters entwickelt hat. Die freie assoziative Verknüpfung von Szenen, die sich an keinen Handlungsfaden, keine Psychologie von Figuren und keine Kausalität gebunden fühlt, versagt sich auch allen üblichen Entschlüsselungsversuchen.[54]

> [[a] reason for the irritation lies in the principle of montage that has developed into the dominant stylistic principle of *Tanztheater*. The freely associative connection of scenes that are not bound to any storyline, character psychology or causality, also break down all the usual attempts at decipherment].

This approach is in contrast with the communicative intent of Keegan-Dolan and Bolger who both consider themselves to be storytellers in the first instance. This is not to imply that they have never made use of montage techniques as described by Servos in their practice, or that their work does not incorporate associative connections in the relation of one scene to another. However, in the pieces that will be discussed in later chapters, their use of narrative, storytelling, and clearly defined characterisation lends their work the power to make pointed and explicit socio-political commentary. This stylistic trait means that their practice is at odds with many of the current trends in contemporary dance. In interview, Keegan-Dolan has spoken of his realisation that his desire for clarity positioned his work outside of mainstream praxis:

> [s]torytelling, that's my instinct. [...] I want to connect with the audience. But when I started making pieces, it really wasn't cool to do anything that was in any way clear or had a narrative; it was considered really naff. Everything had to be weird and incomprehensible. If it was clear, it was considered crap. For a long time I was afraid of being direct. I really do wonder why we've become frightened of clarity.[55]

The productions by Bolger discussed in this book are also strongly driven by the desire to communicate a direct message. Speaking of the creative process behind his work about the Great Irish Famine, *Ballads* (1997), Bolger describes the importance of using dance theatre to practice social commentary.[56] As he explains, this piece represents a turning point in his career, as his use of stories about the Irish famine collected over a two-year research period moved him away from his earlier interest in slapstick and vaudeville: 'I thought there was no way I could make a dance piece about the Irish famine, but I kept being drawn back to the material because it was so powerful and I just felt that dance was the perfect tool to tell a story of such huge catastrophe and loss, but also survival'.[57] Keegan-Dolan's and Bolger's use of explicit social commentary suggests that their work also has some affinity with that of another seminal *Tanztheater* practitioner, Johann Kresnik, whose '*Choreografisches Theater*' (choreographic theatre) has earned him the title of 'the politician of dance theatre'.[58] Kresnik's *Tanztheater*, especially his earlier works, speak directly of specific political events and have been described as agitprop directed against the worldview of the bourgeois ballet audiences who come to his performances. A structural difference between his practice and that of Keegan-Dolan and Bolger is his use of a soloist/corps de ballet organisation and his adherence to a largely classical movement vocabulary. Another difference is that in showing societal breakdown, his pieces allow for no glimpse of hope for betterment. Susanne Schlicher points out that in his pieces, 'Harmonie, und die Utopie einer besseren Welt [...] sind sprich-wörtlich verkrüppelt, rudimentär, verfault, von einer Müllgesellschaft zerfressen' (harmony and the utopia of a better world [...] are literally crippled, inchoate, rotten, eaten away by a waste society).[59] Neither Keegan-Dolan's nor Bolger's works are so bleak. However, despite differences in communicative intent between these choreographers, one important commonality remains: their use of every expressive facet of the body in choreographies that reject any limiting formalist aesthetic, be it the defined vocabularies of techniques such as ballet or modern dance or the conceptual abstractions of 'postmodern' dance, and, most importantly, their use of dance as a tool in the search for aesthetic and social change.

Acts of citizenship

Bausch's choreographies of violent and repetitive depictions of inter-personal struggles are often read, similar to Japanese Butoh, as a response to the devastation of the Second World War. Comparing the work of Keegan-Dolan and Bolger to that of *Tanztheater*, chore-ographers such as Bausch could arguably be seen to confirm a notion that they represent a form of dance theatre that has passed its sell-by date. In the period when the reunification of Germany forced the closure of many dance companies due to the financial strain of re-building the five eastern states, the funding crisis prompted a debate for critics and scholars as to the continuing relevance of Bausch's (expensive) *Tanztheater*. By the year 2000, German dance scholars Claudia Jeschke and Gabi Vettermann were proposing that the 'energy' behind *Tanztheater* had 'passed its peak' and that the 'emotional resources required by the archaeological exploration of the psyche, society and (dance) history seem to be exhausted'.[60] Reporting on the debate originated by the tour of Bausch's Wuppertal company to the BAM Next Wave Festival in New York in 1986, Johannes Birringer outlined the differences between Bausch's devel-opment of *Ausdruckstanz* and the formalist aesthetic of American postmodern choreographers who, in their push against the perceived excessive expression and emotion of Martha Graham, followed Merce Cunningham in a rejection of her use of theatricality, dramatic struc-ture and narrative. Bausch's form of postmodern dance was not well received at the time, and trying to make sense of this reception from an American audience, Birringer (a Bausch fan) proposed that

> [i]mages of pain or fear of death disturb the American landscape; they don't accommodate the rhetoric of beauty, power, and speed in a techno-logical Disneyland. Images of violence are acceptable in films and MTV, where they can be made to look beautiful. As for the dance: why should anyone want to see distorted and victimized bodies that don't even dance most of the time?[61]

Whether or not Birringer's assessment of the American reception was justified, his claim that the US choreographers had less need of a critical response to social and political affairs due to an anaestheti-cised 'Disneyland' existence was soon proved untenable, first with the onset of the AIDS pandemic, and then following the trauma of the terrorist attacks of 9/11. It could be argued that, following these events, Bausch's 'overindulgent' choreographies showing the darker side of society can now be seen to have acquired a new resonance. In the US, dance theatre works such as Bill T. Jones' *Still/Here* (1994) tackled the difficult subject of the destruction of the body through terminal illnesses and AIDS, famously sparking critic Arlene Croce's oft-cited denouncement of the piece (which she refused to see) as 'vic-tim art'.[62] The work of Lloyd Newson, director of the DV8 Physical Theatre Company in England, also stands out due to its engage-ment with explicitly political subject matter. His work is promoted as a challenge, 'to the traditional aesthetics and forms which pervade most modern and classical dance', which stems from his 'personal rejection of abstraction in dance' and a 'concentration on connecting meaning to movement and in addressing current social issues'.[63] The influence of Bausch on Newson's work is often noted[64] and several of his pieces deal specifically with sexual politics, notably *Dead Dreams of Monochrome Men* (1989), *Enter Achilles* (1995) and *To Be Straight With You* (2007).[65] Although Judith Mackrell writes that Newson's brand of physical theatre is rooted in Steve Paxton's postmodern contact improvisation, she proposes that he has created his 'own vocabulary to include not only ordinary movement but often bruis-ingly virtuoso feats of daring and struggle – exploring loneliness, aggression, the oppression of women, and the alienation of gay men'.[66] Germany-based US choreographer William Forsythe's *Three Atmospheric Studies* (2006), which toured to the Dublin International Dance Festival in 2008, represented a shift in his work from conceptual and abstract neo-classical experimentation to theatrical and explicit political commentary. The piece, a modern-day *Green Table* protest of the Iraq war, included a re-enactment of a bomb exploding in an Iraqi market-place and a scene in which dancer Dana Caspersen gave a chilling performance of a speech by the 'Great Decider' – a direct critique of Forsythe's conception of a 'Condoleeza-Rumsfeld-Bush' conglomeration. Hailed as his *Guernica*,[67] the piece marks the Forsythe Company's most explicit foray into political dance theatre, and in a post-show discussion of the performance at the Abbey Theatre in Dublin, he explained that he wanted to make a clear statement about his political stance, and that he views his piece as 'an act of citizenship'. When *New York Times* dance critic Diane Solway gave her review of *Three Atmospheric Studies* the title, 'Is it Dance? Maybe. Is it Political? Sure', she re-articulated the critical anxiety that is caused when dancing bodies move into the political realm. In an interview with Forsythe she asked if he felt that dance and politics 'make good partners'. He replied, '[s]ince when aren't artists citizens?'[68] This sentiment can be found echoed in Keegan-Dolan's affirmation that he is, 'interested in the position of an artist in society, a dancer in society',[69] and Bolger's belief that, 'every choreographer must have a point of view, or an opinion'.[70] It would seem then, that the work of Keegan-Dolan and Bolger has resonance with international artists who are also pushing against the status quo to create 'acts of citizenship'.

Heterogeneous and evolving?

Writing of new developments in the contemporary European dance scene from the 1990s to the present, André Lepecki proposes that, '[s]ome time in the early 1990s, it became transparent for a whole generation of choreographers and dancers that those parameters, notably the isomorphism between dance and movement, and the emphasis on dance's autonomy with regard to the verbal, had set up an ontological and political trap for dance'.[71] Lepecki goes on to describe a 'nameless movement' of contemporary European choreographers, including Jérôme Bel, Xavier Le Roy, Meg Stuart and Jonathan Burrows, whose work is destabilising and rethinking these ontological parameters. Lepecki identifies a grounding in 'minimalism, conceptual art and performance art' and a movement away from a theatrical paradigm to a performance paradigm as some of the linking features of these choreographers' work. Although this would seem to disqualify Keegan-Dolan's and Bolger's work from inclusion, being firmly rooted as it is in the theatrical, Lepecki also claims that the 'truth' of this new European movement 'resides in its performance rather than in its accommodation to previously fixed, established, hermetically sealed aesthetic and disciplinary boundaries' and its realisation of 'the impossibility for dance to stand by itself and to flow in solitary space'.[72] Here a definite link can be made between the interdisciplinary developments in Ireland and developments, as identified by Lepecki, in a broader European context. This link is strengthened when the *Manifesto for a European Performance Policy,* which was signed by many of these choreographers at a meeting in Vienna (2001), is examined. The opening of the statement addresses the difficulty in finding one umbrella term under which to define the anti-disciplinary nature of the work being created by these choreographers, and offers a list of over twenty terms that might be used to describe the many different practices that are emerging. The manifesto states that, '[s]uch a list of terms not only represents the diversity of disciplines and approaches embraced within our practices, but is also symptomatic of the problematics of trying to define or prescribe such heterogeneous and evolving performance forms'.[73] An obvious link can be made here with Keegan-Dolan's difficulty in placing his work within one discipline. This link may still seem rather tenuous, but the following passage from the manifesto allows a firmer connection to be made:

[o]ur practices [...] offer new languages, articulate new forms of subjectivation [sic] and presentation to play with the cultural and social influences which inform us, to create new cultural landscapes. [...] Our practices have proved to be an articulate platform from which to challenge the dominant post-colonial narratives and traditional representations of the 'other'. We consider the borders between disciplines, categories and nations to be fluid, dynamic and osmotic.[74]

This fluidity between disciplines and the ability to create 'new' cultural landscapes and performance languages has great resonance with the practice of the choreographers discussed so far. These issues are also at the heart of the work of choreographers Jean Butler and Colin Dunne, former champion step dancers and *Riverdance* soloists, whose experiments within the competitive step dance genre have allowed for a re-imagining of the creative potential of traditional Irish dance. The final section of this chapter will consider how, in their different ways, they both challenge the stifling postcolonial moulding of a traditional 'Irish' dancing body in dance theatre works that interrogate the traditional form through a contemporary lens.

Developments in traditional Irish dance

Butler and Dunne were both trained in the competitive solo step dancing style, which is distinct from the *sean-nós* style (Gaelic for 'old-style' dance), the Munnix style practised by the performers the National Folk Theatre of Ireland (Siamsa Tíre), and the social forms of set dancing and *céilí* dancing.[75] A radical element of both Butler's and Dunne's work is their creative choreographic approach to step dancing. But why is the notion of pairing artistic creativity with this form so remarkable? As discussed in Chapter One, the modern competitive aesthetic is inextricably linked with its nomination during the Gaelic Revival movement of the late nineteenth century as being representative of 'Irishness'.[76] The founding of the Gaelic League in 1893 saw the renaming of step dancing as 'Irish dancing' and the eventual overt politicisation of this organisation in support of the nationalist cause resulted in the League's version of step dancing, along with its related social form *céilí* dancing, becoming the officially sanctioned danced expressions of national identity and morality. One of the methods used by the Gaelic League to promote preferred expressions of Irish culture was the sponsorship of competitions. The use of competition in the promotion of Irish dance inevitably led to the necessity to narrowly define the form so that it could be adjudicated. In 1927 the Gaelic League set up *An Comisúin le Rincí Gaelacha* (The Commission for Irish Dance), which in 1930 became a centralised organisation with regulatory authority that continues today in its role of creating and enforcing the rules of competition and examination, both in Ireland and internationally.[77] Strictly regulating the form has undoubtedly contributed to the astonishing technical proficiency of today's competitive step dancers. Frank Hall also suggests that there is a belief within the competitive Irish dance world that this system has educative benefits in preparing children for the 'real world' [of a] society and culture with a competition-based economy [...] that produces winners and losers from a material perspective'.[78] Yet the combination of the competitive structure with nationalist ideology can also be seen to have severely limited any scope for creative expression within the form. Although variations in rhythmic stress, weight distribution and movement through space are allowed, any introduction of new movements, or any significant elaborations of existing movements, are strictly policed by the Commission. As Hall writes, '[c]reativity in Irish dancing is guided by selections of movements which emphasize values already inherent in the form. Movements that bring out verticality and "up-ness" or gestures and paths in the forward direction instantiate these values'.[79] He also points out that creative elaborations on allowable steps can result in a considerable degree of controversy as they are seen to pose a potential threat to the stability of the Irish dancing system as a representation of national identity.[80]

The arrival of *Riverdance* marked a shift in the national consciousness towards a consideration of the competitive step dance form as a theatrical dance form. However, as discussed in the introductory chapter, in its spectacularisation of Irish dance and its perpetuation of a nationalist ideology, *Riverdance* arguably continued a reification process of the Irish dancing body that can be traced to the late nineteenth century. Outside of commercial shows there have been several instances in Ireland of theatre dance works that have either included sections of step dance (such as Colin Dunne's choreography of the *Celtic Bitch* routines in Fabulous Beast Dance Theatre's *The Bull* (2005)) or have attempted a merging of contemporary dance with traditional Irish dance forms. Examples of the latter are the collaborations of dancers from the National Folk Theatre, Siamsa Tíre, with various contemporary choreographers (such as Mary Nunan, Cindy Cummings and most recently Fearghus Ó Conchúir). What separates Butler's and Dunne's pieces from the work of other choreographers experimenting with Irish dance is the absence of an encompassing framework of 'Irish dance plus X', or the necessity of having a choreographer that works in a contemporary or postmodern aesthetic applying their concepts from a position outside the traditional form. In contrast to this, both works have emerged from *within* the competitive form, through an anti-disciplinary process of exploration initiated by the dancers themselves. It is interesting to note that neither of these choreographers was born in Ireland. Butler is from New York and was encouraged to take up Irish dancing by her Mayo-born mother at the age of six, and Dunne's Irish parents brought him to his first Irish dance lesson in his hometown of Birmingham when he was three years old. To differing degrees, both choreographers draw attention in their works to the cultural anxiety that arises though their experimentations with the form, the globalisation of Irish dance, and its adoption by non-diaspora communities (in *Out of Time* Dunne creates a jig about the interest in Irish dancing in Russia and China: 'What will they do? What will we do?'). The fact that it is dancers from the Irish diaspora that are at the forefront of these new directions in Irish step dance contributes to a destabilisation of the connection between Irish dancing and nationalist ideology. In both choreographers' works we see instances of a traditional Irish dancing body undergoing a process of change, at times disobeying the impulses dictated by a controlling technique and playfully moving in ways that have not yet been named.

In the intimate and autobiographical solo *Does She Take Sugar?* (2007), Butler stages the explorative process of her choreographic development away from the confines of the competitive Irish step dance vocabulary. As her movement progresses slowly beyond the restrictions of the traditional form during the piece, it becomes clear that the years of training in one idiom have left an inerasable patterning of impulses in her body that must be questioned for every new move to appear. Tracing and erasing drawings and diagrams of her progress in chalk on a large blackboard and showing a film of her daily journey through New York to the dance studio where she practises, she brings the audience inside her rehearsal process and her personal life, exposing and altering a notation of the cartography of her corporeality. In this work, it is as if Butler brings the spectator into the practice studio to observe a process of metamorphosis. The concept of transformation is clearly communicated throughout the piece, beginning with Butler's staging of her rehearsal methods for the performance of a dance choreographed to Vivaldi's *Spring*. This section starts with Butler writing a list of tasks on the blackboard: '1:

mark through and clean, 2: play <u>breathe</u>, 3: Spring!'. Then putting on
the earphones of an MP3 player, she proceeds to methodically follow
this rehearsal schedule, first conducting a walk-through of the spatial pattern, then repeating certain sections focussing on breathing
patterns, before finally removing her earphones to run through the
dance to an external (and finally audible for the audience) playing
of the music.[81] Although the resulting performance is a seemingly
conventional soft shoe dance with intricate footwork, high jumps,
and rhythms dictated by Vivaldi's score, the exposure of the repetitive and sweaty process that went into its preparation changes the
audience's perception of the dance. While Butler rehearses in 'silent
disco' fashion to the music in her earphones, the audience only hears
the sounds of her working body and often labouring breath; the
Irish dancing body is presented without frills in isolation from the
rhythms that are dictating its movements. Due to this, the struggle for perfection of form is highlighted, with the strenuous exertion
that underlies the seemingly effortless leaps and intricate steps being
made apparent. In the latter sections of the work, the difficulty
encountered in her struggle for physical transformation is brought
clearly into focus as she performs movement phrases in a more
contemporary style (still connected to the step dance technique) to
an accompanying soundtrack of garbled language and sounds from
John Cage's *Roaratorio: an Irish Circus on Finnegan's Wake* (1979), the
carefully orchestrated, yet confusing cacophony of the soundscape
lending an aural dimension to Butler's corporeal mixings. Butler tries
to escape the strictly upright posture of Irish dance by bending and
curving her upper body, but the resulting movements are not always
fluid. In the final section of the piece, she abandons the vertical
posture of the traditional technique altogether and performs a passage of floor-work. Aesthetically, this is perhaps the least convincing
section, yet conceptually it is the most enlightening. The condition-
ing of Butler's body through the step dance form has trained it to
always resist rather than give in to gravity and the difficulty of this
final section reveals Butler's willingness to bravely abandon aesthetic
precepts and expectations in order to playfully explore new ways of
moving. In the Irish dance technique, dancers try to land from jumps
on legs held as straight as possible to assist the illusion of a continual
physical state of 'upness'. This contrasts with many dance techniques
in which it is usual to bend the knees on landing in order to lessen

the impact on the knee joint and to facilitate a smooth transition to the next move (in ballet, for example, this bend is called a *plié*). Perhaps unsurprisingly, when Butler began trying to introduce such bends into her technique, her muscles found the unpractised mode of movement difficult to perform and it is this physical strain placed on her body by the transformative process that Butler candidly shows in this work.[82] In the programme she explains that the piece is, 'essentially about the inside of something butting up against the outside of the same thing; the juxtaposition of the interior and exterior life of a dancer; my world inside and out'.[83] *Does She Take Sugar?* demonstrates that the seemingly fixed outer shell of discipline and technique can be made malleable through the playful intervention of a curious and independent inner subjectivity.

The title of Dunne's *Out of Time* already hints at the playful approach he takes to competitive step dance technique, as step dancers must normally never be out of time with their accompanying music. It can also be seen to refer to the dialogue that Dunne engages in between the traditions and corporealities of the past and his own present dancing body, and the space that he creates for his dance outside of the dictates of time-keeping rhythm and the restrictions of form. With microphones taped to his feet, he uses live digital recording technology to dance to the looped, remixed and layered sounds of his own, echoed movements. He also dances with archive footage (projected onto an ever-shifting formation of two white boxes, which he moves around the stage) of the Hayes brothers, Áine Ní Thuaghaigh and Paddy Ban O'Broin as they were recorded dancing in 1935, 1955, and 1972 respectively.[84] Throughout the work, examples of competition and exhibitionism in the traditional form are questioned through a verbal accompaniment that comments on the performance as it is danced. At the beginning of the piece, Dunne dances barefoot to a soundtrack of percussive sounds and canned applause interjected with the words 'lovely', 'thanks', 'beautiful' and 'cheers'. His movements are all based on step dance technique, but he inserts pauses and knee bends, plays with releasing the weight of an extended leg into the ground, and adds expansive arm movements that stem from the impetus created by his lower body. Stepping up onto a small podium, he then looks directly at the audience and asks with a knowing look, 'Do you want to see my hornpipe?' This tongue-in-cheek approach is undercut throughout the work with sections that are more melancholy in tone. One such shift in mood occurs when a film is played of Dunne's performance on the children's show *Blue Peter* when he is 10 years old.[85] Due to the critical framework in which the piece analyses the competitive and exhibitionistic aspects of step dance, the footage of Dunne as a child champion is both endearing and disquieting. Dunne himself has mixed feelings towards it, as he sees it as

> quite a dark piece of footage [...] because of the ridiculousness of a 10-year-old being in the position of a world champion. Where do you go after that? [...] [T]hose early years were so formative and it is such a judgmental form: it's all about, did you do it right? And therefore are you going to win? It takes a long time to get out of it.[86]

Throughout the piece, reflective sections such as this film are often a potent mixture of homage to the form and a concurrent pointed critique of it. Another example of this intermixture is found in a later section in which the white boxes are upended to create lecterns from which Dunne delivers a kind of summation of his thoughts on Irish dance, which he accompanies with the continuous repetition of a simple, grid-like walking pattern: 'OK. This whole dance tradition in Ireland is a virtuoso affair. Its purpose is to amaze, to intrigue, to invite wonder and respect. In a word it is exhibitionistic. Even in informal situations there is an underlying element of competition'.[87]

The experiments of Butler and Dunne challenge the historical connection of the Irish step-dancing body with competition, nationalism and exhibitionism. Their anti-disciplinary approach has not only changed public perceptions of the creative possibilities of the traditional Irish dance form, but has also had a profound effect on how they themselves experience it. Butler says of her process, '[b]y examining my traditional kinetic make-up through a lens of contemporary aesthetics, a new vocabulary has emerged that constantly references Irish dance, albeit in a foreign and sometimes unrecognizable context. To achieve this I had to deconstruct my physical self and put it together again'.[88] Colin Dunne also speaks of how his choreographic research has caused a fundamental shift in the way he approaches his movement, stating, '[w]hereas before my style was very muscular and lifting out of the floor, now it's more released into the floor.

It's like thinking of the body hanging down as opposed to being held up. It's a subtle difference to look at, but a huge shift to find physically'.[89] As mentioned previously, for some spectators in the competitive dance world, Dunne's experimentations will always be a disappointment and possibly even a betrayal to those who expect another display of his virtuosic ability. Jean Butler's uncompromising fidelity to a process of 'un-fixing' her dancing body creates performances that demand a high level of patience and concentration from the spectator; an easily consumed spectacle is also not her goal. In the programme for *Does She Take Sugar?* Butler cites Pina Bausch, 'I come without make-up or hairdo, or costume, or high heels. I have no idea, but I come anyway'.[90] Approaching the traditional form in this inquisitive and creative manner, and being open to transformation, has allowed both choreographers to step outside of the limitations prescribed by genre and discipline. Like the work of Keegan-Dolan and Bolger, these experimentations signal a new landscape of possibility for dance in Ireland.

In conclusion

What has emerged from this investigation into the genre debate is that the choreographers examined in this study are working outside of normative disciplinary categories, which makes their work difficult to place within existing genre definitions. However, a survey beyond the Irish context brings into view certain parallels with similar developments and movements in US and European dance scenes. What is fascinating in the work of these choreographers is their refusal of the notion that interdisciplinary practice contributes to a dilution of dance's autonomy or relevance as an art form. They view every part of their practice as choreography and every element of their work is part of the dance. Also of importance is their commitment to resisting limitations of form (especially in the work of Dunne and Butler) and any boundaries that separate the aesthetic and the political (especially in the work of Keegan-Dolan and Bolger). Instead, they are deftly leaping beyond every 'ontological trap' towards exciting and challenging forms of dance theatre. Although this departure causes anxiety for some, as shown in Chapter Two of this book, it does not represent a radical rupture or tear in the fabric of Irish performance. Similarly, it does not propose a threat to the future of dance (in both contemporary and traditional forms) or the future of theatre. Rather than being divorced from, or rejecting, past or current dance and theatre practice, it represents an interweaving of disciplines that allows for a re-imagining of what is possible in the future while incorporating and commenting on what has gone before. Through their disregard of genre divides and disciplinary rules, these choreographers have moved beyond the limiting separation of dance from other performance disciplines. Importantly, they are also resisting the limiting traditional view of what dance performance 'is' in an Irish context, allowing for practices that are engaged in aesthetic evolution and socio-political change. In so doing, they are developing inclusive and evolving languages of expression that are re-shaping Ireland's performance landscape.

The following chapter begins the second section of this study, which provides detailed readings of five works by Fabulous Beast and CoisCéim. In the first reading, I take a look at how *The Bull* (2005) by Fabulous Beast and *Ballads* (1997) by CoisCéim attempt to re-insert a corporeal perspective into historical and mythical narratives from which the realities of bodily experiences have been forgotten or erased. *The Bull* is a twenty-first-century retelling of the *Táin Bó Cuailnge* (The Cattle Raid of Cooley), an ancient Irish story that has played an important role in the creation of Irish national myth, and *Ballads* is a choreographic exploration of the nineteenth-century Irish famine. Both of these dance theatre works create a space in which the monolithic nature of these narratives can be questioned and challenged through a corporeal re-visioning.

4
Choreographing Narratives: Buried Bodies and Constitutive Stories in *The Bull* and *Ballads*

In *The Bull* (2005) by Fabulous Beast, and *Ballads* (1997, revised version 2000)[1] by CoisCéim, well-known Irish myths and narratives that have played a constitutive role in the formation of national identity are reinterpreted in dance theatre pieces that perform not only a retelling of these stories, but which also highlight aspects of the construction of contemporary 'Irish' identity through their staging of a dialogue between body and text. The narrative of *The Bull* is based on the ancient Irish prose epic, *Táin Bó Cuailnge* (The Cattle Raid of Cooley) and *Ballads* is a work about the Great Irish Famine of the nineteenth century.[2] As is often observed, shared myths and memories play an important role in the development of a national consciousness. Rogers M. Smith, discussing the politics of nation-building and 'people building', proposes that the founding and preservation of communities and political groups requires the creation of 'constitutive stories' that tell of a people's defining traits and characteristics.[3] The creation of national myth through these stories aids the cohesion of 'imagined communities', to use Benedict Anderson's term, and as Arash Abizadeh proposes, '[t]his mythical element in its shared memories is what enables the nation's common history to provide it with a motivating power'.[4] Myths and memories which are preserved in textual form or generated textually, build a 'unified collective history', and have, as Chris Morash argues, 'an ideological function – indeed, they are almost pure ideology, insofar as they create an illusion of complete identity between the individual and society'.[5] However, as Paul Ricoeur asserts, '[a]s soon as a story is well known – and such is the case with most traditional and popular

99

narratives as well as with the national chronicles of the founding events of a given community – retelling takes the place of telling'.[6] In the retelling of these stories and events, *The Bull* and *Ballads* are not challenging any one particular account: there is of course no one 'true' version of the *Táin*, just as there is no single metanarrative of the Famine. Instead, in their different ways, they provoke a rethinking of how these stories and events have been approached in the past and how they are currently used in the formation of subjectivity/identity in contemporary Irish society. In the two works examined in this chapter, the retelling involves not just the narrative content of the story, but also the actual mode in which the story is told. The corporealisation of these stories in *The Bull* and *Ballads* can be viewed as an example of a boundary transgression and an intercultural meeting, as they both employ a meeting of these texts with their traditionally cultural other in a theatrical context, dance. As discussed in the introductory chapter, theatre in Ireland is predominantly a writer's theatre, and dance, especially in the form of contemporary dance, is a relatively marginalised art form. Using the corporeal score of the dancing body in combination with text to tell these 'constitutive' stories, the choreographers of the two works are operating from an in-between position, which they use to present new or forgotten perspectives. Ernest Renan writes that, *'[o]r l'essence d'une nation est que tous les individus aient beaucoup de choses en commun, et aussi que tous oublié bien des choses'* ([t]he essence of the nation is that all the individuals have a lot of things in common, and also that everyone has forgotten many things)'.[7] Both *The Bull* and *Ballads* reveal how certain troubling and unflattering aspects of Irish history have been suppressed in the nation's constitutive stories. These works attempt to create an embodiment of these 'forgotten' and unpalatable aspects. Opening up these stories to critical examination through the medium of dance necessarily places emphasis on the bodies that inhabit them, and through these bodies, the underlying frailty and vulnerability of national identity and social cohesion is brought to the fore. Judith Butler writes

> [e]ach of us is constituted politically in part by virtue of the social vulnerability of our bodies – as a site of desire and physical vulnerability, as a site of publicity at once assertive and exposed. Loss and vulnerability seem to follow from our being socially constituted

bodies, attached to others, at risk of losing those attachments, exposed to others, at risk of violence by virtue of that exposure.[8]

As Butler proposes, socially attached bodies can in fact be viewed as vulnerable due to their need for each other. Constitutive stories construct a defence against the actual frailty of social cohesion in society, yet they also require certain aspects of narratives to be omitted. Bringing the focus of interrogation onto corporealities and highlighting the constructed nature of the constitutive stories that 'attach' bodies to each other, exposes the omitted and forgotten elements of these narratives. It is also a timely pursuit in this period of renewed identity-questioning in Ireland. After introducing the works and the narratives that they are based on, the remaining sections of the chapter will examine specific scenes from each work, paying particular attention to how both works emphasise the gap that exists between official versions of stories and histories and the lived realities of the bodies that inhabit them.

Introducing the works: touching a nerve

Ballads premiered at the Project at the Mint Theatre in Dublin on 24 November 1997, and went on to tour nationally and, in a revised version, internationally.[9] Choreographed by Bolger, it is a piece for five dancers and two musicians (a cellist and an uilleann piper).[10] Compared to his previous works, which were rooted in vaudeville and comedy, Bolger identifies this piece as representing a 'turning point' in his choreographic practice towards a more research-based and socially engaged working method.[11] In contrast with the themes of his first works, which included a piece based on Charlie Chaplin's movement, *Taps with Sax* (1994), and *Temporary Arrangements* (1994), a comic love triangle played out on a living room couch, the subject matter of *Ballads* saw Bolger's attention shift towards much darker and more overtly political material. He had already begun to address social themes in the earlier work *Reel Luck* (1995), which aimed to capture, 'the pace of the transformation in Irish culture over recent decades [...] explor[ing] the changes in the role of women, moral values, symbols of fortune, and the rural/urban divide'.[12] However, Bolger's aim in *Ballads* to address, as he describes, a 'natural calamity and political holocaust which even today historians are keen to ignore', moved his typically lighthearted and humorous approach to social issues into the realm of direct and explicit social critique.[13]

Between 1845 and 1850, potato crops in Ireland were attacked by *Phytophthora infestans* (potato blight), and as the potato was the staple food of the poor, the repeated failure of their crops led to the death through starvation and diseases such as typhoid, of at least 1 million people and the emigration of at least a further million, reducing Ireland's pre-Famine population of 8 million by a quarter. Although the potato blight was the instigating event, it was not the blight alone that caused the Famine. The combination of the potato crop failure with a number of socio-political factors led to the devastating death toll and emigration figures, and an interpretation of these was stated in the programme of *Ballads* in an essay by Charlie O'Neill: '[u]nfair land ownership. The landlord system. Unfair trade. Tenants in debt. Underdevelopment, dependency, political domination. Economic exploitation, cultural repression, lack of education and more'.[14] David Bolger was inspired to create a work about the Famine by the sesquicentennial commemorations of the event that took place in Ireland in 1995–7. One of the original reasons for his interest in the subject was his puzzlement at what he felt to be the almost celebratory tone of the commemorative events. As he explains, '[t]he word celebration kept coming up and I thought it was really strange that the word celebration [was used in connection with] a kind of a holocaust that had happened in our nation.'[15] Bolger is not alone in making this connection between the Great Famine and the Jewish Holocaust within the context of questions of representation and the difficulties inherent in expressing the 'unspeakable'.[16] Terry Eagleton writes of Ireland's Great Famine, 'the event strains at the limits of the articulable, and is truly in this sense the Irish Auschwitz. In both cases there would seem something trivializing or dangerously familiarizing about the very act of representation itself'.[17] Perhaps it is partly due to this fear of trivialisation or over-familiarisation that historical accounts of the famine are often noted as having been written in a detached or overly clinical manner; Colm Tóibín remarks, 'Irish historians, on the whole, do not become emotional about the Famine [...] we remain cool and dispassionate and oddly distant from the events of 150 years ago'.[18] In addition to the emotional distancing found in famine histories, it is important to note that until the explosion of publications that accompanied the Famine's sesquicentennial, there was a dearth of historical publications on the subject.[19] Chris Morash and Richard Hayes suggest, '[t]here is something about the famine which seems to invoke what might almost be called a humility in historians, an unwillingness to venture into one of the largest and darkest areas of Irish history [...]'.[20] Analysing this reluctance, Ó Gráda attributes what he considers a cultural 'amnesia' regarding the Famine to two separate phenomena: survivor guilt and the wish to suppress traumatic memories. As an elderly Cork man interviewed in 1945 suggested, '[s]everal people would be glad if the famine times were altogether forgotten so that the cruel doings of their forebears would not be again renewed and talked about by neighbours',[21] and Ó Gráda writes that for survivors, 'shared memories about the tragedy were very distressing and sometimes traumatic for those who endured it [...] In the Clonmel area famine survivors were taciturn on the matter [...] while in Ballymoe, County Galway, those who had witnessed the horrors of the famine were reluctant to give details, and only an occasional incident was handed down'.[22]

In response to the paucity of survivor accounts and the emotionless historical literature that he encountered during his research, Bolger believed that dance offered the 'perfect tool to tell a story of such huge catastrophe and loss',[23] having the ability, 'to articulate beyond the spoken word'.[24] However the 'desire to come to terms with the emotional aspect' of the Famine, and to explore how this emotion shaped 'the psyche of the Irish people', proved a difficult challenge.[25] Before its premiere in 1997, *Ballads* was in development for two years, and during this time Bolger struggled with the harrowing nature of the research material that he was using: '[t]he piece started to take shape even though I didn't realise it was taking shape because I kept running away from it [...] what we're talking about is people starving to death and how do we do that? [...] But the piece and the research kept coming back to me and saying no you've got to go on, you've got to go on and do it.'[26] In addition to the difficulty of the topic, Bolger was also afraid that he would fail to create a piece 'worthy' of the difficult subject matter. Speaking of the physical effect that the pressures of creating the piece had on him, he explains, 'I used to be really ill when we were working on it, used to have this pain: the piece took us on'.[27] Attempting to physicalise an emotional response to the Famine also took its toll on the performers, and original cast member Liz Roche speaks of the discomfort she experienced during the project: '[i]t's one of the pieces [that] I really don't know what I think about it. David was very well aware that he was taking on something huge: everyone involved was frightened. People would cry on stage'.[28] This corporealisation of the re-imagined suffering of famine victims was also a challenge for the audience, perhaps partly due to the fact that the timbre of the work departed so radically from the fast-paced and humorous style that people had come to expect from CoisCéim and perhaps also due to an inevitable failure of the piece to achieve its aspiration of 'coming to terms' with the Famine. Critical response to the first run in 1997 was noted as being 'mixed', however Carolyn Swift's review for the *Irish Times* was very positive: 'it is a fine piece. The Famine is a subject which could easily lose its emotion in mawkish cliché, but here the use of symbols and multi-purpose props, combined with highly-imaginative choreography, results in excitement and catharsis'.[29]

Fabulous Beast Dance Theatre's *The Bull* also received mixed reviews, and when the work premiered in 2005 at the O'Reilly Theatre in Dublin, it was the cause of much heated debate. A co-production between the Dublin International Theatre Festival and the Barbican in London, Keegan-Dolan retold the *Táin Bó Cuailnge* in a twenty-first-century setting, using the ancient myth as the backbone for a study of contemporary Irish society. Fintan O'Toole's claim that *The Bull* was 'the first great piece of theatre about the new hyped-up 21st-century Ireland'[30] prompted many indignant replies to the contrary in the letter pages of the *Irish Times* for days afterwards. Likewise, the most popular call-in radio show on the national broadcaster (*Liveline*, hosted by Joe Duffy on RTÉ Radio 1), was flooded with callers who alternately argued that it was either 'the most amazing performance' they had ever seen or that it was 'deeply offensive' and a '[l]oad of Bull'.[31] It would appear that Keegan-Dolan had not intended the piece to be controversial and he was taken aback by the negative responses, explaining, 'the shit hit the fan [a]fter opening night, people were ringing up the radio, letters were going to the *Irish Times*. I was really taken by surprise, because I was just telling the story in a modern context'.[32] Despite, or perhaps helped by this controversy, the production was sold out for both its run in Dublin (2005) and at the Barbican in London (2007), going on to win the 2007 Critic's Circle National Dance Award for the best modern choreography performed in the UK.[33] Choreographed by Keegan-Dolan, the production featured a multinational cast of 12 that inhabited the Cúchulainn myth with Slovakian, Nigerian, Italian, Tanzanian, English, Irish and French bodies and was comprised of a mix of dancers, actors and musicians who, as part of the rehearsal process for the piece, trained each other in their respective disciplines.[34]

After the premiere of *Giselle* (2003), the then director of the Dublin Theatre Festival, Fergus Linehan, asked Keegan-Dolan what his next piece was going to be, and he suggested, surprising himself ('it just came out of my mouth'), a reworking of the *Táin*.[35] Interestingly, he also, like Bolger, had significant reservations about taking on such a well-known and meaning-laden story, and his explanation of how he decided to go ahead with the project has a similar sense of ineluctability: 'I spent a while thinking, "What should I do, should I do this?" and then I just started seeing bulls everywhere [...] and I kept noticing those Táin Trail signposts everywhere... and I was like, "Okay, do it!" So we're doing it.'[36] The *Táin Bó Cuailnge* (the Cattle Raid of Cooley) is an ancient Irish prose epic that probably existed in oral tradition long before the earliest surviving manuscript from the twelfth century was written. It is the central story of the Ulster cycle of heroic tales, and tells of the feats of King Conchobar and his famed warrior Cúchulainn (known as 'the hound of Ulster'). In the *Táin* (which means a gathering of people for a cattle raid), Queen Maebh of Connacht invades Ulster and attempts to steal the brown bull of Cuailnge so that she can equal her husband in wealth. Due to a curse, the warriors defending the bull are periodically afflicted with the labour pains of childbirth, and so the defence of the beast falls to the young Cúchulainn, who defeats Queen Maebh's army single-handedly, aided by so-called 'warp spasms' which lend his body the ability to morph into distorted shapes that are terrifying to behold. The story is acknowledged as having played an important role in the creation of Irish national myth[37] and was of particular interest to the writers of the Gaelic Revival, with Lady Gregory writing a celebrated translation, *Cúchulainn of Muirthemne*, in 1902, which Yeats described as, 'the best [book] that has come out of Ireland in my time'.[38] Altering, or simply omitting the immoral aspects of the tale in her, 'determination to ennoble the figures of Irish myth', Gregory romanticised the story, and her version is very different to the translation by Thomas Kinsella that Keegan-Dolan used for the basis of *The Bull*.[39] Kinsella explains that in his translation, which featured commissioned brush paintings by Louis Le Brocquy, he was attempting to provide a 'living version of the story', which would not omit the 'directness in bodily matters: the easy references to seduction, copulation, urination, the picking of vermin, the suggestion of incest'.[40] Le Brocquy also aimed in his illustrations to avoid, 'picturesque images' and the 'social irreality' that usually accompanied the myth's retellings.[41] Keegan-Dolan's danced version of the myth revels in the messiness of the body that Kinsella and Le Brocquy were trying to capture in text and paint. Similar to Bolger's desire to access the 'truth' of the Famine that he felt had been ignored or misrepresented, Keegan-Dolan also felt the need to redress the tamed nature of romanticised versions of the national myth. Explaining why he chose Kinsella's direct approach to the translation, and expressing a frustration with sanitised versions of the story, he explains:

> [w]hat these characters are doing is not very palatable, so we don't accept it, and we change it, and we turn it into 'diddley-eye'. I'm really interested in what happens when you accept it as it is; it's far more liberating than pretending it doesn't exist. [...] We have dark stories in this country, so let's just accept them.[42]

Both Keegan-Dolan and Bolger felt a need to revisit these 'constitutive stories' in order to shed light on aspects that they felt had been muted. Both use the dancing body to highlight these unexpressed facets and seek to re-inject the corporeal excesses, the corporealities, which they believed had been erased in textual versions. Yet their approaches to the retelling of these stories are very different. In order to examine how each choreographer tackled their retellings, the following two sections engage in the analysis of particular scenes from the works. In the first I examine how both works make visible the constructedness of historical narratives, highlighting their omissions and their instability. In the second I take a look at particular instances in both works in which the dancing body, and its ability to simultaneously reflect and critique the stories that shape it, is specifically foregrounded through the use of *mise en abyme* devices. Throughout both sections I will interrogate how the disruptive entrance of the corporeal into these narratives highlights the ever-shifting and malleable nature of constitutive stories and the subjectivities that they shape.

Dancing the unpalatable

The bodies that appear in *The Bull* are all at the mercy of one woman's desires, and the work ends with the entire cast having been sacri-ficed in a myriad of gruesomely violent ways to the insatiable greed of Maeve Fogarty, Keegan-Dolan's re-imagining of the *Táin's* warrior queen, Maebh of Connacht (see Figure 4.1). Following the original narrative, the piece opens with Maeve and her husband Alan – in this version a pair of high-flying property developers living in a city 'mansion' – comparing their financial wealth in bed one evening. Kneeling in opposing stage right and stage left positions and facing out towards the audience, the pair shouts across the gulf between them to engage in pillow talk consumed with one-upmanship. In a rapid *commedia dell'arte* style exchange, delivered in time to an ominous drumbeat, they list and compare possessions until it is dis-covered that Alan is wealthier than Maeve, but only by one item: a prize bull that she gave him for his birthday. There is only one other bull in Ireland that is the equal of Alan's bull, and this belongs to the Cullens, a family of plasterers living in the boglands. However, after overhearing Maeve's son drunkenly declare in a pub toilet that his

Figure 4.1   Beginning of the final scene in Fabulous Beast Dance Theatre's *The Bull* (2005). Photograph: Ros Kavanagh

mother would have their bull whether they gave it willingly or not, the Cullens vow that Maeve will never have their bull, and during the ensuing fight for the beast, the lives of Maeve's son and daughter, her husband, the entire Cullen family, various employees and friends on both sides, and finally her own, are sacrificed. However, it is not just the greed of the nouveau riche produced by the property bubble in the Irish building trade that is lampooned in the work. Along the way, a disparaging eye is also cast over several other Irish institutions including the church (shown to be corruptible when Maeve seduces her parish priest and has him do her bidding) and the health system (critiqued for its inadequacies in a scene in which bribed nurses pick their noses and anuses before rubbing their fingers in Colm Cullen's open wounds). However, it is perhaps the callous and violent behaviour of Maeve Fogarty herself that is the most challenging disruption of a cherished institutional identity: the Irish mother figure. Despite Maeve's best scheming efforts, the Cullens repeatedly refuse to give her their bull and so she resorts to increasingly violent means, which include dispatching her intellectually disabled daughter, Finn, as a sexual emissary to Colm 'the dog' Cullen (*The Bull's* version of Cúchulainn, the 'hound of Ulster', replete with terrifying warp spasms), suffocating Colm's lover with a plastic shopping bag and strangling a troublesome Italian helper, Salvatore, with a telephone cord when he suggests calling the police. The depiction of the mother figure in Irish theatre has, as Melissa Sihra states, 'traditionally been viewed as a personification of the nation.'[43] Viewing the calculating modern Maeve in this light, the nation is bluntly portrayed in *The Bull* as an amoral and grasping victim to capitalist greed.

The action of *The Bull* takes place on a stage covered in 10 tonnes of Irish peat moss against the backdrop of a large white cyclorama. Speaking of the striking *mise en scène* created by bodies lit starkly against cycloramas, which is a recurring feature of his work, Keegan-Dolan explains that he is seeking to lend a certain enhanced definition, or 'hard-edged' quality to the bodies on stage.[44] In his love of hard edges and visual definition he mirrors society's desire for a clearly delineated cultural identity. However, in his reflection of this desire, his heightened definition serves instead to destabilise and warp any fixed identities that are being sought. The use of stark contrast in Keegan-Dolan's approach to the visual quality in *The Bull*

can also be observed in his structuring of scenes in which tragic
or violent moments are often immediately followed by humorous
episodes, frequently in the form of non-diagetic songs whose lyrics
comment on the preceding action obliquely and ironically (for example, following a particularly violent scene in which a man is hacked
to death with an axe in the pouring rain, the cast gathers to sing
Johnny Nash's thoroughly optimistic 'I can see clearly now the rain
has gone'). In this world of constant disruption, the disparity between
notions of 'authentic' Irishness and proposed realities of Irishness
is highlighted. *The Bull* displays a clashing of cultures, being a site
of corporeal meetings that take place in the gap between the narratives of the 'constitutive stories' that form cultural identity, and the
messy, unstable realities of the bodies that create and dance through
them. The sense that visions of a 'hyped-up' Ireland (to use O'Toole's
expression) might be causing damage to the people inhabiting it, was
articulated as early as 2001 by theatre director Garry Hynes:

> [f]rom a wider cultural perspective, and social perspective, I'm
> deeply concerned with what's happening, because I don't know
> what we're losing but I do think we're losing a lot. This town now
> [Galway] seems to be a set for a version of Irishness. [...] There's a
> gap between that and what we are. I don't know what's happen-
> ing in that gap and I don't know how wide that gap is; but it's
> worrying [...].[45]

Hynes proposes that the Celtic Tiger economic boom resulted in a
shiny, new image of a prosperous and pristine Ireland which, to use
her simile, resembles a theatrical stage set in its falsity as a 'true'
picture of the country. She raises issues of authenticity in proposing
that there is a gap between this presentation of Irishness and 'what
we are', and feels that a 'real' and authentic Irishness is being lost.
The Bull plays to this cultural anxiety and troubles the supposition
that there is, or ever was, an authentic singular version of Irishness.
Instead, it deals in multiplicities and presents the intercultural meetings of mythic Ireland (the re-moulded narrative of the *Táin*) with
proposed social realities of contemporary Ireland, and pre-Celtic Tiger
Ireland (represented by the Cullens living in a midlands bog) with
post-Celtic Tiger Ireland (represented by the Fogartys, property developers from the city). In addition to these meetings, its multinational

cast gives rise to a Nigerian parish priest who sings *'as Gaeilge'* (in Irish) and a Slovakian Cúchulainn.

Books and bodies

In the opening scene of *The Bull*, which functions as a prologue to the piece, a man seated at a piano, wearing a bull horn hat and a costume the colour of the peat that surrounds him, pronounces, 'It will all end in death'. As he plays a succession of seemingly atonal chords, the rest of the cast arrive one by one and begin to rhythmically dig into the earth that covers a large mound centre stage. The digging uncovers a coffin, which starts to rattle and shake until its inhabitant – a dead man who will become the narrator of the piece – throws open the coffin lid clutching an old book, which he announces contains the story of *The Bull*. This news is not well received ('not the feckin' Bull!') and the diggers try to beat him back into his coffin, but he explains with exasperation, all the while being interrupted by repeated attacks,

> You can't kill me, I'm already dead! When will you stupid bastards ever learn? Accept it! Accept it! Try and bury it down in the filth and the cold and it will make you sick. And it will make your children sick. And it will make your children's children sick. And it will make your children's, children's children sick and sick for generations. You can't bury poison. You have to burn it. Until you burn it, it won't go away [...] I won't go away until you've swallowed your medicine. Then, we can all move on.

From the outset, this retelling of the *Táin* in a modern setting is put forward as an uncomfortable, yet necessary, review of buried narratives. Digging up 'poisonous' elements from the past for review also means acknowledging that certain stories from contemporary society are likewise being buried and need to be unearthed. The narrator begins his story by standing stiffly to attention and reading from his book in an overly loud manner, exaggerating the enunciation of every word. However, after only a few sentences he pauses, scans through the rest of the opening page with a look of puzzlement that quickly turns into disapproval, and throws the book aside, relaxing his posture and restarting his narration from the beginning, but this time in his own words. The message is clear – the official written version of the story in the book is being abandoned so that it can be retold from the perspective of the body that was buried in its telling. The proposed 'medicine' that will allow for buried societal ills to be aired is a re-embodiment of the story with all its unsavoury elements intact.

Books, as a symbol of the homogenising and sanitising nature of constitutive stories, feature even more prominently in *Ballads*. The piece begins when a dimly lit line of dancers, standing downstage with their backs to the audience, walk upstage into complete darkness. To the sound of distant and distorted bells, wind chimes and a low drone on the uilleann pipes, the face and upper body of a woman suddenly appear out of the dark; the light that makes her visible emanates from the illuminated book she is reading. As she reads, various shadowy figures in frozen positions that will reoccur in motion during the piece are briefly illuminated before they disappear again into the pitch dark. Then a square spotlight shows two arms tapping the strings of a cello that is lying lengthways across an otherwise inert body. The wooden structure of the cello on the supine body brings to mind a corpse in a coffin. The performer (Diane O'Keeffe) who is playing the cello is lying on a large board, which at this point is still invisible due to the dim lighting. As the woman continues reading, the board is slowly lifted from the ground and then pushed upwards from the horizontal to the vertical so that the cellist seems to be floating upwards in the air before being slowly tipped forward so that she is standing upright; through her reading, the woman appears to be raising bodies from the past and from the grave. When the board that supported the cellist crashes to the ground behind her, the reader drops her book in fright and another dim light upstage reveals a group of four dancers processing slowly in a linear formation with their bodies leaning forwards. As the light grows a little brighter, the cello case 'coffin' that they are carrying on their shoulders becomes visible and the line is seen to be a funeral procession. When the reader joins the procession, more light reveals that the performing space is surrounded with stacks and stacks of books and littered with loose pages.

Although this opening scene might seem at first to suggest that experiences from the Famine can be brought to life through the reading of historical accounts, an examination of the use of light leads to a very different reading. The carefully controlled spotlights only ever give a dim, incomplete and frozen view of the action on stage. These flashes of frozen poses bring to mind the iconic images of the Famine from the print media of the nineteenth century: the 'stalking spectre' of famine; the dead man lying in a ditch with a green mouth from chewing grass; or the half-naked mother with her arms around her skeletal children. These images were copied and re-copied as propaganda material in the land ownership campaigns of the 1870s,[46] and as Chris Morash suggests, they became so rigidly defined that they had, 'the boldly defined outlines of religious icons [...] [and] were so widely known that they could be said to constitute a form of collectively maintained "memory" [...] made up of static, iconic tableaux, each existing in a single timeless moment'.[47] Morash proposes that in their iconic form, these images became dislocated from their origin, which allowed for them to be viewed from a detached perspective. In this opening scene of *Ballads*, the use of light to briefly illuminate an image of bodies frozen in a pose that is suspended in the nowhere of darkness, imitates the disembodied iconicity of these famine images. It is only when the reader drops her book and joins the other dancers that the light finally covers the entire stage space, revealing a previously unseen terrain and allowing the bodies moving in it to be placed in a spatio-temporal location and given a grounded materiality and motion. Putting the given story down in both *The Bull* and *Ballads* can be seen to allow the dancing bodies to engage in an example of Michel de Certeau's 'antidisciplinary' acts. Operating on a regulated terrain (the narrative), they simultaneously create space on this terrain for unregulated actions (the reinsertion of the corporeal).[48]

'Stick to your prancing about!': bringing the dancing body to the fore

In the scenes from *The Bull* and *Ballads* discussed so far I have highlighted the ways in which both works call attention to the omission of corporealities from mythic and historical narratives. In the following section I will focus on particular self-reflexive moments in each piece, in which a dance within a dance places heightened emphasis on the role of the dancing body qua dancing body in the performance. In both pieces, the scenes in which the use of a *mise en abyme* device can be observed represent additions by the choreographers to the narrative, that function, superficially at least, as humorous or light-hearted episodes. In *The Bull* it takes the form of the dance routines of a *Riverdance* parody, 'Celtic Bitch', an 'Irish music Irish dance extravaganza' that Maeve Fogarty has invested in, and in *Ballads* it occurs in an episode in which people begin to dance to Irish music in a potato field.

In *The Bull*, the dance routines of 'Celtic Bitch' show the Irish dancing body to be a slave to Maeve Fogarty's desires. We are told that 'Celtic Bitch' tells the story of the Warrior Queen Maebh of ancient myth (the same queen from the *Táin*), and that Maeve Fogarty was not only keen to support a show in which her namesake 'dances circles' around her warrior enemies and lovers, but that she also 'liked the idea of being made love to by every dancer that danced the male lead'. The personal identification of contemporary Maeve with this commercialised version of mythic Maebh and the fact that she is able to 'buy' the myth and bend it to her desire underlines the malleable nature of the constitutive story and its ability to be remoulded to suit the needs of changing economic climates. The Celtic Bitch troupe makes four appearances throughout *The Bull*, and their first 'show' serves as the blueprint for their subsequent appearances in the manner of a running gag. Accompanied by Robbie Harris on the bodhrán,[49] four chorus dancers, two men and two women, dressed in satin costumes of green, white and orange (the colours of the Irish national flag), perform synchronised faux Irish step dance moves with fixed, inane grins, overly exaggerated 'sexy' arm gestures and self-encouraging whoops and cries of 'go on ya good thing'. After their introductory sequence, the male lead, Fergus (played by ex-*Riverdance* lead Colin Dunne, who also choreographed these sections), enters wearing a Michael Flatley-esque[50] open shirt and leather trousers to deliver his step dance solo. In each appearance the group perform downstage on a narrow, grey strip of flooring that was cleared of peat in the opening scene to resemble a concrete pathway or road. During the same opening scene, a cement mixer is rolled onstage and sits perched on a mound of peat upstage left for the duration of the performance. The presence of both the mixer and the 'road' in the peat landscape can be read as a constant reminder of the steady progression of housing developments into rural Ireland, which is further underlined by the intrusions of property developers Maeve and Alan into the lives of the Cullens.

Peadar Kirby proposes that, 'under the Celtic Tiger, economic success correlates with social failure', and the 'actions of the state have favoured market forces to the detriment of social well-being'.[51] The social failure being brought to attention here is the economic changes that have led to physical changes in the rural Irish landscape, with the sprawl of poorly designed and badly serviced housing estates into the so-called 'commuter belts' around larger cities. The image of the cement mixer could also be seen to symbolise the control and sanitisation of that which is 'wild' and 'untamed'. Reading this in combination with the performance of the Irish dancing body in 'Celtic Bitch', it can be argued that the pouring of concrete into the boglands to make them even and smooth for the progress of the Celtic Tiger is being linked with the re-fashioning of the Irish dancing body to bring it in line with the efficient streamlined vision of a modern Ireland. As discussed in the introduction, this is exemplified by the rows of dancers advancing forward in perfectly synchronised lines in *Riverdance*, whose sleek, uniform, upright bodies corporealise the national project of modernisation.

Probing the link of the geographical landscape with the cartography of the dancing body further, the use of bog, with its layer upon layer of sediment, could be seen as comparable to the palimpsestic layerings and redefinitions of the Irish dancing body that are made visible in the *mise en abyme* device used in *The Bull*. As the name suggests, 'Celtic Bitch' shows the commercialised form of Irish dance to be a slave to a reinvented version of 'traditional' Irish culture. The exaggerated 'sexy' arm gestures used in the choreography parody the addition by the *Riverdance* choreographers of arm movements to the traditional style of Irish competitive step dancing, which requires the arms to be held stiff and immobile at the sides of the body. However, the 'traditional' style that is supposedly being reinvented is, as discussed earlier, itself an invention. In contrast with the regimented movement of the 'Celtic Bitch' choreography, the impulses for the rest of *The Bull* stem from Keegan-Dolan's reading of the *Táin*, and the resulting dance and language are as coarse and graphically violent as the battles described in Kinsella's text. The parody of *Riverdance's* Celtic Tiger version of Irish dance can therefore be viewed in contrast with both the straightjacketed dancing body of recent history and the imagined free and anarchic movement of the ancient bodies that inhabited the *Táin*. The inclusion of 'Celtic Bitch' within *The Bull*, then, becomes an intercultural meeting of dance traditions moving across three temporal planes of cultural identity. It can also be viewed as a demonstration of the way in which notions of 'authentic' traditions are revised to suit the needs of the current authorities.

Criticising recent revisionist readings of Irish history that serve to redefine national identity in order to make it coincide with hegemonic views, Kirby proposes that Irish identity has been 'sanitised' in its assimilation into multinational capitalism. He argues that Irish identity has thus been 'robbed of reference points from a rich and subversive history' and due to this, is characterised 'by a "high degree of deference" '.[52] In creating a contemporary version of the *Táin*, Keegan-Dolan is tapping into elements of this rich and subversive history that have been erased. John Frow, speaking of the heritage industry, points out that the creation of national history, 'involves a ritualistic staging of heroic narratives in such a way as to deny their active historicity – their usability for the present'.[53] *The Bull's* at times structurally chaotic retelling of the *Táin*, with its emphasis on the greedy and violent aspects of the story, its copious use of foul language and its eclectic mix of performance media, challenges this reification of heroic narratives. *The Bull* revels in the messy, dirty side of the national myth and in so doing, contrasts greatly with another theatricalised version. A production of the story by Galway based theatre company, Macnas,[54] was chosen to represent Ireland at the 1992 Expo in Seville and Martin Drury and Christopher Murray describe this non-verbal version as 'a celebration and dramatisation of one of Ireland's oldest and most important legends, [which] was quintessentially Irish [and] able to "speak" to our European neighbours'.[55] Expressly chosen to promote the country abroad, this 'quintessentially Irish' version is put forward as an authentic representation of the cultural values of Ireland. Keegan-Dolan's celebration of the 'foul-mouthed, violent, sexual, preChristian and amoral'[56] elements of the *Táin* and his linkage of these to societal ills in contemporary Ireland would perhaps preclude its ever being chosen by the body politic to represent the state and 'speak to our European neighbours', and it was arguably the fear of the piece being seen to represent that which is supposedly 'quintessentially Irish' which caused such a negative reaction from some quarters when it premiered. However, I would argue that Keegan-Dolan's focus on these 'dirty' aspects of Irish cultural identity is a reaction to its sanitisation, and that his attempt at subverting bowdlerised versions is long overdue.

Over the course of the 'Celtic Bitch' appearances, Fergus's dancing becomes increasingly ragged and insecure. We have been told that his knees are damaged from the relentless touring schedule of the show (at one point he is described as 'knee-fucked Fergus') and in the final 'Celtic Bitch' sequence, he quickly becomes dishevelled and breathless, finally stopping his movement altogether, doubling over and holding his damaged knees in pain. André Lepecki uses the term 'still-act' to describe such moments in dance where movement is suspended and 'a subject interrupts historical flow and *practices* historical interrogation'.[57] Stopping the movement of the Celtic Bitch machine ruptures the vision of the untroubled and uninterrupted progress of the pristine 'new' Ireland. It enacts 'a corporeally based interruption of modes of imposing flow' and in retrospect seems a curiously prescient warning of the ensuing collapse of the Irish economy in the recent recession.[58] The extraordinary closing scene of *The Bull*, in which the entire cast perform an almost 10-minute long percussive, stamped and yelled finale, moving in the closing moments into a *Riverdance*-esque line across the stage, is an impassioned and vehement rejection of the Celtic Tiger values embodied in the commercialised form. The representation of a dancing body that stops or rejects a flow of movement in this way is challenging the incorporation of the Irish dancing body into the homogenising project of the state.

In his presentation of the Irish dancing body in 'Celtic Bitch', Keegan-Dolan inhabits the 'traditional' dance form so as to subvert it. The sanitised body politic is made visible and through the use of parody, made absurd. In the original version of *The Bull* for the 2005 Dublin Theatre Festival, actor Conor Lovett played the role of the narrator and in the revived version at the Barbican, this role was given to Colin Dunne. Giving the role of narrator to a dancer rather than an actor positions the Irish dancing body in the centre of Keegan-Dolan's critique, lending it not only a heightened visibility, but also an increased power of articulation. In a scene towards the end of the work, Fergus offers Maeve some advice to which she replies, 'stick to your prancing about and leave the serious business to me'. Here Keegan-Dolan points out the usual marginalised placement of theatrical dance in Ireland, and, again, as is ultimately shown through the disastrous consequences of Maeve's actions, also demonstrating that a refusal to 'listen' to the body can have damaging consequence for society ('it will all end in death'). Viewing the performances of 'Celtic Bitch' as a *mise en abyme* device, the 'dance within a dance' is an encapsulation of Keegan-Dolan's critique of Irish society and its relation to the dancing body, embedded in a parody of commercialised Irish traditional dance. Functioning in this way, 'Celtic Bitch' would seem to highlight the dislocation, or 'gap' (to recall Hynes' term) between Irish society's past notion of its cultural identity, for example traditional dance in a form propounded to be historically 'pure', and the 'false' image of Celtic Tiger Ireland indexed by commercial cultural productions such as *Riverdance*.

The instance of a dance within a dance in *Ballads* (see Figure 4.2) is very different from the *mise en abyme* device used in *The Bull*, both in terms of its tone of delivery and its intended purpose within the piece as a whole. The scene begins with one dancer downstage scrambling along the ground, hurriedly arranging loose book pages into neat parallel lines ordered to resemble the furrows of a potato field. Behind this labouring body, four upright figures wearing heavy, bustled dresses or dress suits and holding illuminated wine glasses, perform a slow-moving, stately dance to a Bach gavotte played faintly and in slow motion on the cello. As their dance progresses from upstage left to right, the movements of the figure working in the field in front of them become more abject as her body begins to contort and twist and she struggles to move. The sharp disparity in how the Famine was experienced by the different classes in Ireland is clearly communicated here and the extremely slow playing of the Bach gavotte, added to the visual divide between the actions, levels and postures of the two groups, lends the scene a mournful and disquieting tone. It is important to note that all social classes were vulnerable to being affected by the diseases that accompanied the Famine, although there were inevitably far more deaths through disease in the cottager class. When the high-living landlords exit, more workers arrive at the field and help the distraught woman in the potato field back on her feet. The dancers then begin a concentrated phrase of weaving in and out of the furrows in a linear formation, using arm, leg and upper body swings to create synchronised movement phrases that are reminiscent of farming activities such as harrowing

Figure 4.2   Simone Litchfield in CoisCéim's *Ballads* (1997). Photograph: Kip Carroll (www.kipcarroll.com)

and ploughing. A recorded soundtrack of clapped rhythms, birdsong and a low drone accompanies this section. The mood then changes rather abruptly when a traditional Irish dance tune on the uilleann pipes is played offstage. Lining up at the edge of the 'field', the workers begin a playful dance across the furrows, engaging in brief flirtatious duets and duels, stamping in counterpoint to the rhythm of the tune (with rhythms reminiscent of traditional step dancing), and calling and laughing to an accompanying soundscape of children playing schoolyard games ('concentration, are you ready, if so, let's go'). As it progresses, the dance becomes increasingly wild, and when the music stops the neat rows of book pages have been messed up so that the furrows are indistinguishable. In the silence that follows, the dancers exit the space leaving the original woman labourer back on the ground, contorted amidst the devastation.

Unlike in *The Bull*, in which the acerbic humour of the 'Celtic Bitch' episodes follows the general tone of ironic satire in the work, the mood of the potato field dance in *Ballads*, with its humorous tone, is conspicuously contrastive to the sombre mood of the rest of the piece. Bolger explained that in this dance, '[t]he humour for me basically signifies our will to survive and that maybe our sense of humour is not always killed straight away'.[59] Although Bolger set out to oppose what he felt to be the celebratory tone of the Famine sesquicentennial, his sentiment here echoes many of the feelings expressed at the time of the commemorations. President Mary Robinson, for example, suggested that the Famine had more influence on Irish identity than any other event, as it, 'shaped us as a people. It defined our will to survive'.[60] Bolger's use of a *mise en abyme* device to emphasise these qualities of humour and survival in a dance, places the dancing body once again in a position of central importance. Within the context of 'coming to terms' with the Famine tragedy, the dancing body would seem to be imbued here with reparative qualities. However, on closer inspection, certain aspects of this scene are quite problematic. Linking the recorded sound of children's games to the dance connects childlike qualities with the actions of the people working the potato field. This would seem to perpetuate a colonial patriarchal social order, also making it possible to read the destruction of the potato field at the end of the dance as having occurred through the actions of careless 'children' at play. This scene also appears at first to be at odds with Bolger's attempts throughout the rest of the piece to redress misconceptions about the Famine and to undertake a re-visioning of the social and emotional realities of the times. In Cormac Ó Gráda's discussion of contemporary accounts of the Famine found in Irish language ballads written during the period, he examines a Kerry song, *'Amhrán an Ghorta'* (The Famine Song), that gives an insight into the effect that starvation was having on behaviour and social relations:

[t]he famine not only did away with the usual enthusiasm for music and socializing: people hardly recognized one another any more; there were no marriages, *'ná suim ina dhéanamh'* (nor any

interest in arranging them), and those young people who might normally be considering marriage now wanted to spend their dowries on a passage to America instead. Young men had lost their vigor (*tréine*), so that '*ní miste spéirbhean bheith amuigh go déanach*' (it is safe for young beauties to be out alone late).[61]

In light of this account and others of a similar nature, the energetic and carefree dance in the potato field becomes at best incongruous and at worst inappropriate. Yet, it can be argued that what this dance within a dance actually highlights has nothing to do with the 'reality' of the Famine or with the celebration of some national characteristic that was made manifest through adversity. Rather, what this scene is actually drawing attention to is the continued need of contemporary society for constitutive stories that provide some sort of cohesive narrative for a community or nation. As discussed in the introductory chapter, the 1990s was a period of rapid social change in Ireland, which led to a questioning of social and moral values. I would argue that in this work, and particularly in this *mise en abyme* section, the story of the Famine is in fact allowing for an expression of the fears and desires brought about by the experience of a *contemporary* rather than historical subjectivity. Publications at the time of the sesquicentennial commemorations would seem to support this argument. Kevin Whelan, for example, writes

> [t]he frail famine voices now reach us across an aching void. We need to amplify that acoustic: in hearing them attentively we might reclaim our famine ghosts from their enforced silence and invisibility. In doing so, we can rescue them from the enormous condescension of posterity, paying them the respect which their lonely deaths so signally lacked. *That very gesture of reconnection may alleviate a cultural loneliness we do not even know we have and liberate us into a fuller and more honest sense of ourselves,* showing us how we got to be where we are, even as we leave it behind.
>
> [emphasis added][62]

It would seem that remembering the Famine has as much, or more, to do with tackling the sense of dislocation and 'cultural loneliness' that arrived with the social shifts of the 1990s, as it does with a desire to 'rescue' the memory of the famine victims. In light of this, the potato field dance in *Ballads* becomes less incongruous. Read this way, the playful, childlike dance and the use of children's voices and games in the soundtrack connect the story with nostalgic notions of innocence, simplicity and honesty; qualities that are projected onto these bodies from the past and whose perceived lack in contemporary society provokes the need for a re-appraisal of identity to achieve an 'honest sense of ourselves'. *Ballads* attempts not only to lend materiality to Famine narratives, but also to recover, through the body, a lost sureness of identity and confidence in the existence of supposedly 'Irish' qualities such as humour in the face of adversity and a strong will to survive. In this example, the dance within a dance demonstrates that constitutive stories pertaining to national characteristics still have currency in contemporary Ireland. The critique embedded in *Ballads* is of a different nature to the critical incisiveness of *The Bull*'s social commentary, yet an examination of the choreography of the dancing body in *Ballads* is equally enlightening in terms of the insight it can provide into the function of these narratives in current society.

Sick and well, living and dead

Peggy Phelan writes that, '[o]ur "own" body is the one we have and the history of the ones we've lost. Our body is both [...] sick and well, living and dead. Full of jerks and rears, the body moves like an awkward dancer trying to partner someone she can never see or lay full hold of'.[63] In both *The Bull* and *Ballads* the unpalatable jerks and rears of bodies that are rendered invisible in the creation of national myths and memories are brought to 'life' in works that attempt an embodied questioning of constitutive narratives. An examination of the choreography of the dancing bodies in these works shows that cultural identity is always in flux, slippery and shape-shifting, simultaneously looking backward and forward. At the opening of *The Bull*, a dead body from the past refuses to remain buried and re-emerges from the bog with the warning that the corruptions and ills of society may be covered up, but in their decaying they will poison the future. Keegan-Dolan's attempt to highlight the darker side of contemporary Irish society through his choreography of the awkward 'jerks and rears' of the dancing body may not have made for the most palatable of productions for some; the relentless repetition of cartoon-like violence is perhaps at times in danger of appearing to be as nonchalant and casual, in its seeming indifference to human life, as the unfeeling aspects of the society it is trying to critique. Yet it is undoubtedly a site of cultural resistance to the hegemonic order, challenging stereotypical and sanitised portrayals of Irish society and the Irish dancing body. Bolger's attempt to redress the shortcomings of textual accounts of the Famine through an embodiment of, 'the emotion of the real people who were caught up in [it]', also has its difficult elements.[64] Nonetheless, *Ballads* succeeds in creating a retelling that highlights the stifling of bodily realities in textual accounts. The re-appropriation of these constitutive stories by the resistive dancing body in both works allows for their interrogation from an otherwise erased corporeal perspective.

In the following chapter I also consider the relationship between bodies and narratives, however the focus shifts from a consideration of how dance theatre can highlight the repression of the corporeal in constitutive stories, to a discussion of how well-known narratives of gender and sexual oppression can be reshaped and transformed through the choreography of unanticipated moves. Both *Giselle* and *The Rite of Spring* by Fabulous Beast engage in a critique of the socio-political moulding of corporealities, highlighting the continued oppression of certain femininities and masculinities in modern Irish society and the perpetuation of a culture of shame and taboo surrounding corporeal issues.

5
Choreographing the Unanticipated: Death, Hope and Verticality in *Giselle* and *The Rite of Spring*

In this chapter I develop my discussion of narrative and storytelling in dance theatre works to consider how certain choreographies not only function to reinstate a corporeal perspective into mythical/historical narratives, but how they also gesture towards a transformation of the traditional 'bad endings' for certain oppressed corporealities. In Fabulous Beast's reworkings[1] of *Giselle* (2003) and *The Rite of Spring* (2009) there is a radical departure from the usual endings of the ballets' original librettos. In both instances, an unexpected twist in the narrative occurs in the closing moments, leaving the spectator with a surprising final image that allows for a questioning of seemingly hermetic narratives of oppression. This chapter will examine the potential political efficacy of these unanticipated endings, examining how these alterations transfigure the relationship between a feminine corporeality and death. Dancing dead bodies appear in several of Keegan-Dolan's works for Fabulous Beast; in *The Bull* (2007), for example, exhumed corpses signal the poisoning of a community by suppressed societal ills or, as seen in the finale of the same work, reanimated slain bodies vent an anger provoked by the excesses of the Celtic Tiger era. In these instances, the dead bodies' dances can be seen to function allegorically in a chiefly condemnatory capacity. Yet, in the works analysed here, it will be argued that a linking of dance and death is employed for a transformative rather than censuring effect and paradoxically gives rise to expressions of hope and potential agency. To examine this proposed transformative effect, this chapter will focus primarily on the striking images presented in the final scenes of the two works, in which a dancing dead woman and a woman dancing in defiance of death perform critiques of gendered spatiality in their disruptions of traditional narratives.

Tackling classics

Giselle, the first work of the *Midlands Trilogy*, was choreographed by Keegan-Dolan and a multinational cast of 10 dancer-actors in a converted barn on a dairy farm in County Longford, over an intensive eight-week period of devising. This radical reworking of the original ballet was Keegan-Dolan's fifth work for Fabulous Beast and is the production that secured his status as a choreographer of international renown.[2] As in most of his work for Fabulous Beast, Keegan-Dolan's choreography in *Giselle* utilises an eclectic blend of song, theatre, and a variety of movement techniques that harness every expressive facet of the dancing body in order to tell a story. Stylistically, this piece marks a watershed in his choreographic development, as it is the first work in which the spoken word is used.[3] As previously discussed, Keegan-Dolan's disregard for genre boundaries stems from his desire to clearly and effectively communicate ideas. Speaking of his inclusion of speech in *Giselle* he explains

> [i]n the years preceding the creation of *Giselle* I had become increasingly frustrated by my attempts to tell stories through the wordless medium of dance. As the choreographer George Balanchine pointed out, 'it is impossible to say, *this is my mother in law*, in the language of dance'. I decided that I could not successfully tell the story of Giselle with all its details and quirks in complete silence [emphasis in original].[4]

Typical of all Fabulous Beast productions examined here, *Giselle* is an example of dance theatre that uses a reworking of well-known narrative to serve as a platform for a critique of Irish society. Despite its roots in a traditional ballet narrative, the overwhelmingly positive critical reviews of *Giselle* invariably make reference to its 'originality', 'radicalism' and 'uniqueness' of style. Identifying it as 'brazenly and triumphantly new', Karen Fricker claims that the piece 'challenges and extends the definitions of all the words with which it is necessary to describe it: "Irish", "dance" and "theatre".'[5]

The Rite of Spring, Keegan-Dolan's eighth piece for Fabulous Beast, premiered at the London Coliseum in November 2009. In terms of scale, this production is the company's most ambitious work to date. Presented in co-production with the English National Opera in a double bill,[6] the piece brought together a cast of 25 dancers accompanied by an expanded ENO orchestra of over one hundred players conducted by Edward Gardner.[7] As is often noted, responding to Stravinsky's *The Rite of Spring* has become something of a rite of passage for choreographers. Speaking of his decision to join his own response to the long list of reworkings, which includes acclaimed versions by practitioners such as Kenneth MacMillan (1962), Pina Bausch (1974), Martha Graham (1984) and more recently Shen Wei (2003), Keegan-Dolan suggests that Stravinsky's score is, 'an iconic work, one that chooses you rather than you choosing it' and that the opportunity to create a production with live orchestra, offered to him by the artistic director of the ENO, John Berry, fulfilled a long-held ambition.[8] Critical reaction to Fabulous Beast's *Rite* from dance critics in the UK was overwhelmingly positive,[9] and following in the footsteps of *Giselle* and *The Bull*, the piece was also nominated for an Olivier Award. Interestingly there is no spoken word used in *The Rite of Spring*, yet the strong narrative of the libretto positions this work, alongside *Giselle* and the other pieces in the *Midlands Trilogy*, as belonging to Fabulous Beast's works of storytelling dance theatre.

Images of verticality

It is the striking expression of an unexpected verticality in the final images of *Giselle* and *The Rite of Spring* that deviates so radically from the librettos of the original ballets, and which serves as my point of departure for a discussion of their potentially transformative effect. In the final scene of Fabulous Beast's *Giselle*, the heroine (in keeping with Théophile Gautier's original libretto) rescues her lover Albrecht from being murdered by the vengeful spirits of women who have died through the selfish acts of men. But after their final *pas de deux* – a fluid interplay of weight and weightlessness that moves through tender embraces and exquisitely controlled, slow, revolving lifts – Giselle does not disappear by descending gracefully into her grave, leaving

Albrecht in sole possession of the stage. Instead, as the lighting on the scrim behind her brightens, indicating the return of daylight, she starts to jump, rising higher and higher in a seemingly effortless verticality created by the weight of her own body. Underneath the accompanying soundscape composed of a mixture of Philip Feeney's modern score and the closing strains of Adolphe Adam's original score from 1841, are the squeaks of the springs on the concealed trampoline beneath her. All around this jumping Giselle, the captive women's spirits start to ascend the noose-like ropes that have chained them to the earth and as Albrecht's figure backs away downstage right into shadow, the entire scene describes a powerful upward motion of hope and joy (see Figure 5.1).

Similarly, the final scene of Fabulous Beast's reworking of *The Rite of Spring* begins in a manner very close to the original libretto for the ballet composed by Stravinsky: a young woman, the Chosen One, is dancing centre stage surrounded by a community who are performing a ritual of sacrifice to ensure the return of spring. But this woman does not dance to death. Instead, as snow falls, her emphatic and authoritative movements rooted in a low centre of gravity induce a dance to the point of collapse in a group of men who, influenced

Figure 5.1   Image from the final moments of Fabulous Beast Dance Theatre's *Giselle* (2003). Photograph: T Charles Erickson

by the power of the ritual, have stripped themselves naked and put on floral print dresses. One by one the men join the Chosen One in her dance until the entire group jumps in unison, the large circular motions of their arms helping to propel the bodies upwards, and the whole stage picture seems to pulse to the music's pounding rhythms. In the closing moments the woman starts to spin on the spot, and in the final bars of Stravinsky's score the men collapse to the ground creating splashes of colour in the snow. As the scrim turns a bright yellow signalling the rising sun and the return of spring, the Chosen One remains standing, her body a stark silhouette against the yellow light, feet planted in a wide, open stance, her face and arms raised upwards (see Figure 5.2).

In the two scenes described above, the anticipated endings are transformed. In both instances the death of a woman, which leads

Figure 5.2 Image from the final moments of Fabulous Beast Dance Theatre's *The Rite of Spring* (2009). Photograph: Johan Persson/ArenaPal

to the re-establishment of a threatened status quo in a community, is either denied completely or reframed so that the woman's spirit acquires agency in death. Both pieces end with striking images of a verticality that is in direct opposition with the traditional horizontal conclusion for the female body in the original works. My use of the term verticality connects the reconfiguration of the choreographed space in the final images with a gendered reading of planes of representation. As Lepecki argues, choreo-political reconfigurations of the planes of representation in dance can allow for a critique of gendered spatialities and 'colonialist territorializations'.[10] Rendered passive in death and consigned to the horizontal plane, the women's bodies in the two original ballets remain a 'territorialised domain'. A reclaiming of the vertical plane for the feminine body in Fabulous Beast's reworkings challenges an ordering of spatiality that, as Henri Lefebvre proposes, 'bestows a special status to the perpendicular, proclaiming phallocracy as the orientation of space'.[11] However, shifting the spatial order of the original ballets does not negate the presence of their traditional narratives. Indeed, the images in these reworkings are only especially striking due to their being haunted by both the anticipated original endings that they depart from and the particular historical events in Ireland (which will be discussed later) that they are commenting on and critiquing. Furthermore, the upending of a gendered spatial order must also be read in relation to the linking of a feminine corporeality with death in both works. What, if anything, is transgressed when joy and hope for a community is expressed through the dance of a dead body or when a sacrificial victim does not die, but instead causes all around her to collapse? In order to understand the complexity of resonances created by the palimpsestic nature of these final images, this chapter will first examine these alternative endings in the context of their dialogue with the original works. It will then examine how they critique the repression of certain corporealities in Irish society and in conclusion it will interrogate how the choreographing of unanticipated spatial disruptions in the endings of the works potentially opens up new landscapes of possibility.

In dialogue with Gautier and Nijinsky

Giselle premiered in Paris in 1841 and quickly became the most celebrated romantic ballet of the mid-nineteenth century. Taking inspiration from Heinrich Heine's account of a Slavic folk tale, Gautier's libretto tells the story of a young peasant girl, Giselle, who goes mad and dies of a broken heart when she discovers that her fiancé, Albrecht, has been concealing his real identity and is, in fact, a prince engaged to marry another woman. The second act of the ballet moves the action to Giselle's grave and the realm of the 'Wilis' – vengeful spirits of women who died before their wedding night and whose desire for dancing remains unsatisfied. To avenge their deaths and fulfill this desire, the Wilis lure unsuspecting men into the forest and force them to dance to their deaths. As Susan Foster proposes, although these spirits were probably intended to warn young women of the dangers of indulging in excessive corporeal pleasure, the fact that they constituted an exclusively feminine community that expressed aggressive sexual desire was not only a, 'thrilling embodiment of violated social codes [but also] offered a scandalous [and] intriguing alternative social organization'.[12] Yet as subversive as this glimpse of an autonomous feminine community would seem to be, the conclusion of the ballet ensured a reinstatement of the reigning patriarchal social order. After selflessly challenging the queen of the Wilis to save the life of the man who caused her death, Giselle returns to her grave. Albrecht is left standing centre stage, exhausted and grief-stricken, but back in control of his destiny and ready to continue in his ordained position in the social hierarchy.

In Keegan-Dolan's one-act reworking, the pastoral setting of the traditional first act is retained. However life in the fictional midlands village of Ballyfeeney is portrayed as barbaric and backward rather than bucolic. As with *The Bull* and *James Son of James* (the other two works from the *Midlands Trilogy*) the midlands setting holds particular significance for Keegan-Dolan. In addition to his ancestral links to this area, which stretch back several generations,[13] he interprets this location 'in the very centre of an island' as having a psychosomatic influence on its inhabitants, resulting in an inwardness and desire for stasis: '[t]he world I have invented for *Giselle* is a place where it rains everyday, where it is mucky, where things change incredibly slowly, where people are terrified of change'.[14] His treatment and understanding of this landscape as representing 'the heart of Ireland', goes beyond a topographical/geographical perception, to a somatic reading of the 'body' of the Irish landscape that connects with, and shapes, the corporealities of the people living in it.[15] It is interesting to note that the Irish playwright Marina Carr has also based a substantial amount of her work in the midlands (e.g. *The Mai* (1994), *Portia Coghlan* (1996), *By the Bog of Cats* (1998)). Melissa Sihra's insightful analysis of the influence of this location on Carr's use of language, in which she argues that Carr's attempt to represent the landscape in words results in 'the corpus or "body" of standard English [being] fractured, ruptured and defamiliarised as conventions of syntax are radically broken', has, despite the difference in medium, a significant degree of resonance with the influence accredited by Keegan-Dolan to the landscape in his shaping of corporealities for the *Midlands Trilogy*.[16]

Similar to the way in which Gautier's original rural setting is reworked in Fabulous Beast's *Giselle*, familiar character names from the original libretto also reappear in an altered guise. Many of the relationships between original characters have been modified considerably and the addition of several important roles such as the sexually confused Pat Dunne the Butcher's Son, the domineering and ambitious Nurse Mary, greedy Fat Mary (Nurse Mary's daughter) and the outsider Tommy McCreedy (Giselle's father), results in a shift from the soloist/corps structure of the original to a much more ensemble-oriented model. Giselle, who has been mute and asthmatic since her balletomane mother committed suicide one Christmas Eve, is treated with scorn by most of the community. She lives with her mentally disturbed brother, Hilarion (a significant reworking of the original jealous gamekeeper) whose implied incestuous love for her is expressed through violence, and whose comi-tragic attempt at joining in a line-dancing class replaces the traditional mad scene at the end of act one. Adding to this twist and firmly relocating the element of madness in the original ballet from its traditional locus in the feminine, it is Giselle's father Tommy McCreedy, introduced as a recluse who has chosen to live on top of an electricity pole, who functions in a non-dancing role as narrator of the piece. This wonderfully literal physical rendering of the elevated position of the patriarchal into an image of absurdity is further underlined by the fact that Giselle, danced by the only female performer in a cast of 11 (Daphne Strothmann), appears as arguably the most eloquent member of her community. Being mute, her corporeal communications are thus placed in opposition with the supposed logic and order of the patriarchal word and law. As in the original ballet, the social order is shown to be under threat, but now the subversive sexual elements that were lurking under the ethereal surface of the so-called 'white act'[17] are brought to the fore. In Keegan-Dolan's version, Albrecht is a bisexual line-dancing teacher from Bratislava, at once doubly other in his transgression of the community's outwardly narrow definitions of sexual and ethnic norms. Albrecht's dance class, a flamboyant blend of country-western and Eastern European styles of line-dancing, becomes a site of relative freedom and sanctuary for Giselle, and her blossoming sexual relationship with him seems to present a possible route of escape from her tortured life. Yet, throughout the piece, Giselle's asthma functions as an ominous reminder of the stifling and constricting oppression exerted by the community on its members. After falling in love with Albrecht, Giselle dies of an asthma attack after she witnesses him having sex with Pat Dunne the Butcher's Son. While she is struggling to catch a breath, two white balloons (exo-corporeal lungs) are inflated and when she dies they are let go. The usually comical sound of air rushing out of balloons combined with the image of her lifeless body creates an uncomfortable moment between bathos and pathos, which functions to underline the futility of her death. In the following graveyard scene the Wilis emerge from trapdoors and use noose-ended ropes to sweep across the stage in an aerial dance accompanied by countertenor Angelo Smimmo singing *Libere me Domine*. During the transition to the graveyard Giselle's father tells us that she has had to be buried outside of the church walls of the Ballyfeeny graveyard because she has 'fornicated with a stranger, a bi-sexual man'. Similar to the original ballet, Giselle's dead body becomes a site for the projection of the community's fear of the repressed and the unknown. In the original, Albrecht's 'violation of class boundaries'[18] functions as the pivotal point of betrayal, but in Keegan-Dolan's version, it is a fear of change and the stubborn cultivation of an environment of secrecy and shame in relation to sexual expression outside of permissible heteronormative boundaries that leads to a whole community betraying a young woman.

Although Nijinsky's choreography of Stravinsky's *The Rite of Spring* for Diaghilev's Ballets Russes would seem to have nothing in common with the romantic ideology of *Giselle*, parallels can nevertheless be drawn between both ballets' portrayal of an immolated feminine body as an instrument of societal redemption. The disturbance created by protesting audience members at the premiere of Nijinsky's *Rite* in Paris on 29 May 1913 is legendary and undoubtedly helped secure its status in dance and theatre history as being 'emblematic of the shock of the new'.[19] A collaboration between composer Stravinsky, choreographer Nijinsky and ethnologist and designer Nicholas Roerich, *The Rite of Spring* took as its inspiration Slavonic myth, iconography and imagined folk rituals to construct a danced primal scene in which a community sacrifices a young girl to ensure the return of spring. However the historical elements that created the backdrop also functioned on a metaphorical level as 'a vehicle for conveying the tragedy of modern being',[20] and as Lynn Garafola proposes, Nijinsky created in his choreography of shockingly angular, violent and repetitive group movements, 'a biologic order that designed the body into both an instrument and object of mass oppression'.[21] Brendan McCarthy also observes the links between the ballet's mythic foundation and its modernism, writing, '[a]lthough Nijinsky's creatures are primitives, they are the automata of an industrial age'.[22] It is interesting to note that the sacrifice of the 'Chosen One', the virgin girl selected by the community to be killed in Stravinsky's libretto, has no foundation in Slavonic folklore. Pointing out the synthetic nature of the myth at the ballet's core, Garafola connects the feminisation of the sacrificial victim, represented by a young girl, with a need to make 'safe' the threatening androgynous sexuality of the *fin-de-siècle* 'feminised artist', proposing that the 'Chosen Virgin is, above all, a creation of twentieth century male sexual anxiety'.[23]

Fabulous Beast's reworking of *The Rite of Spring* remains loosely connected to Stravinsky's libretto, but, as with *Giselle*, departs radically from the original ending. Similar to the way in which Nijinsky's use of distorted faux-pagan movement was seen to reflect the modern brutality of mass oppression in the newly industrialised Western world, Keegan-Dolan's intent was to create a 'faux pagan world of rubber and plastic'[24] that would nevertheless speak of what he views to be problematic issues in contemporary Western society, in particular the disconnection of body and mind and the subjugation of the feminine. Stating, 'women have had a raw deal in Ireland',

Keegan-Dolan has spoken of how his close relationship with his mother, grandmother and grand-aunt influenced the choreography of his *Rite*, and his desire to combat the potentially ambivalent and misogynistic original ending of the piece.[25] While recognising the inevitably synthetic results produced by any search for 'authentic' movements from pagan times, Keegan-Dolan was able to find inspiration in the notion of ritual, explaining that for him, ritual is

> essentially about *doing*, reconnecting with the body and acknowledging its interrelation with the earth and its surroundings. Ritual is about disconnecting with the miasma of the mind and recognizing the bones, the body and the blood, our essential physicality that so much of the modern world dissociates us from.[26]

Similar to Pina Bausch's famous reworking of the ballet, which staged an epic and violent struggle between men and women, Keegan-Dolan also structures his *Rite* around issues of gender.[27] Yet, in his version, it is the societal control of masculine and feminine energies, rather than the difference between man and woman, that produces the site of conflict. In the community portrayed in Fabulous Beast's *Rite*, the feminine, linked to a force of change and growth, has been oppressed in a male-dominated society that is in a state of imbalance. The stage is covered in what appears to be hard, frozen earth and in the upstage left corner, a large, white statue of the Virgin Mary watches over the proceedings. The rite begins with the appearance of the black-robed Cailleach, or Hag, played by Olwen Fouéré, who strides in circular patterns through the space, trailed by cigarette smoke and her boy acolyte. Drawing inspiration from myths of the winter goddess Demeter and the Irish *cailleach*, a repulsive hag who transforms into a beautiful young woman if she can persuade a young man to sleep with her, Keegan-Dolan and Fouéré conceived of the Cailleach as an outsider and a powerfully subversive figure, who embodies both masculine and feminine desires and has the power to initiate the ritual of the sacrifice. In stark contrast to the foreboding presence of the Cailleach, three women dressed in stereotypically feminine, floral-patterned dresses enter on bicycles; one of them, danced by Daphne Strothmann, will later become the Chosen One. Similar to his positioning of the Cailleach on the periphery of the community, Keegan-Dolan's interpretation of the Chosen One also underlines a quality of otherness inherent in the role prior to the beginning of the rite, explaining, 'she's an unmarried woman and that character in a certain community has a kind of power. There's a question hanging over her because she doesn't fit into the community's expectations'.[28] The rest of the community is made up of a group of 18 bearded men led by a Sage (played by Bill Langfelder), the original 'Oldest and Wisest One' from Stravinsky's libretto. However, in this version the Sage's authority is physically destabilised when the table he has been standing on is lifted into the air, leaving him desperately clinging on to its sides as the men whisk him around the stage in a deliberately wild and shaky manège. Dressed like farmers in heavy, dark-coloured winter clothing, the men's costumes lend their group a mask of homogeneity and at the beginning of the piece the movement of this male group is strictly dictated by the shifting rhythms of Stravinsky's score. Clutching large cardboard boxes with 'fragile' printed on the side (perhaps a forewarning of the later fracturing of the libretto and shattering of a patriarchal hegemony), their small, pulsing motions, and tight, tense shifts of weight with perfectly synchronised abrupt half-turns describe a stifled energy that is simultaneously bizarre and menacing in its fiercely concentrated inward focus. The group's tension finds an early outlet in the violent chase and mock sacrifice of a young man who is stripped naked and hunted by the group, who are brandishing long knives. Later, when the women drink a potion prepared by the Cailleach and enter a trance state that induces deep pliés in second position and frightening convulsions, they put on the realistic hare masks and are held aloft, totem-like, on the shoulders of the men. Following this, the men drop their trousers and copulate furiously with the barren earth, but a post-coital snow-fall seems to underline their impotence. The piece progresses deeper into a dreamlike, visual surrealism when the Cailleach gives the men bull-terrier dog masks with lolling tongues and the hunt for the Chosen One begins. These eerily naturalistic masks, like the stereotyped clothing, serve to further reify and fix gender divisions in the frozen landscape. They also alter the actions of the wearers by magnifying certain movement qualities; the women/hares crouch and incline their heads in a watchful anticipation while the men/hounds shift their upper bodies forward in a predatory curve. After the frightening chase and capture of the sacrificial victim, all masks are removed. But here Keegan-Dolan's libretto begins its most marked departure from the original. The Chosen One appears for the final dance of sacrifice with what seems to be a long, colourful rope. In a beautiful moment of transformation, the unwinding of the umbilical-like rope by the men reveals that it is made up of a large number of floral dresses, all wound together. The men slowly shed all of their winter clothes until they are completely naked, and during Stravinsky's 'Ritual Actions of the Ancestors', solemnly put on the dresses. As the Chosen One begins the 'Sacred Dance' centre stage, the men surrounding her are initially motionless, but as her dance progresses, they join in ever-increasing numbers and with intensifying energy. Near the end of this rite, the dancers' euphoric stamps and jumps emphasise the polyrhythms of the timpani in Stravinsky's score, and as described earlier, the piece ends with the Chosen One standing over the group of men who lie collapsed at her feet. As Fouéré explains, this version of the *danse sacral*, 'is not a literal sacrifice: it's a death and rebirth, suggesting that you can transform reality'.[29] The dominance of an enforced, monolithic masculinity that represses the feminine is physically collapsed, and in this image of frozen earth covered in the bodies of men wearing brightly coloured dresses, the ground seems to be strewn with flowers. Collocating 'death' and life in this closing moment underlines Keegan-Dolan's reading of the sacrifice in *Rite* as 'innately optimistic', and his understanding that the piece offers, 'a way of processing the terrible finality of death, [...] encourag[ing] us not to be so frightened, to see death as the equal and opposite of birth'.[30]

Questions of relevance

The portrayal of gender and sexual oppression in *Giselle* and *The Rite of Spring* narrates a strict control of bodies by church and state powers and the perpetuation of a culture of shame and taboo surrounding corporeal issues. As discussed in the introduction, the ideology of the Irish state has historically been closely intertwined with the teachings of the Catholic Church, promoting the repressive control of an 'Irish' corporeality to a 'strictly enforced sexual code'.[31] Yet in a twenty-first-century Irish culture of supposed confidence in sexual expression, can this portrayal of oppression in *Giselle* and *The Rite of Spring* claim socio-political relevance, and is the social reality in

Ireland in need of transformation? In his recent publication chart-
ing a history of sexuality in Ireland from the late nineteenth century
up to 2005, Diarmaid Ferriter asserts that, 'a concern with outward
conventions, a decidedly middle-class discourse about sexuality [and]
deep strains of homophobia and misogyny [...] cannot be regarded
as only belonging to the first half of the twentieth century'.[32] In fact,
he argues, 'conflict, guilt, uncertainty and anger over sexuality' and
a 'preoccupation with what is sexually acceptable' have not 'ceased
to exist' in twenty-first century Ireland, but rather continue to be of
great relevance.[33] Speaking of the position of women in contemporary Ireland, Melissa Sihra argues that 'in the last two hundred years it
has not changed significantly [...]. Women are still under-represented
in all political, professional and religious structures and [t]he dominant cultural ideology by which women are repeatedly defined is
that relating to reproduction and the family'.[34] In many of his works
for Fabulous Beast Dance Theatre, Keegan-Dolan approaches issues of
gender and sexual identity with a remarkable fluidity. Both male and
female dancers perform feminine and masculine roles, and gender
swapping is not only used to subversively comic effect, such as in the
sex scene between grasping Nurse Mary and Pat Dunne the Butcher's
Son played by two men in *Giselle*, but can also portray the heartbreak
of an ill-fated relationship between two teenage girls in his reworking
of *Romeo and Juliet*, *The Flowerbed* (2000, revived 2006). Keegan-Dolan
explains that in his choreography he is interested, 'not so much in
men and women but the masculine and feminine in both men and
women'[35] and proposes that the masculine and the feminine are to be
found in varying degrees in everyone. Interrupting any fixed notions
of identity with a fluid choreography of both gender and sexuality
allows unpredictable configurations to be corporealised, positing a
potential for the appearance of an infinite number of shifting identities. Centring on the broader tropes of betrayal and forgiveness in
Giselle and ritual and sacrifice in *The Rite of Spring* arguably brings the
focus away from any specific site of contestation regarding identity
politics and strives towards a broad critique of all forms of oppression,
and the destabilisation of any reified notion of a singular identity.
Furthermore, due to the fact that the primary medium of expression is dance, the socio-political critique in his work assumes an
even greater significance in the context of the rooting of these dance
theatre works in Ireland.

Haunted bodies

In situating the site of feminine agency within the realm of ghosts in *Giselle*, and a sacrificial dance in *The Rite of Spring*, a link is created between feminine corporeality and death. This notion has great resonance with the repression of the feminine deemed necessary in the postcolonial formation of a national identity in Ireland. As is often noted, and as Eibhear Walshe summarises, '[c]olonialism [...] generates a gendered power relationship and, inevitably, casts the colonizing power as masculine and dominant and the colonized as feminine and passive'.[36] Walshe points out that the ensuing 'unease with the shifting and "unstable" nature of sexual difference' and 'narrowing of gender hierarchies' led to a silencing of sexual difference in Ireland due to a perceived connection between homosexuality and a feminised masculinity.[37] As discussed in the introduction, this silencing of any association between the feminine and the masculine can also be observed in the linking of dance and femininity and consequently, dance and homosexuality. It is important to note that in the establishment and maintenance of a stable postcolonial masculine identity and patriarchy in Ireland, the creation and definition of a hegemonic masculinity inevitably also functioned to repress other masculinities. In her examination of the diversity in, and relations between, masculinities, R.W. Connell points to 'relations of alliance, dominance and subordination [...] constructed through practices that exclude and include, that intimidate [and] exploit', which she argues constitutes a 'gender politics within masculinities'.[38] As Brian Singleton points out, in an Irish context this led to the dominance of a hegemonic masculinity that, 'not only lorded itself over women, but also subjected subordinated groups of men to its authority and control'.[39] It is perhaps not surprising then, that theatrical dance – as threatening as it is to the hegemonic masculine – has remained such a marginalised practice in a society that, in its creation of an 'Irish' corporeality, was obliged to performatively reject any feminine associations and to uphold such an oppressively narrow definition of the masculine. Perhaps it also sheds some light on why dance was only officially recognised as a named arts form in Ireland in the government's Arts Act of 2003.[40] This repression of problematic feminine and masculine bodies also has resonance with the discussion in Chapter One of Francis Barker's notion of the 'dead flesh' of the modernised (and in the Irish context, the postcolonial) body. Resisting death and the horizontal plane in the revised endings of *Giselle* and *The Rite of Spring*, the women's dancing bodies are also resisting the relegation of a dancing feminine corporeality (and repressed masculinities aligned with the feminine) to a state of 'dead flesh'.

However, this is not the only aspect of social history that haunts the final images. In choosing *Giselle* as a platform for his challenge to the hypocrisy of a community, Keegan-Dolan brings the focus onto the muting of a feminine corporeality. But his piece is not only in dialogue with broader parallels between the repressive combination of church and state powers in Ireland and the ultimately conservative ideology of the romantic ballet. Keegan-Dolan locates the original source of inspiration for the work in a specific event that occurred in his midlands home county of Longford when he was 15 years old. In the town of Granard on 31 January 1984, Ann Lovett, also 15, was found haemorrhaging on the ground in a grotto near her school by two passing schoolchildren. She had given birth to a baby boy who she had placed on a stone under a statue of the Virgin Mary, and her red schoolbag and the scissors she had brought with her to cut the umbilical cord were found nearby. Both Ann and her baby died. This family tragedy was propelled by the media to the status of national trauma; however the uncomfortable question as to why Ann gave birth alone in the rain has never been satisfactorily addressed. The Granard townspeople directly involved in the case have maintained an unwavering silence towards the media, and the Lovett family has never spoken publicly on the matter. The unwillingness in Granard to speak about the circumstances surrounding Ann's death has been interpreted by some as an understandable effort to shield the Lovett family from the glare of media attention. Making the Lovett family, or indeed the townspeople of Granard, the whipping boys for the failures of Irish society as a whole is clearly unjust. However, it can also be argued that this resistance towards a questioning of the matter is evidence of a perpetuation of the social conditions that led to Ann's need for secrecy in the first place, and a substantiation of the community's wilful blindness to her situation. Occurring so soon after the divisive abortion referendum of September 1983, which resulted in a pro-life amendment to the Irish constitution,[41] the Lovett tragedy became a focus for feminist anger and Angela

Bourke writes that, '[Ann's] silence about the pregnancy was inter-preted in the context of the silencing of women's experiences'.[42] Further disturbing elements connected to the event were the tussles between the media and the school authorities over the legal distinc-tions between 'knowing' and 'suspecting' in relation to the school's knowledge of her pregnancy, and the maddeningly predictable 'no comment' response from members of the religious order connected to the school, who also acted as social workers in the town and were alleged to have visited Ann's family.[43] As current ombudswoman Emily O'Reilly pointed out in an article written shortly after the tragedy, '[m]ore effort has been expended in defending the social superstructure than in defending the basic unit'.[44] This example of institutions feigning ignorance in order to escape potential blame has great resonance with the recent findings of the *Commission on Clerical Child Abuse in Dublin* (2009) also known as the Murphy Report, which concluded that

> the Dublin Archdiocese's pre-occupations in dealing with cases of child sexual abuse, at least until the mid 1990s, were the mainte-nance of secrecy, the avoidance of scandal, the protection of the reputation of the Church, and the preservation of its assets. All other considerations, including the welfare of children and justice for victims, were subordinated to these priorities.[45]

The church was, of course, not the only state authority guilty of per-petuating a culture of secrecy, and as Ferriter proposes, there is a long history of desperate attempts by various authorities in Ireland to, 'keep uncomfortable truths behind closed doors [...] [as] the most important thing was to keep souls, not bodies, safe'.[46] Ann Lovett's death prompted the disclosure of further shocking stories from all over the country and radio presenter Gay Byrne ded-icated his high profile morning show to the reading out of letters from the public. Commenting on this outpouring, Colm Tóibín pro-poses that it was at that time, 'the most relentless assault which has ever been presented to a mass audience [in Ireland] on the accepted version of reality in this country'.[47] This event would appear to have succeeded in creating a gap in a given perception of social reality. The intolerability of the mental image of the grotto scene and the alterna-tive reality it represented revealed reactions ranging from blindness and aversion on the one hand, to an acknowledgement of the difficulty of comprehending and processing such an event on the other. Perhaps due to this, the memory of the tragedy remains a contentious and unsettled matter. On the 25th anniversary of Ann's death in January 2009, a Granard resident told a reporter, '[n]o one wants talks about that anymore. It's completely blocked out'.[48] Accepting the discomfort involved in contemplating the event, yet acknowledging the haunting presence of Ann's memory, O'Toole possibly comes closer to the truth when he states, '[i]t is not that Ann Lovett's awful death stayed at the forefront of our collective consciousness, but it did take up residency in the back of our minds'.[49]

When asked what inspired him to do a midlands version of *Giselle*, Keegan-Dolan has simply replied, 'Ann Lovett', and he has spoken and written of the central importance of this event to his reworking of the piece.[50] Although there is no explicit reference within the work to the event, it could be speculated that an explicit visual reference is to be found in *The Rite of Spring* in the form of the tall statue of the Virgin Mary placed upstage left; perhaps functioning as a reminder of the oppressive petrification of idealised femininity in Irish society, or as an image of defunct 'verticality' presiding over a dysfunctional community's sacrifice, rendered silent and unmoving. Read as an idealised image of boundless maternal generosity created by the Catholic Church, the inaction of this frozen figure in the face of the violence occurring in front of her and the emptiness of the embrace promised by her outstretched arms, could be seen to underline the impotence of the phallocratic order she represents. During *The Rite of Spring* the dancers never acknowledge the presence of the statue, and in the final image of the piece, the vertical body of the Chosen One is in direct opposition to an archetypal suppliant body, kneeling at the foot of a statue to pray. It is interesting to note that the Lovett tragedy is not mentioned in the programmes for the two Irish productions: the premiere in the Samuel Beckett Theatre in 2003, and the tour to the Galway Arts Festival in 2008. However, in the programme for the most recent tour to Sydney, Australia in 2010, the story of Ann Lovett's death constitutes the opening paragraph of Keegan-Dolan's statement about the piece and is related in some detail.[51] Perhaps this is coincidental, but it certainly raises the speculative question as to whether the subject is still so sensitive that the disclosure of the source of the piece's inspiration can only be safely told in a distant land.

Like Avery Gordon's description in *Ghostly Matters* of the 'improperly buried bodies'[52] of the past who return to haunt the sociological imagination, the Lovett tragedy haunts both *Giselle* and *The Rite of Spring*, just as O'Toole suggests it haunts the 'back of our minds'. The ghost, according to Gordon, is 'that special instance of the merging of the visible and the invisible, the dead and the living, the past and the present'.[53] As asserted earlier, the problem of sexual and other forms of corporeal oppression continues to be a relevant issue in contemporary Irish society. Due to this, the citing of a tragedy that occurred almost a quarter of a century ago as the motivation for a critique of present-day issues, results in the haunting presence of a past event in works such as *Giselle* functioning not merely as a requiem, but also as a prism through which the continued subordination of certain corporealities in contemporary society can be highlighted. This can then produce what Randy Martin describes as a 'rehistoriciz[ation of] that moment's effect on the present'.[54] Yet in Fabulous Beast's *Giselle* and *The Rite of Spring*, these events from the past, which are interwoven with the narratives from the original ballets, are not brought to their tragic conclusions.

Returning to the final scenes described at the beginning of the chapter and re-examining them in light of their socio-political context in Ireland, what might these reworked endings achieve? In exhuming oppressed corporealities from their enforced horizontal resting place, the dancing bodies of Giselle and the Chosen One could be seen to challenge the phallocracy of verticality, both in the original narratives and in the contemporary social context. Reading beyond the formal limits of the dance, this verticality comes to represent church and state institutions that have traditionally been, and continue to be, dominated by men in Irish society. The women's bodies dance the femininity whose oppression has, in part, led to a discrimination against sexual difference and the promotion of a culture of shame and taboo surrounding corporeal issues. However, as in the example of the blurring of boundaries between the masculine and feminine in the Chosen One's dance in *The Rite of Spring*, a rise of the feminine dancing body to a position of verticality does not propose a simple replacement of the masculine with the feminine.

It proposes instead a utopian ideal in which expressions of both masculinity and femininity can co-exist in every man and woman. However, this utopia is simultaneously destabilised by the staging of these dances within a narrative framework of death. This complicates the representation of a simple upending of existing power structures, and functions as a reminder that these utopian bodies are a fiction constructed in the choreographed space between the reality of the repressed corporealities of history that haunt them, and their unexpected escape from the narrative that allows them to appear. Speaking of the haunting spirits of dead women in the grave scene in *Giselle*, Keegan-Dolan explains that for him, 'ghosts are people who left this world unwillingly and remain stuck in a limbo state'.[55] Interrogating the liminal ambiguity inherent in the ghostly figure, Gordon proposes that

> [h]aunting always harbors the violence [...] and *denial* that made it, and the *exile of our longing*, the utopian. [...] The ghost always registers the actual 'degraded present' in which we are inextricably and historically entangled *and* the longing for the arrival of a future, entangled certainly, but ripe in the plenitude of non-sacrificial freedoms and exuberant un-foreseen pleasures.
>
> [Gordon's emphasis][56]

What is particularly interesting in the choreography of the final images in *Giselle* and *The Rite of Spring* is that Keegan-Dolan does not leave his ghosts in limbo, and does not resign the longed-for utopian to exile. Instead he lends (living) flesh to these 'non-sacrificial freedoms' in exuberant dances of forgiveness and hope. This complication leads me to a final question. If these works are in response to the social conditions that led to tragedies such as the death of Ann Lovett and her baby, what capacity for social change can these dances of alternative realities have? In not performing the difficult endings of the tragic narrative, does the reversal of the anticipated outcome undermine their potential power for critique?

Emancipated encounters

In *The Emancipated Spectator* (2009) Rancière proposes that a 'classic' employment of intolerable images for political purposes presupposed a 'straight line from the intolerable spectacle to awareness of the reality it was expressing; and from that to the desire to act in order to change it'.[57] However, following Guy Debord's analysis of the 'spectacle' and discourse surrounding questions of representation and the unrepresentable, a scepticism now exists regarding the political capacity of any image. To avoid this anaesthetisation of political art, Rancière suggests that it is necessary to rethink the hierarchy of passivity and activity as normally described in the theatrical relationship between the passive spectator and the active performer. A spectator is always active in that she 'observes, selects, compares, interprets' and 'links what she sees to a host of other things that she has seen on other stages'.[58] This then allows spectators to be understood as composers of their own stories who refashion elements of a performance with what they have personally experienced or dreamt. Acknowledging the emancipated spectator, then, allows for an approach to the representation of the intolerable which avoids the 'stock reaction' of scepticism or aversion. In order to reawaken the capacity for political art to inspire social change, it must then 'sketch new configurations of what can be seen and what can be thought and, consequently, a new landscape of the possible' in such a way that the meaning and effect of the performance is not anticipated.[59] This 'resistance to anticipation' creates 'dispositions of the body and the mind where the eye does not know in advance what it sees and thought does not know what it should make of it'.[60] In re-choreographing the traditional endings of *Giselle* and *The Rite of Spring*, Keegan-Dolan creates a space for a multiplicity of alternative readings of corporealities in Ireland. Harnessing the political potential of the unanticipated allows for an element of uncertainty to appear in these well-rehearsed narratives. Instead of expiring quietly at the end of these works, the women take control of their own deaths. However, what the spectator is to make of a Giselle that jumps for joy or a Chosen One who chooses her own destiny is undetermined, and what political efficacy these destabilising choreographies with their open-ended conclusions might have beyond their performance is, of course, also questionable. As Peter Hallward cautions in relation to a Rancièrean politics of emancipation, 'emphasis on division and interruption' risks 'confinement to the "insubstantial kingdom of imagination"', due to its seeming lack of regard for what might sustain or organise the political after its disruptive appearance.[61] Yet, I would argue, within an Irish context the imagining and performance of new realities through the medium of dance is always already an active form of political resistance, in a theatrical landscape dominated by the literary. Furthermore, in combination with the disarming and liberating potential of the unanticipated, an examination of the spectator's possible kinaesthetic responses to these final moments of verticality may also shed light on their political efficacy. In her discussion of the application of architectural and philosophical theory to the experience of space in performance, Victoria Hunter suggests a 'model of influence' that accounts not only for the influence of a chosen site on the performers interacting with it, but also for the lasting influence of a work on the ways in which the site itself is experienced after the ending of the performance event. Hunter writes that

> [t]he active role played by the audience in the reading and interpretive process [...] [is] a process which can carry resonances of the performance forward after the event, in turn serving to 're-inscribe' the original space with a variety of meanings.[62]

Hunter's discussion focuses on transformations of space and place in site-specific performance, yet an application of her idea might also be useful when considering the shifts in representational planes that occur in the reworking of traditional narratives (both mythic and social) of *Giselle* and *The Rite of Spring*. In this way, it could be argued that the disruption of the expected ending calls not only for an analytical reinterpretation (following Rancière), but also, I would suggest, a 'rewiring' of the spectator's kinaesthetic response that, following Hunter's model of influence, affects all future experiences of the narratives in question, linking situations of oppression with the possibility of agency.

The following chapter continues my examination of dance theatre works that highlight and challenge the oppression of certain corporealities in Irish society through a reading of the intersection of the choreography of spatiality, the social choreography of the cityscape, and the politics of citizenship as they are presented in CoisCéim's *Dodgems* (2008). Ireland is still adjusting to being a destination for immigrants, and in the current climate of economic recession, the question of the rights of non-citizens has become a critical issue. *Dodgems* stages the meeting of citizen body and non-citizen body on a full-sized fairground bumper-car track, and makes visible many sides of the political divides in Irish society as they collide or swerve in and out of each other's paths. This chapter examines the possibilities for dispute and resistance to the status quo that are opened up by the convergence of dancing bodies in the interval of a choreographed space of difference.

6
Choreographing Dissensus: Dodgems and Roundabouts

Continuing my analysis of how the choreography of spatiality can lend visibility and agency to oppressed corporealities, this chapter conducts a reading of CoisCéim Dance Theatre's *Dodgems* (2008), interrogating how the work stages the politics of citizenship in Ireland. Whereas Chapter Five focussed on the transformative reconfigurations of gendered planes of representation in narratives of oppression, my interest here is in the links that can be found between the choreography of space in performance and the social choreography of space in everyday life. It is perhaps not so unusual to find the seductive, yet oftentimes empty, promise of 'transportation to another world' in the promotional material for a dance or theatre performance; however, the hyberbole arguably came close to realisation in the case of *Dodgems*, which premiered at the 2008 Dublin Theatre Festival. In a curious merging of the site-specific with the 'painted stage', the production involved the transplantation of a dodgems (or bumper-car) track, replete with 12 fully functioning dodgem cars, into Dublin's O'Reilly Theatre in a bid to 'captur[e] the lights, smells and sounds of the funfair'.[1] *Dodgems* boasted one of the most highly anticipated and imaginative designs of the festival, yet I will argue that the concept resulted in more than just a crowd-pulling scenographic coup. This chapter examines how the interaction of the performers and the audience with the scenography in *Dodgems* succeeded in creating a 'world within a world' that allowed for the emergence of previously invisible bodies in a choreographed space of difference and disagreement. To interrogate how this was achieved, I examine the intersection of the choreography of the dancing body with the social choreography of the cityscape and the politics of citizenship, as they are made visible in the piece. Building on Rancière's concept of 'dissensus', which he describes as 'putting two worlds in one and the same world' so that the framing of a 'given' or 'common sense' notion can be disputed and an interval for politics[2] can be opened, I will discuss the functioning of the dodgems track as a metaphor for the collision of citizens and non-citizens in Irish society.[3] In particular, I will examine the ways in which the work creates a choreographed space that allows for a corporealisation of silenced political dispute. Reaching beyond a reading of the internal structure of the piece to include a consideration of its cultural context, I will also discuss the resonance *Dodgems* has with a recent incident involving the encampment of an immigrant family on a roundabout of Dublin's busiest motorway, the M50. In conclusion, a reading of a closing scene in *Dodgems* will hopefully illustrate how the choreography of dissensual space has the ability to highlight the dangers of the depoliticising project of social consensus in society, and how in this piece it is employed to protest against the censorship and ghettoisation of 'invisible' non-citizen bodies.

Introducing *Dodgems* and Ireland's citizenship laws

Directed and choreographed by David Bolger, *Dodgems* is the most ambitious collaborative project undertaken by CoisCéim to date. It featured a script by Charlie O'Neill, set design by Paul O'Mahony, live original music composed by Ellen Cranitch, and a multinational cast of 19 dancers, actors and musicians who hailed from Poland, Nigeria, France, Serbia, England, Israel, the Philippines, Slovakia, Norway, Spain, Russia, the US and Ireland.[4] The inspiration for the work sprang from Bolger's desire to create a piece about his childhood fascination with visiting circus troupes and fairground shows in the Dublin coastal suburb of Sandymount, and his decision to commission a script from O'Neill resulted from their conversations about O'Neill's experiences growing up in a travelling fairground family. Before studying design and working in theatre of the clown, street theatre, cabaret theatre and as a playwright, O'Neill operated his family's fairground dodgems, and it was his connections to the travelling fairground trade that secured the dodgem track for the production.[5]

Bolger and O'Neill were particularly interested in exploring the potential of a dodgem track to represent the encounters in Irish cities between 'insiders and outsiders' (both Limerick and Dublin are named during the piece). Early ideas about investigating the 'outsider' position of travelling fairground families within Irish society were soon expanded into a consideration of the many kinds of 'othered' people that inhabit contemporary Ireland. O'Neill notes that one of the significant 'narrative drives' behind *Dodgems* is an exploration of the displacement of people:

> [a]ll over the world, millions cross physical and political borders every week. Millions of others cross social and cultural ones. The driving will to survive leaves people vulnerable. [...] Because of Ireland's haphazard and misguided immigration, health, economic and social systems we have grown a race of outsiders inside our own borders – a balmy, bawdy and beautiful mixture of new arrivals and indigenous misfits.[6]

Although many kinds of marginalised and 'outsider' bodies are represented in the piece – for example otherly-abled bodies (such as dancer David Toole, a three-foot-two-inches-tall amputee) or religiously garbed bodies (represented by a 'flock' of acrobatic nuns and a woman wearing a burqa) – the main focus in *Dodgems* is on a group of immigrants as they arrive in Ireland and try to make their way in an unfamiliar, and oftentimes unwelcoming and exploitative, society. *Dodgems* explores the theme of 'avoidance and collision' in the encounters between these outsiders (immigrants) and insiders (citizens), and the use of a fairground dodgem track within a proscenium arch setting stages the meeting of non-citizen body and citizen body in a simultaneously exotic and domestic site. This allows for an intertwining of divergent socio-political landscapes and the bodies that inhabit and create them. In their interactions in this electrically charged setting, the dodgem cars and performers, metal and flesh, persistently highlight both society's categorising and grouping of bodies into permissible roles and positions and the ensuing invisibility of bodies that do not belong to the 'legitimate' socio-cultural framework.

A common thread running through all CoisCéim productions is Bolger's interest in telling 'human stories' and the company's manifesto expresses a desire to, 'demonstrate and articulate stories and emotions that are relevant to the landscapes in which we live'.[7] With its long history of emigration, twenty-first century Ireland is still adjusting to being a destination for immigrants. During the unprecedented financial boom years of the Celtic Tiger economy, which (as discussed in the introductory chapter) began in 1993 and lasted for roughly a decade, Ireland boasted the fastest growing economy in Europe, and the number of economic migrants to the country rose sharply. From 1990–4 Ireland was the only EU member state to have a higher level of emigration than immigration and the percentage of non-nationals in the country in 1990 was 2.3 per cent. Yet by 2007 Ireland had the third highest immigration rate of the 27 member states, and the 2006 census showed that the percentage of non-nationals living in Ireland had increased to just over 10 per cent (414,512 of 4,025,010).[8] Now that the country is in economic recession, the question of the rights of those on the margins of society, especially those who have no right to citizenship, has become an increasingly pressing issue. After a referendum that succeeded in abolishing *jus soli* in 2004, children born in the territory of Ireland to non-citizens are no longer given automatic citizenship of the Republic.[9] In 1956, the Irish Nationality and Citizenship Act had provided an inclusive access to citizenship through the principle of both *jus soli* (Latin for 'right of the soil' – citizenship by birth in a territory) and *jus sanguinis* (Latin for 'right of blood' – citizenship by descent). At this time, *jus soli* allowed for citizenship laws to cut across the North/South division of the island, and the *jus sanguinis* provision was introduced to help stem the depopulation that was occurring due to emigration. However, as Siobhán Mullally notes, this inclusive approach to citizenship was not 'all-embracing', and '[f]rom the beginning, debates on the meaning and significance of citizenship in Ireland were deeply racialised'.[10] As an example, Mullally cites a speech made by Deputy John Esmonde in 1956, who noted that the *jus soli* entitlement, 'carried with it a "certain amount of danger" ', as there were ' "a great number of people [in the world] who would be undesirable to us in Ireland" '.[11] With the large increase in the number of immigrants after 1994, the Irish government again looked to change citizenship law, but this time with the emphasis firmly shifted towards keeping 'undesirable' migrants out of the country. In April 2004, the twenty-seventh amendment to the Irish constitution proposed an addition to Article 9:

9.2.1 Notwithstanding any other provision of this Constitution, a person born in the island of Ireland, which includes its islands and its seas, who does not have, at the time of his or her birth, at least one parent who is an Irish citizen or entitled to be an Irish citizen is not entitled to Irish citizenship or nationality, unless otherwise provided for by the law.[12]

At the constitutional referendum on 12 June 2004, a four-to-one majority voted for the amendment. This change to the citizenship laws fixes a divide in Irish society, and as has recently been argued, could be seen to have transformed Ireland into a 'gated community'.[13] In making visible the exploitation of immigrants when they arrive in an affluent city hoping for a better life, *Dodgems* stages the world of their exclusion inside the protected world of the citizen. Cities, as James Holston and Arjun Appadurai propose, have always been 'stages for politics' that are also 'especially privileged sites for considering the current renegotiations of citizenship'.[14] In representing the city, the dodgems track, with its boundaries and rules, becomes a stage for the interrogation of the discrepancy between the supposed equality of Irish society and the lived realities of its citizenship laws.

Before proceeding with my reading of the work, it is important to note that any attempt to conduct an analysis of scenes from *Dodgems* presents a dilemma, as the choreographic structure of the piece continued evolving well beyond the premiere, and changes made over the course of the festival run included such drastic alterations as the condensation of two acts into one act and the erasure of entire scenes.[15] As a result, audience members who saw a preview would have experienced quite a different show to those who saw a performance near the end of the two-and-a-half-week run. Bearing this in mind, the description and movement analyses of episodes from the piece that follow are confined to scenes that remained largely (if not wholly) unchanged throughout the run.

Tactical ruptures

An important feature of *Dodgems* that remained unchanged for every show was the beginning of the performance, which occurs long before the cast assume their pre-set positions. Already recreating the ambience of the funfair in the foyer, the smells and tastes of the free candyfloss and popcorn work to elicit an evocative and nostalgic sensory experience. On entering the auditorium, the intimate atmosphere of this world is sustained by performers strolling around, stopping to greet audience members and welcoming them into the communal space. Ten minutes into the performance proper, the smell of the popcorn still lingers as the location represented by the dodgems track transforms once more. A small space upstage-left becomes a room where people wait to board a boat. One by one, dancers enter the space carrying large, battered suitcases and begin a patient dance of sitting, standing and turning movements to mark the time. The space becomes crowded as each new arrival causes everyone to shift their cases and their positions once more. Elbows and knees jut and bend, heads duck and bow, as the bodies pile in. A blast of a foghorn sounds and through a cloud of dry ice the awaited boat emerges from the darkness. It is a dodgem car with a dirty white and tattered sail attached. Amidst a disconcerting cacophony of sound and flashing lights the dancers 'board' and cling to the sides of the dodgem-ship as it describes large circles in the space. The voyage around the track is slow at first, but as the speed increases, the passengers find it harder to hold on. Their screams of terror cut through the accompanying soundscape of foghorns as they lose their grip and are violently flung off. When the dodgem-ship finally arrives at its destination, the track is strewn with seemingly lifeless bodies. Slowly, the passengers pick themselves up, but some bodies remain motionless on the ground. Making their way to form a queue facing the audience at the dodgems track buffer, the passengers perform an identity dance one at a time, changing the audience's role from passive popcorn munchers, to judging immigration officials. Contorting themselves into convulsive and slightly frantic gestural phrases of introduction and explanation of occupation, some of the passengers' dances provoke nervous laughter from the audience. While this is happening, one of the prone bodies, a young woman, still has not moved. The immigration ordeal continues stage right as a little girl goes to the body, and echoing movements from an earlier scene, starts to tenderly comb her mother's hair with her fingers. As the passengers continue to present themselves to the audience for inspection, the dead mother's body is reloaded unceremoniously back onto the dodgem-ship and removed offstage.

In this early scene, the sense of familiarity and community generated by the funfair setting and the choreography of the pre-show
experience is ruptured. Within the funfair world, another world
becomes visible when a division between citizen and non-citizen is
made physically manifest. Portraying the violent arrival of a group
of immigrants in a city port, this scene stages their first meeting
with Irish citizens in the form of immigration officials, who, through
Bolger's spatial tactics, are played by the audience. Throughout the
piece, the spectator/performer relationship often positioned the audience as the citizen body that is confronted with its other. In so doing,
Dodgems repeatedly demonstrated the discrepancy between the citizen's perception of the world and the immigrant's perception of
the same world in city spaces that, due to their transposition to a
dodgem track, were at once both foreign and familiar: an immigrant
mother's baby is given by nuns to a barren but wealthy Irish couple who whisk it away in a dodgem car; an unaccompanied minor is
stalked by a pimp, who forces trafficked immigrant women to balance
on the perimeter buffer of the dodgem track in forced erotic poses for
his cruising Irish clientele; and two Muslim men on their way to a
dance performance are urged to try a bit of bacon by a Dublin taxi-
dodgem driver, who also warns them to keep their backs to the wall at
the show so that they can protect themselves from 'those gay dance
types'. In all of these encounters the city and its citizens are shown
through the eyes of the non-citizen, disrupting the usual framework
of perception in Irish society.

Dissensus: a world within a world

Rancière proposes that communities are governed by a so-called 'distribution of the sensible' which controls the perception of what
is allowed to be visible and what is excluded from all forms of
visibility.[16] This ordering of perception organises bodies into fixed
roles and parts according to what they have in common with the
established order of a community. Bodies that do not fit into the
legitimate groupings are thereby rendered voiceless and invisible.
In *The Politics of Aesthetics* (2004), Rancière argues that artistic practices have the ability to disrupt the given perception and framing
of bodies in a particular system. A project of political aesthetics
could then be understood as the perceptual reorganisation of the

relation between bodies that are seen and unseen, included and excluded. To achieve this disruption, Rancière proposes the political process of 'dissensus', which, in its 'putting two worlds in one and the same world', confronts the habitual framework of perception with those bodies that are normally excluded and invisible.[17] Placing the world of the non-citizen into the world of the citizen allows the given 'outside' placement of the non-citizen within the political order to be reframed. In reading *Dodgems* as a staging of scenes of dissensus, it then becomes possible to examine the potential for dispute and communication that is opened up by the convergence of dancing bodies in the interval of a choreographed space of difference.

In *Dodgems*, the scenography that stages this 'world within a world' is a site of collisions in its own right. The dodgems track transforms itself throughout the performance into various city locations: a port and immigration office, a Limerick city park, a lap-dancing club, inner-city streets, a grimy bedsit in Dublin, a hotel ballroom and (as a spatial leitmotif) the transient space of the fairground.[18] As Bolger explains, the overarching theme in *Dodgems* is 'avoidance and collision [in a] space of opposites'.[19] The staging of a space of opposites within the piece functions at various levels, and the scenography beyond the dodgems track itself also creates a collision. Both the track, with its 12 fully functioning cars, and the audience seating are enclosed within the partly physicalised, but mostly suggested, 'belly' of a tiger. The red eyes and gaping mouth of this beast were woven into the stage-left side of the multi-levelled set surrounding the track. These spectral hints of an engulfing body served as a constant reminder that all proceedings were taking place within the underbelly of Ireland's recently extinct 'Celtic Tiger' economy. The scenographic space thus helped to underline a tension of opposition between the seductive thrill of the fairground for citizens seeking pleasure in a visit to an 'other' world, and the decidedly less pleasurable precariousness of life as experienced by non-citizens.

Although they arrive as heterogeneous individuals with various professional qualifications (doctors, scientists, engineers), due to their common status as 'foreigners' the immigrants are quickly categorised and grouped together as 'other' and must take whatever menial work is offered to them.[20] In a following scene, which builds to a crescendo of sound and repeated group movement formations, everyone is persuaded to join in the cleaning of the dodgem track and cars. In transforming the track into an operational space, the immigrants are seemingly creating a legitimate role and home for themselves. Their movement, which began with small, hesitant gestures, becomes increasingly more confident and expansive. Synchronised phrases with cleaning cloths and brushes to the driving rhythms of the music lends the working, dancing bodies the appearance of having joined a community and the dance ends in a mood of joyful optimism. Yet after scrubbing and polishing and righting everything for the opening of the fairground, the group finds that they have no access to the better world they have helped create. At a ticket box ominously located inside the tiger's gaping mouth, they purchase a token to ride the cars, a ticket to a better life, but when they seat themselves in the machines, the generator is heard shutting down. Their initial disbelief turns to anger as they are left with no option but to move on from the dodgem track. Unable to participate in driving them, it is implied that they will forever be left clinging to the outside of the dodgem cars, in danger of being thrown aside. In *Dodgems*, the choreography of space with the 'bodies' of the dodgems cars is as integral to the politics of the piece as the choreography of the performers' bodies. The dodgem cars in this scene show how the partitioning of roles in the community determines the positioning of bodies in relation to each other. Like the legitimate groupings in Rancière's 'distribution of the sensible' that order the community, the dodgems are off-limits for the immigrants. Their inanimate forms and impenetrable metal exteriors are a physical manifestation of Irish society's exclusion of immigrants from having any part in the running of the community.

Social blindness

Turning to the choreography of this space, the movements of the dancers and cars on the electrically charged dodgems track can be seen to harness the close proximity between bodies, and between bodies and traffic, produced by city encounters. Speaking of the hazards of moving through the city, Walter Benjamin writes that it 'involves the individual in a series of shocks and collisions [and] [a]t dangerous intersections, nervous impulses flow through [the individual] in rapid succession, like the energy from a battery'.[21] However, Benjamin points out that in order to survive these jolts and collisions, citizens have learned to ignore their fellow human beings, and citing Paul Valéry, writes that

> the inhabitant of [...] urban centres [...] reverts to a state of savagery – that is, of isolation. The feeling of being dependent on others which used to be kept alive by need, is gradually blunted in the smooth functioning of the social mechanism.[22]

In order, then, to achieve this smoothness, the awareness of our need for others and of the needs *of* others is blunted; the reiterated routines of our everyday operations in the city would seem to cause a certain blindness as to how our bodies are interacting with other bodies in the ordered space. In her study of bodies and cities, Elizabeth Grosz writes that the relationship between the two is often described as either causal or representational.[23] In the first instance, a 'one-way relation' positions the city merely as a product/effect of human thought and action, and in the second, the relationship is isomorphic, with a reflection of each to be found in the other, but with a bias towards viewing the city's 'culture' as paralleling, yet superior to and an improvement on, the body's 'nature'. Grosz finds both of these approaches to be lacking, suggesting instead that the relation between body and city is one of mutual definition, an 'interface' in which 'the form, structure, and norms of the city seep into and affect all the other elements that go into the constitution of corporeality'.[24] Due to this interface, she argues that the city 'affects the way the subject sees others'[25] and that this occurs because

> the city's form and structure provides the context in which social rules and expectations are internalized or habituated in order to ensure social conformity or, failing this, position social marginality at a safe distance (ghettoization). This means that the city must be seen as the most immediate locus for the production and circulation of power.[26]

Ghettoisation, then, becomes the paradoxical naming of the marginalised as a group so that they are accounted for by the community; yet, due to their assigned placement, rendered voiceless. The city, and through this the political body, is ordered in such a way that its structure controls the 'seeing' of itself, and the positioning of itself to marginal bodies; another form of 'blindness' employed to aid the smooth functioning of society. The circulation of power is safeguarded due to the placing of bodies that do not or cannot achieve social conformity at a 'safe distance'. In other words, bodies that do not fit are placed at the margins of the locus of power, where they have no ability to interrupt the circuit and no longer have to be in the line of sight.

This protection of the circulation of power is made visible in a scene in *Dodgems*. A Roma man, Stanislav, enters the empty track dressed in overalls, and walking over to a dodgem car, smiles and starts to run his hand along its side. This quiet moment is roughly interrupted by the entrance of the dodgem track owner who yells at Stanislav to get away from his dodgem cars. Protesting that he meant no harm, Stanislav explains that he is looking for a job. The dodgems owner replies in Palari (the cant slang of fairground workers): 'What clubs and spades have you? Can you hans blix a haddock and bloater?' ('What trades have you? Can you fix a motor?'). During their exchanges Stanislav tries repeatedly to explain that he cannot understand what is being said, and the owner gets increasingly annoyed at having to explain his language, the language of his world. After delivering a lengthy tirade at high speed that was probably just as incomprehensible for the audience as it was intended to be for Stanislav, the owner finally orders him to leave his dodgems track, as he has no interest in employing someone from a 'far away dodge and bass' ('far away place'). Due to his inability to comprehend a language specifically designed to be incomprehensible to the uninitiated, the Roma man is not permitted to work, even though he tells the owner that his language, Romani, shares many expressions with Palari. Ordered to step off the dodgems track, he is returned to his position of voicelessness in the topographical arrangement. In this scene, the raised platform of the dodgems track becomes the definition of the societal boundaries that are experienced by immigrants. Policed by the owner, the body that does not fit into the communicative exchange is prevented from stepping into and disrupting the circuit of power.

Roundabout choreographies

Dodgems engages in direct socio-political commentary, and links can be traced between the choreography of space and bodies in the piece and the social choreography of 'dangerous intersections' between bodies in everyday life. *Dodgems'* staging of the non-citizen's world within the citizen's world has a strong resonance with a recent event involving the encampment of an immigrant family on a round-about of Dublin's busiest motorway. Over the course of nearly two months from May to July in 2007, a large extended Roma family lived on a roundabout and slipway of the M50 in Dublin.[27] Clear-ing an area in the centre of the shrubbery that formerly covered the roundabout, the family used whatever materials they could find to construct makeshift lean-tos around their tents. Children as young as two camped with their parents and grandparents, and during the family's time there, one of the women gave birth in a Dublin mater-nity hospital, returning after the birth of her new born (non-citizen) baby back 'home' to the roundabout encampment. The Rostas came from Romania in search of a better standard of living. However, although Romania (along with Bulgaria) joined the EU in January 2007, Romanians do not have the same rights as other EU citizens: they may enter Ireland on a holiday visa and stay for a maximum of three months, but are not allowed to work without a permit, and have no social welfare entitlements.[28] Ironically, because of their sta-tus as EU citizens, they also have no right to seek asylum. Motorists were startled by the appearance of children crossing their paths as they made their way to and from the encampment. The children also weaved in and out of cars on the slipway approaching the round-about, tapping on windows to beg for money. As they negotiated the traffic, the movement of their fragile bodies in such close prox-imity to fast-moving vehicles was a disturbing sight. As the weeks went by, the sanitary conditions of the encampment deteriorated and two children were brought to hospital with severe vomiting and diarrhoea.[29] Public opinion was divided between those who saw the situation as a humanitarian crisis and those who felt that the predica-ment was of the family's own making and that so-called 'welfare tourists' should be deported. The incident quickly became a point of dispute and debate locally, and the story of Ireland's 'Roundabout Stand-off' was taken up by the international media.[30] Yet despite all the media attention, the standoff continued for many weeks before the situation was finally resolved when the family agreed to fly back to Romania.

The use of the roundabout as a home defied its intended purpose and ideological construction as, to cite Michael McKinnie, 'a physical space that enable[s] capitalist economic transactions'.[31] The main artery of the city's transport system was in threat of being clogged by foreign bodies that were not obeying the spatial distribution. And yet, the authorities were unable to remove these deviant bodies, since to do so would require the acknowledgement of a responsibility to provide alternative accommodation. The Roma had the right to travel as EU citizens, but paradoxically, this citizenship excluded them from accessing any assistance on arrival. In Ireland, the Roma are normally positioned in a ghettoised state in which their invisibility poses no threat to Valéry's 'smooth functioning of the social mechanism'.[32] Ireland has its own indigenous population of nomadic people known as 'travellers' who also live in encampments and some of whom also travel around the island and internationally from site to site.[33] A marginalised minority, travellers, along with immigrants, belong to the excluded and the invisible in Irish society. A question that was often asked during the two months of the 'Roundabout Standoff' by people shocked at the lack of intervention by the government and police authorities was, 'what if those children were Irish?' Perhaps a more obvious question, and one that was not so readily asked was, 'what if those children were Irish travellers?' The incident of the Roma encampment highlighted the way in which Irish travellers have been positioned by the authorities into a non-threatening ghettoised state. Although they are seemingly free to follow their customs and travel the country, their freedom is in fact strictly monitored and their movement is curtailed to journeys between designated halting sites. It is reasonable to assume that if a traveller family had tried to camp where the Roma did, they would have been swiftly moved on by the *Gardaí*.[34]

However, the unexpected appearance of the Roma family on their roundabout 'stage' created a rupture in the social topography that seemed to suspend the rules. It also made visible the gap that exists between what it means to be an EU citizen from Ireland and what it means to be an EU citizen from Romania. Unaware of, or just disregarding the laws of place and social order, the Roma did not behave as they should in the Irish system. They did not adhere to their 'proper' positioning of invisibility within the community. As a result, the Roma encampment on the M50 roundabout succeeded in bringing forth dispute and political debate because it stepped outside the pre-constituted model of communicative exchange. Having no legitimate position in the social topography, the encampment brought a new world, with its alternative perspective and rules, into the existing world. Creating dissensus, and through that, a scene for the emergence of politics, it '[made] visible that which had no reason to be seen, it place[d] one world in another'.[35] Unfortunately, the incident cannot be seen to have directly benefited the Roma family involved at the time. However, it did succeed in forcing a necessary acknowledgement of, and creating debate about, the social inequalities in Irish society, and in a broader frame, the inequalities of European citizenship.

A place for us?

This incident on the roundabout exposed the social choreography of bodies in the city. In breaking the topographical rules, an interval was created in which the hegemonic social order became visible and was challenged. Similar to the real life example of the roundabout, the bumper-car track in *Dodgems* becomes a site of dispute where a clashing of worlds is staged. An extraordinary scene near the end of the piece is perhaps an example of how choreography can gesture towards a scene of dissensus. In this episode, which is performed to a version of the Bernstein/Sondheim song *Somewhere (A Place for Us)*, the elective mute Hoppy, and the Polish labourer Marek, both find sanctuary from their troubles in a weekly ballroom dance lesson where they are partners. Standing in a slowly revolving dodgem car in the frozen formal embrace of the Viennese waltz, they look into each other's eyes as refracted pinpoints of light move across the back wall of the theatre. The stage picture has a curiously frozen, fairytale-like quality. While the couple hold this pose, the rest of the cast stand in a semicircle around the dodgem car, looking directly at audience members. They use sign language to 'sing' the lyrics of the song[36] to the audience and after a few stanzas, start to process into the audience's space (see Figure 6.1).

Figure 6.1 Somewhere (a place for us): Hoppy and Marek dance on a dodgem car in CoisCéim's *Dodgems* (2008). Photograph: Pat Redmond

While this is happening, the house lights come up and the fun-fair world is merged once more with the audience's world. Coming after a relentless, yet often humorous, cataloguing of the wrongs and humiliations endured by those marginalised by society, this scene is a shockingly sentimental picture of a harmony that is at odds with reality. There currently exists no legitimate 'place for us' of agency within Irish society for non-citizens. And yet this scene is simultaneously a precise reflection of the depoliticising project of social consensus, and of the blunted perception required for the smooth running of the social order; an order in which contradiction may not occur (e.g., the triply signified song lyrics that are sung *and* danced *and* signed). When compared with preceding scenes highlighting the injustices experienced by the non-citizen, and the following scene, which presents a rather saccharine, mixed-genre 'dance of diversity',[37] this scene succeeds much more powerfully in making visible Ireland's fantasy of being a society that is accepting of cultural and racial diversity. Joining performers and audience together in this imagined dancehall community of inclusion and universal visibility, the only place, we

are told, that you can 'let yourself love yourself', posits an integration that is pleasing to the citizen, but essentially hollow.[38] If the
'common sense' requires the belief that everyone has a place 'somewhere' in the community, yet the community can only function if
certain groups remain on the peripheries, then placing these two
worlds in the same kinaesthetic moment of a dance performance creates a clash: a bodily dispute. Due to its ability to lend corporeal form
and visibility to the ways in which bodies are regulated and ordered
in the community, dance would seem to have the ability to stage
scenes of 'dissensus'. In *Dodgems*, a sign on the track states: 'The less
you bump, the faster you go', but the piece continually highlights the
need for dispute in society and the dangers, as were made evident in
the shocking incident of the Roma encampment, that arise from a
'bump free' consensual perception that sustains a blindness towards
those who are marginalised. Choreographing the space of the interval, *Dodgems* harnesses the energy of corporeal collisions to allow for
the appearance of the silenced and the invisible.

In the next chapter, I conclude this study by investigating thematic
connections between the readings of works across the individual
chapters, and also highlighting how these works function as nodal
points that allow collisions between different points of view to be
danced into visibility. The chapter also takes a look at the work of the
latest generation of dance theatre choreographers.

7
Concluding Thoughts and Future Moves

On her return to Ireland in 1995 after dancing for several years with Pina Bausch in Wuppertal, Irish choreographer and dance scholar Finola Cronin was struck by the isolation of dance from other art forms in Ireland:

> [...] dance in Ireland was so marginalised and for me the crossovers were just so evident between drama and dance as performance [...] I always had difficulty dealing with those sorts of separations in Ireland, and also between dance and the visual arts where there are so many connections. For me it is weird that people can't transfer those same sets of principles in looking and perception and all the rest of it to dance [...] that people are so mystified by dance.[1]

This sentiment is similar to that expressed by Joan Davis in Chapter Two, who also felt that the task of Dublin Contemporary Dance Theatre in the 1980s was to 'demystify' theatrical dance in Ireland. The dance theatre works that I have discussed in this book have wrested the dancing body from its enforced marginalised position, and have made the connections between different artistic disciplines that Cronin found so obvious and yet so lacking in the Irish performance landscape before their emergence. Especially in contemporary works, dance theatre pieces exhibit an exuberant celebration of 'demystified' physicality, exposing in their movements both the surprisingly beautiful and the unsettlingly ugly aspects of Irish society. These works all speak of a society that has yet to come to terms with its history of oppressing corporealities that do not fit the hegemonic norm, and I have argued that they function as important sites of questioning, experimentation and critique in which both aesthetic and socio-political issues are addressed through the choreography of the dancing body. As Gerald Siegmund notes, 'Tanz erzeugt mit dem Körper Orte' ('dance generates sites with the body').[2] Emerging between dance and theatre, these works create a site in which 'antidisciplinary' (to use de Certeau's term) acts allow dancing and speaking bodies to lend visibility and motion to marginalised, silenced, and oppressed corporealities. In the context of the Irish performance landscape, dance theatre achieves a heightened significance and an increased potential for political efficacy due to the traditional dominance of the word and the neglect of the body's communicative capacity. In my readings of these pieces I have been interested in examining the connections between the choreography of the body, and the political and social choreography of bodies in everyday life. In several chapters my interrogation of how the organisation of bodies in time and space in a performance can resonate with, or reflect, how bodies are organised in communities has further led to a consideration of how the patterns of movement in everyday life can be read through the lens of choreography. Conducting readings of the links between the movement of bodies in a dance work, and the movements of bodies beyond and surrounding the performance, has allowed for a consideration of the functioning of social choreographies. As shown in the reading of CoisCéim's *Dodgems* and the Roma encampment on the roundabout in Chapter Six, calling attention to these links can provoke a recognition of manufactured 'blind spots' in the social fabric. Similarly, the unanticipated escape of the oppressed feminine in Fabulous Beast's *Giselle* and *The Rite of Spring* allowed for a dialogue to emerge between past real-life tragedies, and the continued present subjugation of certain corporealities in contemporary Irish society.

A further significant component of this study has been its interrogation of how dance theatre works function as nodal points that allow connections and/or collisions between differing frames of reference and points of view to be danced into visibility. In addition to the meeting of the corporeal and the textual, all the works discussed, from Yeats' dance plays to those from the present day, have enabled the creation of dialogues between various artistic disciplines and genres. They also allow for dialogue between the confines of a restricting technique and the freedom of playful movement in Butler's *Does She Take Sugar?* and Dunne's *Out of Time*; between stories from the past and myths of the present in Fabulous Beast's *The Bull* and CoisCéim's *Ballads*; between well-rehearsed negative outcomes for oppressed bodies and the danced possibility of unanticipated optimism in Fabulous Beast's *Giselle* and *The Rite of Spring*; and between the harsh realities of the non-citizen's world and the 'fairy-tale' notions of social equality in the citizen's world in CoisCéim's *Dodgems*. In each case, the destabilisation of hegemonic narratives has allowed for a dissensual approach that engenders debate and a rethinking of previously accepted norms.

On a more intimate level, these works also allow for connections and collisions to appear between the shapers of the choreographies themselves: the dancing bodies. Following Martin's perception of dance as the coming together of bodies to put problems into motion, 'whose momentary solutions we call dancing', a reading of the phys-ical negotiations between the many different bodies in these pieces has uncovered a further site of danced dialogues.[3] In addition to the fluid and multiplicitous approach to issues of gender and sex-ual identity (as in Fabulous Beast's *Giselle* and *The Rite of Spring*), intercultural meetings between bodies of different race and ethnic-ity within Irish stories, myths and traditional dance techniques also function to expel any lingering notions of the existence of a mono-lithic 'Irish' corporeality. Take for example the Japanese, Slovakian, Nigerian, Italian, Tanzanian, English and French bodies that inhabit the Cúchulainn myths in *At the Hawk's Well* and *The Bull*, or the hybrid American-Irish and English-Irish bodies that explore tradi-tional Irish step dance in *Does She Take Sugar?* and *Out of Time*. A look at the many dance techniques and genres practiced by these dancing bodies also shows dance theatre in Ireland to be a site of interdisci-plinary and intercultural physical negotiations: Michio Ito's mixture of Kabuki and Dalcroze techniques and Ninette de Valois' experience with the Ballets Russes shaped the development of Yeats' dance plays; Erina Brady's training with Dalcroze, Laban and especially Wigman brought a German modern dance aesthetic to her dance theatre at the Abbey; Joan Davis' study of the Graham technique and contempo-rary dance in London was brought together with the US postmodern dance experience of Robert Connor and Loretta Yurick in the work of Dublin Contemporary Dance Theatre; CoisCéim's aesthetic emerged from David Bolger's blending of slapstick, physical theatre, jazz and tap with contemporary dance and ballet; Michael Keegan-Dolan's search for a more 'comfortable' movement practice combines his foundational ballet technique with a study of yoga and martial arts; and the work of Jean Butler and Colin Dunne positions their hybrid bodies in an experimental zone between a traditional, ethnic technique and contemporary postmodern dance. The international influences that can be traced through the works of these choreographers, and the multinational bodies that dance them, show that any geographical or ideological borders that may have notionally isolated the island of Ireland and its inhabitants in the past are truly obsolete in the practices considered here. Similarly, in her critique of 'border keeping' between artistic disciplines in 2009, Peggy Phelan spoke of the limiting nature of genre divides, suggesting that instead of thinking in terms of defining work as dance 'or' any other discipline, scholars and artists should instead take the approach of viewing works as dance 'and' theatre 'and' performance 'and' whatever other disciplines any particular work may relate to.[4] As discussed in Chapter Three, and as the various sites of interconnection listed above show, the practice of these dance theatre choreographers exemplifies contemporary developments in *Tanztheater* that are politically and socially engaged, that celebrate inclusivity and heterogeneity, and that resist reductive notions not only of genre, but also of identity.

In the first section of this book I argue that the work of the contemporary choreographers discussed follows in the dancing footsteps of earlier dance theatre practitioners. Taking a look at the future of dance theatre in Ireland, a new generation of dance theatre practitioners are emerging, who are continuing the experimentations of the choreographers considered in this study to create exciting work that speaks of contemporary Ireland. In 2004 co-artistic directors Jessica Kennedy and Megan Kennedy founded their company Junk Ensemble with the aim of creating 'brave and imaginative dance theatre' that enters into collaborations with artists of different disciplines 'to produce a rich mix of visual and performance styles that seeks to challenge the traditional audience performer relationship'.[5] In *Five Ways to Drown* (2010), a dance theatre piece for five performers representing different age groups, the Kennedys play with an exploration of memories (a leitmotif that can be traced through all of their work), woven into a thematic framework of 'drowning in the everyday'. In a carefully constructed world that made use of a multilevelled set design, the everyday was jumbled with the dreamlike, and common household items such as a couch, a bath and a wall doubled as combat zones in which the boredom of routine was battled with risk-taking activities: in one scene a 70-year-old woman with a stopwatch supervised a young boy as he tried to hold his breath underwater; in another a trampoline added thrilling precariousness (and a great deal of hilarity) to the humdrum task of wallpapering. Further recent works include *Bird with Boy* (2011), which touched on issues of institutional violence and child abuse, bringing audiences on an evocative journey through the basement spaces and courtyards of Dublin's Kilmainham Gaol (a former prison), and *The Falling Song* (2012), which examined 'male physicality' through themes of 'flying and falling [...] self-destruction, invincibility and failure'.[6]

Choreographer Emma Martin's debut work, *Listowel Syndrome* (2010), was inspired by a real-life incident at a rape trial case in Kerry, in which 50 members of the Listowel community queued up to show their support for a convicted rapist by shaking his hand. A multidisciplinary cast of dancers, actors, musicians and a humming and whispering choir of singers examined the functioning of belonging and exclusion in tight-knit communities. The narrative of the work was divided into four stages of 'predation', showing a rape victim being singled out from a group, being stalked and cornered, and finally being 'consumed' by a sexual predator. Moving from community dynamics to a study of the intimate dynamics of a couple's relationship, Fidget Feet Aerial Dance Theatre's *Hang On* (2010) was an indoor work for two performers (Chantal McCormick and Lee Clayden), a musician (Jym Daly), and a single trapeze. McCormick, an aerial artist and contemporary dancer, founded Fidget Feet with musician Jym Daly in 2000, and the company's indoor and outdoor works attempt a fusion of dance theatre and contemporary circus. In *Hang On*, McCormick and Clayden communicated the stress of living in a profit-driven world, suggesting in the final beautiful image of the couple suspended in a precarious embrace on the trapeze, that the current disintegrating economic and social structures in Irish society can be countered through a return to basic human connections.

The cleverly titled *The Ballet Ruse* (2010) was another duet choreographed and performed by two of Ireland's best-known contemporary dancers, Muirne Bloomer and Emma O'Kane (both regular performers and choreographers with CoisCéim). Bridging the ballet/contemporary divide in this alternately humorous and critical examination of their experiences of ballet training and performance, the pair demonstrated a deft ability to puncture and manipulate the iconicity of the ballet world. Donning tutus and *pointe* shoes and dancing to a soundtrack of music from *Giselle, Swan Lake* and pop star Lady Gaga's single, *Just Dance*, ballet steps such as *bourrées* and *échappés* became boxing drills and corps de ballet members smoked to kill the tedium during lengthy onstage posing sessions (later downing pints of Guinness with an alarming rapidity at sessions of another sort). Amidst the humour, Bloomer and Kane also highlighted some of the more tragic survival tactics associated with the profession. In a scene reminiscent of the *Kingdom of the Shades* from the romantic ballet *La Bayadère*, lengths of toilet paper were substituted for the usual gauze, and after some wafting around, were held in the mouth and eaten, before being vomited out in the wings by Bloomer, who later speaks directly to the audience of her 10-year struggle with bulimia. Body image issues and autobiographical narratives are also tackled in the work of Emma Fitzgerald and Áine Stapleton, who founded their company Fitzgerald and Stapleton in 2008. Influenced primarily by the US postmodern choreographer Deborah Hay,[7] they play with quotidian movement and sound, and their choreography is based on a pre-written score that is then interpreted during performance. Past scores have been based on the narrative of *Swan Lake* (*Starvin'* (2009)) and the ceremonies of a Catholic mass (*Dog of All Creation* (2008)), and more recent pieces, such as *The Work The Work* (2010), are based on the everyday experiences of the choreographers themselves recorded over a set period of time. An important element of Fitzgerald and Stapleton's work is their use of nudity as a critical response to the portrayal of female bodies in the media. This might seem a little paradoxical, but as they explain, their commitment to fully inhabiting their 'normal women's bodies' (during *The Work The Work* Fitzgerald asks, 'what does it feel like to be a woman in Ireland today?' and states later on, 'my body is my own') is intended as an intervention into a world full of airbrushed images of unobtainable corporeal perfection.[8]

As these examples show, the newest wave of dance theatre choreographers in Ireland are continuing to expand the possibilities for dance theatre practice. As with the work of the choreographers discussed in earlier chapters, they are resisting the separation of the political and the aesthetic to create choreographies of change that speak directly of current socio-political and cultural issues, and which contribute to a new understanding of corporealities in Ireland. Throughout this book I have highlighted practitioners who are telling stories of the body through the body, creating moving histories that dance a dialogue, as Elizabeth Grosz suggests, 'between bodily inscription and lived experience'.[9] In the wake of the Celtic Tiger's collapse, Ireland is once again entering a period of change and uncertainty. Speaking of the need for choreographers and dancers to always be ready to improvise and find 'new choreography to fit the moment', Susan Foster proposes that, 'like democracy, the dance must be made, struggled over, negotiated, reconciled, and reconfigured in perpetuity'.[10] With its inclusive, adaptive and boundary-testing ethos, dance theatre practice will continue to function as an important site of innovation, where choreographers, performers and audiences can engage in an embodied questioning of the socio-political and cultural ideas that are shaping their lives. The increasing number of dance theatre practitioners in Ireland and their challenging choreographies of both lived and wished-for worlds, presents an exciting and ever-growing body of work for future research.

Notes

1 Introduction

1. Brian Singleton, *Irish Theatre Magazine*, Winter 2003, p. 47.
2. See for example Bernadette Sweeney, *Performing the Body in Irish Theatre* (Basingstoke: Palgrave Macmillan, 2008), Michael Seaver's interview in Deirdre Mulrooney, *Irish Moves: an Illustrated History of Dance and Physical Theatre in Ireland*, (Dublin: The Liffey Press, 2006) and Karen Fricker's essay, 'Traveling Without Moving', in Dermot Bolger (ed.), *Druids Dudes and Beauty Queens* (Dublin: New Island, 2001).
3. Conall Morrison, cited in Deirdre Mulrooney, *Irish Moves*, p. 190. Although this recognition of a strong bias towards literary expression in Irish theatrical practice seems to produce an opposition between the written word and the body, it is important to note that any live performance of a playwright's text inevitably involves some form of physical expression, as the text is voiced and actioned through the body. Similarly, the work of poststructuralist philosophers in the 1960s such as Jacques Derrida and Roland Barthes has resulted in an expanded notion of 'text', whereby it no longer merely refers to a written or printed body of writing, but can also be used to designate 'not only coherent and complete series of linguistic statements, whether oral or written, but [...] every unit of discourse, whether verbal, nonverbal, or mixed, that results from the coexistence of several codes [that possess] the constitutive prerequisites of completeness and coherence' (Marco de Marinis, *The Semiotics of Performance* (Bloomington: Indiana University Press, 1993), p. 47). It is possible then, to view or 'read' dance as a 'text' that assembles codes into coherent readable systems, and also to read the movements of the body as acts of writing (see Goellner and Shea Murphy (eds), *Bodies of the Text: Dance as Theory, Literature as Dance* (New Jersey: Rutgers University Press, 1995)). In discussing the choreography of dancing bodies that speak, it is important to acknowledge both the materiality of linguistic expression and the linguistic materiality of the body (see André Lepecki, *Exhausting Dance, Performance and the Politics of Movement* (New York: Routledge, 2006), p. 55).
4. Susan Foster, *Choreography and Narrative: Ballet's Staging of Story and Desire* (Indianapolis: Indiana University Press, 1998), pp. xv–xvi.
5. Examples of other companies and practitioners who have produced works of this nature include Finola Cronin, John Scott's Irish Modern Dance Theatre, Cindy Cummings, Ríonach Ní Néill, Megan Kennedy and Jessica Kennedy (with their company Junk Ensemble), Fearghus Ó'Conchúir, Fitzgerald and Stapleton, Ella Clarke and Emma Martin.
6. Terence Brown, *Ireland: a Social and Cultural History 1922–2002* (London: Harper Collins, 2004), p. 360.

7. Fianna Fáil is a centrist, liberal-conservative republican party, and the largest political party in Ireland. It has been elected to government seven times since 1932, making it the most dominant political party in Ireland since the establishment of Dáil Éireann (the Irish parliament).

8. Robinson represented Mary Magee in the Supreme Court in 1972 in a family planning case that challenged the state's 1935 law prohibiting the importation and sale of contraceptives. The challenge was successful and in 1979 a bill was finally passed that allowed contraceptives to be sold on prescription to married couples in chemist shops (see Brown, *Ireland*, pp. 290–2). Twenty years later, in response to the world AIDS crisis, another bill was passed that relaxed these laws further.

9. Robinson represented future senator David Norris in his case to the Supreme Court in 1980. When this case was rejected, she brought it to the European Court of Human Rights in Strasbourg in 1988 where it was finally successful. A bill decriminalising homosexuality for consenting adults was passed in 1993.

10. Diarmaid Ferriter, *The Transformation of Ireland 1900–2000* (London: Profile Books, 2005), p. 744.

11. The GAA (Gaelic Athletic Association) promotes the indigenous Irish sports of hurling and Gaelic football, and is a community-based organisation run by volunteers.

12. Brown, *Ireland*, p. 29.

13. Brown, *Ireland*, pp. 372–3, and Kenny, cited in Brown, p. 373.

14. Joe Cleary, *Outrageous Fortune: Capital and Culture in Modern Ireland* (Dublin: Field Day Publications, 2007), p. 95.

15. The Eurovision song contest is an annual song competition for participating Europe Broadcasting Network countries. The show is broadcast live on television (and since 2000 on the internet) in countries both within and outside of Europe. Broadcast since 1956, recent television audiences for the show are estimated as being at least 100 million viewers and possibly as high as 200 million (see Karen Fricker, Elena Moreo and Brian Singleton, 'Part of the Show: Global Networking of Irish Eurovision Song Contest Fans', in Karen Fricker and Ronit Lentin (eds), *Performing Global Networks* (Newcastle: Cambridge Scholars Publishing, 2007) p. 140).

16. Flann O'Brien, 'The Dance Halls', in *The Bell*, February 1941.

17. The official *Riverdance* website supplies a host of statistics related to the show. These include the number of Irish dancers who have performed in it (over 1,500) and the number of performances (over 10,000), the number of people globally who have watched the show on television (claimed to be over 2 billion), the number of miles travelled by the three *Riverdance* troupes (over 563,000 'or to the moon and back!'), and the number of marriages between cast members (35). See www.riverdance.com (accessed 4 February 2010).

18. Liam Fay cited in Ferriter, *The Transformation of Ireland*, p. 743.

19. Natasha Casey, 'The Importance of Being Irish-American', *New Hibernia Review*, 6 (4), Geimhreadh/Winter 2002, p. 12.

20. André Lepecki defines the choreo-political as, 'all kinesthetically performed programs of subjectivation and counter-subjectivation embedded in ideological structures of command or resistance'. Lepecki, 'Stumble Dance', in *Women & Performance: a Journal of Feminist Theory*, 14(1), (2004), p. 48.

21. Moya Doherty cited in Casey, 'Riverdance: the Importance of Being Irish American', p. 12.

22. See Helena Wulff, *Dancing at the Crossroads: Memory and Mobility in Ireland* (Oxford: Berghahn Books, 2007), p.113.

23. John Tiller, who worked in the cotton industry, was a musical theatre enthusiast, and the original Tiller Girls troupe were young working-class girls from Manchester who Tiller recruited and trained to perform in chorus line formations. The precision achieved by Tiller's methods (he is credited with the innovation of having the dancers hold each other by the waist to increase their synchronicity) proved extremely popular, and by the time of Tiller's death in 1925, Tiller Girls troupes were performing in London, New York, Paris and Berlin.

24. See Siegfried Kracauer, 'The Mass Ornament' in *The Mass Ornament: Weimar Essays*, edited and translated by Thomas Y. Levin (Cambridge: Harvard University Press, 2005), pp. 75–86. Ramsay Burt points out that Kracauer's reading of the Tiller Girls within the framework of American capitalism as exemplified by the car manufacturing industry is 'factually inaccurate', as they 'were not from ultra-modern, industrialised America but from declining cotton spinning towns in the north of England' (Ramsay Burt, *Alien Bodies: Representations of Modernity, 'Race' and Nation in Early Modern Dance*, London: Routledge, 1998; p. 99). Nevertheless (and as Burt also observes) Kracauer's analysis continues to be of theoretical interest.

25. Aoife Monks, 'Comely Maidens and Celtic Tigers: *Riverdance* and Global Performance', *Goldsmiths Performance Research Pamphlets*, No. 1, (London: Goldsmiths University of London, 2007), p.10.

26. See the *Gaelforce* website: www.gaelforce-dance.com. Originally based in Australia, but now based in Ireland, the *Gaelforce* production is not currently touring.

27. Michael Flatley cited in Seaver, 'Stepping into Footprints', in Sherry Shapiro, *Dance in a World of Change: Reflections on Globalization and Cultural Difference* (Champaign, Illinois: Human Kinetics, 2008), p. 11. Flatley has also choreographed, produced and danced in *Lord of the Dance* (1996) and *Feet of Flames* (1998).

28. A detailed biography of Michael Flatley can be found on his official website: www.michaelflatley.com.

29. In an article on the relationship between the development of dance in Ireland and Arts Council policy up to 2002, Paul Johnson notes that Brinson had recommended that funding to Dublin City Ballet be cut, and that funding to the Irish National Ballet be reduced, but not cut completely. A funding cut to the Dublin Contemporary Dance Theatre was not one of Brinson's recommendations. Johnson writes that the

1989 cuts represented, 'a sudden and deeply surprising partial reversal of their previous wholesale embrace of the Brinson Report's advice.
By cutting funding over that short span of time to three of the country's
most firmly established companies, the Council dramatically under-
mined many years of work' (Paul Johnson, 'Dancing in the Dark', *Irish
Theatre Magazine*, 3(12), (Summer) 2002, p. 36.)

30. See the 1980 Arts Council Annual Report, Note 4: General Expenditure
    on the Arts: http://www.artscouncil.ie/Publications/An_Chomhairle_
    Ealaíon_1980.pdf (accessed 4 January 2008). In this year, the total
    expenditure on the arts was £2,946,928 (Irish punts), with £1,506,115
    allocated to drama and £216,709 awarded to dance.

31. See the 1989 Arts Council Annual Report: http://www.artscouncil.ie/
    Publications/An_Chomhairle_Eala%C3%ADon_1989.pdf (accessed 4 Jan-
    uary 2008).

32. Reflecting Brinson's emphasis on dance-in-education, community dance
    and vocational training, several dance organisations and companies
    continued to be supported. These included Cathy O'Kennedy's Bare-
    foot Dance Company in Wexford, Thomond College, and Daghda Dance
    Company.

33. Tanham was appointed as a full-time Arts Council officer for 'Dance and
    Youth Arts' in 1996.

34. Playwright Conor McPherson proposes that Friel 'wrote the rulebook
    for the modern Irish monologue with *Faith Healer*' ('Will the Morning
    After Stop Us Talking to Ourselves', *Irish Times*, 3 May 2008, p. 6.). Brian
    Singleton, however, suggests that it was Friel's *Molly Sweeney* (1994) that
    'supplied a template for these new writers' ('Am I Talking to Myself?',
    Irish Times, 19 April 2001).

35. Brian Singleton, 'Am I Talking to Myself?', *Irish Times*, 19 April 2001.

36. Raymond Williams, *The Sociology of Culture* (Chicago: University of
    Chicago Press, 1995), p. 142.

37. Conor McPherson, 'Will the Morning After Stop Us Talking to Our-
    selves', *Irish Times*, 3 May 2008, p. 6.

38. The 2003 Arts Act changed the 1951 and 1973 definition of 'the arts'
    to include dance. The original definition defined the expression 'the
    arts' as including, 'painting, sculpture, architecture, music, the drama,
    literature, design in industry and the fine arts and applied arts gener-
    ally'. The Arts Acts can be accessed online: http://www.irishstatutebook.
    ie (accessed 7 March 2009).

39. DanceHouse is one of the very few custom-built spaces for dance, and
    the recently published Arts Council report on the building-based infras-
    tructure for dance in Ireland, *Giving Body to Dance* (2010), concludes
    that despite a high level of dance activity throughout the country, there
    exists a 'serious lack' of suitable rehearsal and performance spaces. The
    report is available online (accessed 2 September 2010): http://www.
    artscouncil.ie/en/publications/research_publications.aspx.

40. Quoted from the programme for the 1995 Dublin Theatre Festival.

41. Carolyn Swift, '*Dances With Intent*', *Irish Times*, 21 February 1995.

42. Quoted from the CoisCéim online archive (accessed 20 January 2010): http://www.coisceim.com/reelluck.html
43. Bolger cited from an interview with Theodores, *Dancing on the Edge of Europe: Irish Choreographers in Conversation*, (Cork: Institute for Choreography and Dance, 2003), p. 48. *Ballads* is discussed in detail in Chapter 4 of this book.
44. Ibid, p. 54.
45. Quoted from CoisCéim Dance Theatre's website (accessed 12 November 2008): http://www.coisceim.com/aboutus.html
46. Directed by John Comiskey, choreographed by Bolger and co-produced by Rough Magic Films, some of the awards won by *Hit and Run* include the Paula Citron Award for Choreography for the Camera 2002, the Jury Prize at the Moving Pictures Festival, Toronto 2002, and the Award for Creative Excellence at the Dance on Camera Festival, New York 2003.
47. CoisCéim also performed at the opening ceremony of the 2006 Ryder Cup held in Kildare, and Bolger has choreographed and directed opera productions such as Gluck's *Orfeo ed Euridice* (2006), Handel's *Imeneo* (2005), and Benjamin Britten's *A Midsummer Night's Dream* (2008), all for Opera Ireland.
48. This work was a co-production with the Abbey Theatre and featured a script by Gina Moxley.
49. *Dodgems* will be discussed in detail in Chapter 6 of this book.
50. *DruidSynge* was a cycle of six plays by John Millington Synge performed back to back, which premiered in Galway in 2005. Bolger was also the movement director for three John B. Keane plays produced by Druid (*Sive, Sharon's Grave* and *The Year of the Hiker*).
51. The other regularly funded dance organisations are Dance Theatre of Ireland, Fabulous Beast Dance Theatre, Irish Modern Dance Theatre, Rex Levitates, and, until 2009, Shawbrook Dance Trust (a youth dance centre and studio and retreat for dance companies in Longford). CoisCéim supplements its Arts Council funding with income generated from dance classes and workshops given in the studio of their Sackville Place premises in Dublin. Their successful 'Broadreach' programme, established in 2006, is a community outreach and 'dance awareness' programme that runs several courses throughout the year catering for different dance styles and age groups. CoisCéim are one of the few dance companies in Ireland who have their own premises. This was made possible by the award of a capital grant from the Arts Council in 2001.
52. Tour destinations have included the 10 Days On the Island Festival in Tasmania (2000), Jacob's Pillow Dance Festival in Massachusetts, USA (2001), the Ireland China Festival of Arts and Culture in Beijing and Shanghai (2004), the Edinburgh Fringe Festival in Scotland (2005, 2006), and the *Internationale Tanzmesse* in Düsseldorf, Germany (2010).
53. Members of *Aosdána* are entitled to apply for *Cnuas*: 'a stipend which is designed to enable them to devote their energies fully to their work'. See the Arts Council website: http://aosdana.artscouncil.ie/ (accessed 14 March 2008).

54. The encounter with MacMillan, one of the most celebrated British choreographers of the twentieth century, seems to have had quite an impact on the 23-year-old:

> [s]omehow Kenneth Macmillan and Nick Hytner saw through my limited technique as a dancer and gave me a job. [...] Macmillan seemed to like me – and to see something in me that didn't show externally. With people from the Royal Ballet around me [...] I felt really out of my depth. I bumped into Macmillan. He looked at me – I looked at him – and then he said 'When are you going to stop pretending that you're not as talented as you are?'
>
> (Keegan-Dolan cited from an interview with Brendan McCarthy, 'Celtic Tiger', *Dance Now*, 16 (4), (Winter) 2007/2008, p. 50).

55. Rice has subsequently danced in several Fabulous Beast shows.
56. Keegan-Dolan has since choreographed several opera productions including Stravinsky's *The Rake's Progress* directed by Robert Lepage (2007), and works for the Royal Opera House, the English National Opera, the Royal Flanders Opera, Cologne Opera and the Bavarian State Opera.
57. The Institute of Choreography and Dance closed in 2006.
58. Quoted from the 'history' section of the Fabulous Beast website (accessed 14 March 2009): http://fabulousbeast.net/about/history/.
59. Mary Leland, 'Leaps and Bounds of Anarchic Humour', *Irish Times*, 28 September 1998, p. 12.
60. See Michael Seaver, 'Fringe Reviews', *Irish Times*, 25 September 1999, p. 3.
61. For example, the programme for *Fragile* describes the action thus: '[w]hen cutting an umbilical cord requires a large saw and taking a shower turns into a physical impossibility, life can be a continual heartache. In the world of *Fragile* owning a piece of fruit can be a killing matter. And who does the fat blue Buddha think he is? God?' (cited in Stephen Benedetto, 'Guiding Somatic Responses within Performative Structures', in Sally Banes and André Lepecki (eds), *The Senses in Performance*, p. 128).
62. *Giselle* is discussed further in Chapter Five of this book.
63. Keegan-Dolan cited in Mulrooney, *Irish Moves*, p. 162.
64. Keegan-Dolan cited in an interview with Brendan McCarthy, 'Celtic Tiger', *Dance Now*, Winter 2007/2008, p. 50.
65. From the Fabulous Beast manifesto on the company website (accessed 12 November 2007): http://fabulousbeast.net/site.html.
66. Ibid.
67. Keegan-Dolan's father was from County Longford, and Keegan-Dolan now lives there himself.
68. Keegan-Dolan cited in McCarthy, 'Celtic Tiger', p. 47.
69. Ibid.
70. *The Bull* is discussed in detail in Chapter Four of this book.

71. Culture Ireland is a government-funded organisation that supports the promotion of Irish arts internationally. The Dance Touring Partnership is a network of theatres in the UK that work together to bring dance productions to a broader audience.
72. *The Rite of Spring* in discussed in detail in Chapter Five of this book.
73. Keegan-Dolan cited in an interview with the author, 'Sharpening a Sensibility for Truth', 2011 Dublin Theatre Festival programme for *Rian* (unpaginated).
74. Keegan-Dolan cited on the Barbican website (accessed 2 March 2008): http://www.barbican.org.uk/25/we-say/partners.
75. Fabulous Beast have no permanent 'home' in Ireland, and must resort to using different locations for rehearsal periods; these have included the Shawbrook retreat in Longford (significantly for the *Midlands Trilogy*), the Samuel Beckett Theatre in Dublin, and the Black Box Theatre in Galway.
76. A recent publication by Victoria O'Brien contributes a valuable record of four decades of Irish ballet history: *A History of Irish Ballet from 1927 to 1963* (Bern: Peter Lang, 2011).
77. It must be noted that Wulff's project of discussing how 'Irishness' is expressed through various dance forms is operating from an essentialist basis that is at odds with the aims of this book. Based on interviews with over 100 interlocutors from various dance sectors, *Dancing at the Crossroads* nevertheless provides very useful information.
78. This essay is published in Nicholas Grene and Patrick Lonergan (eds), *Interactions: Dublin Theatre Festival 1957–2007* (Carysfort Press: Dublin, 2008).
79. For example Joe Cleary, *Outrageous Fortune: Capital and Culture in Modern Ireland* (2007).
80. For example Coulter and Coleman, *The End of Irish History? Critical Reflections on the Celtic Tiger* (Manchester: Manchester University Press, 2003).
81. Elizabeth Grosz, *Space, Time and Perversion: Essays on the Politics of Bodies* (London: Routledge, 1995), p. 232.
82. Ann Cooper Albright, *Choreographing Difference: the Body and Identity in Contemporary Dance* (Connecticut: Wesleyan University Press, 1997), p. 3.
83. Bryan S. Turner, from *Regulating Bodies: Essays in Medical Sociology*, quoted in Helen Thomas, *The Body, Dance and Cultural Theory* (Basingstoke: Palgrave Macmillan, 2003), p. 29.
84. Ibid.
85. Maurice Merleau-Ponty, *The Primacy of Perception* (Illinois: Northwestern University Press, 1964), p. 3.
86. Ibid, p.5.
87. Ibid.
88. Taylor Carman, *Merleau-Ponty* (Oxford: Routledge, 2008), p. 124.
89. See Judith Butler's essay in Taylor Carman and Mark Hansen (eds), *The Cambridge Companion to Merleau-Ponty* (Cambridge University Press, 2005).

90. Iris Marion Young, *On Female Body Experience: 'Throwing like a Girl' and Other Essays* (Oxford University Press, 2005), p. 8.
91. Elizabeth Grosz, *Volatile Bodies: Toward a Corporeal Feminism* (Indiana University Press: Indianapolis, 1994), pp. 94–5.
92. Philipa Rothfield, 'Differentiating Phenomenology and Dance', *Topoi*, 24 (2005), p. 46.
93. Ibid, p. 5.
94. Thomas Csordas cited in Thomas, *The Body, Dance and Cultural Theory*, p. 63.
95. Jane Desmond, *Meaning in Motion: New Cultural Studies in Dance* (London: Duke University Press, 1997), p. 1.
96. See, for example, André Lepecki's consideration of the 'parallels habit and language have forged between dance and writing [...] and between dance and femininity', in *Of the Presence of the Body: Essays on Dance and Performance Theory* (Middletown: Wesleyan University Press, 2004), pp.124–39.
97. Many dance scholars have highlighted dance's marginalisation in academia and 'poor relative' status in relation to other art forms. This phenomenon is often explained as stemming in part from the difficulty of translating movement into written text. See for example Ellen W. Goellner's and Jacqueline Shea Murphy's introduction to *Bodies of the Text* (1995) or Susan Foster's introduction to *Choreographing History* (1995).
98. Michel Foucault, 'The Body of the Condemned', in Paul Rabinow (ed.), *The Foucault Reader* (London: Penguin, 1986), p. 173.
99. Ibid.
100. Elizabeth Grosz, *Volatile Bodies*, p. 122.
101. In *Reading Dancing* (1986), for example, Susan Foster proposes that the movement of the body can be viewed as an 'act of writing' (see *Reading Dancing: Bodies and Subjects in Contemporary American Dance* (California: University of California Press, 1986), p. 237). She supports her argument with an interpretation of the semiological studies of Barthes and his post-structuralist approach to the body 'as a locus of mindful human articulations' (ibid., p.237).
102. Susan Foster, *Choreographing History*, p. 15. Foster is commenting on Foucault's *Discipline and Punish, Madness and Civilization* and *The Order of Things*.
103. Susan Foster, *Corporealities: Dancing Knowledge, Culture and Power* (London: Routledge, 1996), p. xi.
104. Ibid, p. xiii.
105. Foster, *Choreographing History*, p. 15.
106. Ibid.
107. Randy Martin, *Critical Moves: Dance Studies in Theory and Politics* (London: Duke University Press, 1998), p. 6.
108. Martin, 'Overreading *The Promised Land*: Towards Narrative of Context in Dance', in Foster, *Corporealities*, p. 178.
109. Martin, *Critical Moves*, p. 3.

110. Ibid., p. 10.
111. Several performance and dance scholars have highlighted the useful-ness of de Certeau's work in approaching cultural politics. For example, his theory is used by Susan Foster in her study of improvisational performance (*Dances That Describe Themselves: the Improvised Choreogra-phy of Richard Bull* (Middletown CT: Wesleyan University Press, 2002), Gabriele Brandstetter in her examination of choreography as cartog-raphy ('Choreography as a Cenotaph: the Memory of Movement', in Brandstetter and Völckers (eds), *ReMembering the Body* (Ostfildern-Ruit, Germany: Hatje Cantz, 2000), and Dwight D. Conquergood in his study of research methodology in performance studies ('Performance Studies: Interventions and Radical Research', in *The Performance Studies Reader* (2007)).
112. Michel de Certeau, *The Practice of Everyday Life* (London: University of California Press, 1988), p. xiv.
113. Ibid., p. 36.
114. Ibid., p. 37.
115. Ibid.
116. Declan Kiberd, *Inventing Ireland: the Literature of a Modern Nation* (London: Vintage, 1996), p. 1.
117. Bernadette Sweeney also discusses the postcolonial relationship to lan-guage in Ireland with reference to a 'repression of the body as dictated by the state-sponsored identification with the Catholic Church', *Performing the Body in Irish Theatre*, p. 3.
118. Patricia Palmer writes that these English sanctions from the sixteenth century, 'recognized all too well the intersection between the liter-ary and the political in Gaelic society'. See ' "An headlesse Ladie" and "a horses loade of heades": Writing the Beheading', in *Renaissance Quarterly*, 60 (1), Spring 2007, p. 29.
119. Kiberd, *Inventing Ireland*, p. 3.
120. For a discussion of the patriarchal oppositional structuring of a masculine/feminine dichotomy in which the feminine represents the negative to a masculine positive, see Hélène Cixous, 'Sorties: Out and Out: Attacks/Ways/Forays', in Hélène Cixous and Catherine Clement, *The Newly Born Woman* (Manchester: Manchester University Press, 1986).
121. Kiberd, *Inventing Ireland*, p. 25.
122. Helen Brennan, *The Story of Irish Dance* (Dingle: Brandon, 1999), p. 31.
123. Ibid, p. 36.
124. See Gearóid Ó'hAllmhuiráin, 'Dancing on the Hobs of Hell: Rural Com-munities in Clare and the Dance Halls Act of 1935', in *New Hibernian Review*, 9 (4), (Winter 2005), pp. 9–18; also Helen Brennan, *The Story of Irish Dance*, Barbara O'Connor, 'Sexing the Nation: Discourses of the Dancing Body in Ireland in the 1930s', *Journal of Gender Studies*, 14 (2), 2005, pp. 89–105, and Frank Hall, *Competitive Irish Dancing: Art, Sport, Duty* (Madison: Macater Press, 2008).
125. André Lepecki, *Of the Presence of the Body*, p. 124.

126. Ramsay Burt, *The Male Dancer* (London: Routledge, 1995), p. 9.
127. Gearóid Ó'hAllmhuiráin, 'Dancing on the Hobs of Hell', p. 9.
128. See Brennan, *The Story of Irish Dance*, p. 57. Breandán Breathnach also writes of the perceived need for restraint by Irish step dance teachers who 'discouraged flinging the hand about or flourishing them at the level of the head. [...] The good dancer, it was said, could dance on eggs without breaking them and hold a pan of water on his head without spilling a drop', (Breathnach, *Folk Music and Dances of Ireland* (Cork: 1996), p. 53).
129. See Barbara O'Connor, 'Sexing the Nation: Discourses of the Dancing Body in Ireland in the 1930s', *Journal of Gender Studies*, 14 (2), 2005, pp. 89–105.
130. Diarmaid Ferriter, *The Transformation of Ireland 1900–2000*, p. 101. Ferriter argues that the ban was not solely motivated by Anglophobia and political nationalism, but was also necessary for 'administrative' reasons to allow for distinct forms of Irish sports to emerge.
131. Edward Said citing Thomas Flanagan, *Culture and Imperialism* (London: Vintage, 1994), p. 285.
132. Declan Kiberd, *Inventing Ireland*, p. 118.
133. Francis Barker, *The Tremulous Private Body: Essays on Subjection* (Ann Arbor: University of Michigan Press, 2005), p. vi.
134. Ibid, p. vii. Barker uses the diaries of Samuel Pepys as an example of the emerging modern body's guilt in relation to its sexuality, and James Grantham Turner has pointed out that the version of Pepys that Barker uses to base his argument on is bowdlerised (see Grantham Turner, 'Pepys and the Private Parts of Monarchy', in Gerard MacLean (ed.), *Culture and Society in the Stuart Restoration*, p. 96). However problematic this makes Barker's argument in relation to Pepys, the notion of the 'two bodies' created by modernity still has resonance with the emergence of the 'Irish' body in the early twentieth century.
135. L. P. Curtis quoted in Ferriter, *The Transformation of Ireland*, p. 96.
136. For a discussion of different aspects of neo-colonialism see Philip G. Altbach, 'Education and Neocolonialism', in *The Postcolonial Studies Reader*, p. 381.
137. There are reports of parish priests bursting uninvited into house dances and chasing the dancers out onto the street with sticks. Parishioners caught dancing were also denounced from the pulpit. For a discussion of these stories and specific legal cases and prosecutions under the Act, see Brennan, *The Story of Irish Dance*, pp. 121–33.
138. Barker, *The Tremulous Private Body*, p. 91.
139. De Certeau, *The Practice of Everyday Life*, p. 128.
140. Joseph Roach, *Cities of the Dead* (New York: Columbia University Press, 1996), p. 55.
141. Benedict Anderson, *Imagined Communities* (London: Verso, 2006), p. 6.
142. Bolger cited in Mulrooney, *Irish Moves*, p. 149.

2 Danced Precedents from Yeats to Davis

1. Lady Cunard was a dedicated patron of the arts and Lynn Garafola documents her support of the Ballets Russes in *Diaghilev's Ballets Russes* (1998). The audiences at these London drawing room gatherings were not always small in number. The second performance of *At the Hawk's Well* was given as a charity benefit in Lady Islington's drawing room, which held more than three hundred people (See Caldwell, *Michio Ito: the Dancer and his Dances* (Berkeley: University of California Press, 1977), p. 49).
2. Yeats, W. B. *Autobiographies*, (London: Papermac, 1987), p. 493.
3. Declan Kiberd, *Irish Classics*, (London: Granta Books, 2000), p. 440.
4. Kiberd, *Inventing Ireland: the Literature of a Modern Nation*, (London: Vintage, 1996), p. 127.
5. Susan Foster, 'The Signifying Body: Reaction and Resistance in Postmodern Dance', *Theatre Journal*, 37 (1), 'Theory', (March) 1985, p. 62.
6. André Lepecki, *Exhausting Dance: Performance and the Politics of Movement* (New York: Routledge, 2006), p. 23. Here Lepecki is referencing an observation made by Susan Manning in her book *Modern Dance, Negro Dance: Race in Motion* (University of Minnesota Press, 2004).
7. Seamus Kelly writing as Quidnunc in 'An Irishman's Diary', *Irish Times*, 7 June 1948, p. 5.
8. Yeats writes of this notion in the 1902 edition of *Samhain: an Occasional Review*, a publication of the Irish Literary Theatre which ran from 1901–8 and of which Yeats was editor.
9. Ibid.
10. Mary Fleischer, *Embodied Texts: Symbolist Playwright-Dancer Collaborations* (New York: Rodopi, 2007), p. 154.
11. See Elizabeth Bergmann Loizeaux's *Yeats and the Visual Arts* (London: Rutgers, 1986) for a detailed discussion of the influence of the Pre-Raphaelite painters on the development of Yeats' aesthetic.
12. A set of Craig's moveable screens were first used in the Abbey Theatre for re-written versions of *The Countess Cathleen, The Land of Heart's Desire* and *The Hour Glass* in 1911 and Craig provided Yeats with a working model of the set, which Yeats writes, 'allowe[d] the scene to give the words and the words the scene' (Yeats cited in Fleischer, *Embodied Texts*, p. 162).
13. Yeats, *Four Plays for Dancers* (London: Macmillan & Co., 1921), p. 8.
14. See Edward Gordon Craig, 'The Actor and the Über-marionette', *The Twentieth Century Performance Reader* (2nd edn, London: Routledge, 2002), p. 159.
15. Ibid., p. 161.
16. Mary Fleischer suggests that, 'Fuller's art demonstrated for the symbolists how the dancer's movement could theatricalize space and transform the perception of time' (Fleischer, *Embodied Texts*, p. 18).

17. Stéphane Mallarmé, *Oeuvres Complétes*, p. 306, cited in Bate, 'Yeats and the Symbolist Aesthetic', *Modern Language Notes*, 985, (December) 1983, p. 1218.
18. Stéphane Mallarmé, 'Ballets', in Marshall Cohen and Roger Copeland (eds), *What is Dance?: Readings in Theory and Criticism* (Oxford University Press, 1983), p. 115.
19. For a comprehensive history of Diaghilev's achievements, see Lynn Garafola's *Diaghilev's Ballets Russes* (Oxford University Press, 1989).
20. Yeats in a letter to Lady Gregory, 8 March 1913 cited in Sylvia Ellis, *The Plays of W. B. Yeats: Yeats and the Dancer* (London: Macmillan, 1995), p. 202.
21. Helen Caldwell, *Michio Ito*, p. 42.
22. W. B. Yeats, 'Certain Noble Plays of Japan', in *Essays and Introductions*, (London: Macmillan, 1961), p. 230–1.
23. In addition to the remaining three of the *Four Plays for Dancers* – *The Dreaming of the Bones* (1919), *The Only Jealousy of Emer* (1919) and *Calvary* (1921) – the later works *The Cat and the Moon* (1926), *The Resurrection* (1931), *A Full Moon in March* (1935), *The King of the Clock Tower* (1935) and *The Death of Cuchulain* (1939) can also be considered as belonging to Yeats' dance plays.
24. See Richard Taylor, *The Drama of W. B. Yeats: Irish Myth and the Japanese No* (New Haven: Yale University Press, 1976), p. 120.
25. This ceremony involved the musicians ritualistically unfolding and refolding a large cloth while singing the opening and closing verses of the play. Supposedly inspired by Noh rituals, this was used as a device by Yeats to help transport the viewers into the imagined world of the play.
26. Mary Fleischer, *Embodied Texts*, p. 201.
27. Helen Caldwell, *Michio Ito*, p. 45.
28. Ibid., pp. 49–50.
29. Yeats cited in Caldwell, *Michio Ito*, p. 48.
30. Yeats cited in Mary Fleischer, *Embodied Texts*, p. 181.
31. See Shelley Sharp Dirst, 'From *The Hour Glass* to *At the Hawk's Well*: Revisions Toward an Idealized Theatre', *The South Carolina Review*, 36 (2) (Spring 2004), p. 126.
32. See Helen Caldwell, *Michio Ito*, p. 38.
33. Hedwig Müller and Patricia Stöckemann (eds), '...*jeder Mensch ist ein Tänzer' : Ausdruckstanz in Deutschland zwischen 1900 und 1945*, (Giessen: Anabas, 1993), p. 10.
34. Ito, cited in Mary Fleischer, *Embodied Texts*, p. 183.
35. Ito, cited in Mary-Jean Cowell, 'East and West in the Work of Michio Ito', *Dance Research Journal*, 26 (2) (Autumn 1994), p. 11.
36. See Yutian Wong, 'Artistic Utopias: Michio Ito and the International', in Susan Foster (ed.), *Worlding Dance*, (Basingstoke: Palgrave Macmillan, 2009), p. 148.
37. Cowell, 'East and West in the Work of Michio Ito', p. 20.
38. Yeats cited in Ellis, *The Plays of W. B. Yeats*, p. 130.

39. Mallarmé writes: 'I mean that the ballerina *is not a girl dancing*; [...] *she is not a girl*, but rather a metaphor which symbolizes some elemental aspect of earthly form: sword, cup, flower, etc., and that *she does not dance* but rather, with miraculous lunges and abbreviations, writing with her body, she *suggests* things which the written work could *express* only in several paragraphs of dialogue or descriptive prose. Her poem is written without the writer's tools.' Cited in Roger Copeland and Marshall Cohen (eds), *What is Dance?: Readings in Theory and Criticism* (Oxford University Press, 1983), p.112.

40. James Brandon (ed.), *The Cambridge Guide to Asian Theatre* (Cambridge University Press, 1997), p. 145.

41. Ellis, *The Plays of W. B. Yeats*, p. 147.

42. David Holdeman, *The Cambridge Introduction to Yeats* (Cambridge University Press, 2006), p. 72.

43. Christopher Murray, *Twentieth Century Irish Drama: Mirror up to the Nation*, (Manchester University Press, 1997), p. 26.

44. See Fleischer, *Embodied Texts*, p. 203.

45. Alain Badiou, *Handbook of Inaesthetics* (Stanford: Stanford University Press, 2005), p. 68.

46. See Noreen Doody in Mulrooney, *Irish Moves: an Illustrated History of Dance and Physical Theatre in Ireland*, (Dublin: The Liffey Press, 2006), p. 65.

47. Christopher Murray, *Twentieth Century Irish Drama*, p. 25. Murray explains that Horniman withdrew her funding as she felt that the Abbey productions were too political.

48. Ninette de Valois cited in Katherine Sorley Walker, 'The Festival and the Abbey: Ninette de Valois' early choreography 1925–1934, Part One', *Dance Chronicle*, 7(4), (1984–5), p. 385.

49. De Valois engaged teachers from her London school to run the Abbey School of Ballet full-time, as her own visits there were short. See Victoria O'Brien, *A History of Irish Ballet from 1927 to 1963* (Bern: Peter Lang, 2011).

50. De Valois, *Come Dance With Me: a Memoir 1898–1956*, (London: Dance Books, 1973), p. 104.

51. See Sorley Walker, 'The Festival and the Abbey: Ninette de Valois' Early Choreography, 1925–1934, Part One', p. 408.

52. *Bad Boy of Music* is the title of Antheil's autobiography.

53. Fleischer, *Embodied Texts*, p. 237.

54. J. J. Hayes, 'Mr Yeats Plans an Experiment', *The New York Times*, 25 August 1929 (cited in Fleischer, *Embodied Texts*, p. 245).

55. Yeats, *Letters*, pp. 767–8.

56. Joseph Holloway in Robert Hogan, and Michael O'Neill (eds), *Joseph Holloway's Irish Theatre*, (Dixon California: Proscenium Press, 1968), p. 51.

57. *Irish Independent*, 14 August 1929, cited in Sorley Walker, 'The Festival and the Abbey: Ninette de Valois' Early Choreography, 1925–1934, Part One', p. 410.

58. Chris Morash, *A History of Irish Theatre: 1601–2000* (Cambridge University Press, 2002), p. 189.
59. Anonymous reviewer, *The Times*, 31 March 1930, p. 9.
60. De Valois cited in G. M. Pinciss, 'A Dancer for Mr. Yeats', *Educational Theatre Journal*, 21 (4) (December 1969), p. 389.
61. Yeats, 'Preface', *Four Plays for Dancers*', p. v.
62. Yeats, *Letters* (London: Rupert Hart-Davis, 1954), pp. 767–8.
63. Samuel Beckett cited in Katherine Worth, 'Enigmatic Influences: Yeats, Beckett and Noh', in Christopher Murray and Masaru Sekine (eds), *Yeats and the Noh: a comparative study*, (Gerrard's Cross, Buckinghamshire: Colin Smythe, 1990), p. 149.
64. See Fleischer, *Embodied Texts*, p. 306.
65. Ibid., p. 307.
66. A significant contemporary production of *At the Hawk's Well* was staged in 2010 by Blue Raincoat Theatre Company as the second work of their Yeats Project, which commenced in 2009.
67. This is how Brady was described by her pupil Jacqueline Robinson (Robinson, *Modern Dance in Dublin in the 1940s (yes, there was ...)* (Dance Ireland archive, 1999), p. 12).
68. Larraine Nicholas, 'Dancing in the Margins', in Alexandra Carter (ed.), *Rethinking Dance History: a Reader*, (London: Routledge, 2004), p. 120.
69. Robinson founded the first professional modern dance school in France, L'Atelier de la Danse, in Paris in 1957. See Geneviéve Piguet's essay on Robinson's significance in the development of French modern dance in Robinson's book, *Modern Dance in France: An Adventure 1920–1970* (Amsterdam: Harwood Academic, 1997), pp. 240–50.
70. 'Spectator', 'Leader Page Parade', *Irish Independent*, 29 November 1941, p. 2.
71. Robinson, *Modern Dance in Dublin*, p. 13.
72. Robinson confirms that when she herself met Mary Wigman in Germany, Wigman confirmed that Brady had taught for her in her Dresden school.
73. Robinson, *Modern Dance in Dublin*, p. 12.
74. Number 39 also housed many other artists and craftspeople during Brady's tenancy. These included the founders of Dublin's Gate Theatre Hilton Edwards and Michael Mac Liammóir, who lived above her studio, and the filmmaker Liam O'Laoghaire who lived below (see an interview with June Fryer, another of Erina Brady's pupils, in Mulrooney, *Irish Moves*, p. 108).
75. In Germany, for example, the Freikörperkultur (Free Body Culture) that began to establish itself at the turn of the twentieth century, 'spiegelte [...] die Sehnsucht des modernen Menschen nach dem ungebundenen Ausdruck des Körpers in der Natur wider' (mirrored modern man's longing for the free expression of the body in nature) (Müller and Stöckemann, *Jeder Mensch ist ein Tänzer*, p. 9).
76. It must be noted, however, that the electrification of rural areas was miserably slow. In 1945 only 2 per cent of rural households in Ireland

had electricity, in comparison with 85 per cent in Denmark and 98 per cent in Holland (see Diarmaid Ferriter, *The Transformation of Ireland 1900–2000* (London: Profile Books, 2005), p. 425.

77. Melissa Sihra, *Women in Irish Drama: a Century of Authorship and Representation* (Basingstoke: Palgrave Macmillan, 2007), p. 88.

78. Hannah Sheehy Skeffington cited in Sihra, *Women in Irish Drama*, p. 87.

79. Catríona Beaumont, 'Gender, Citizenship and the State in Ireland 1922–1990', in Scott Brewster et al. (eds), *Ireland in Proximity: History, Gender, Space* (London: Routledge, 1999), p. 98.

80. This is how Brady was described by June Fryer, one of Brady's two 'professional' students (cited in Mulrooney, *Irish Moves*, p. 107).

81. Concurrent to their dance studies, senior students who worked towards a professional 'Diploma' (such as Robinson and the other senior student of the school, June Fryer) also pursued a course in the History of Art at Trinity College Dublin, taught by François Henry (see Robinson, *Modern Dance in Dublin*, p. 19). This model of dance education was very similar to that of the Mary Wigman school.

82. Unknown author, 'Barefoot Dancer at the Mansion House', *Irish Times*, 6 December 1941, p. 6.

83. Anonymous reviewer cited in Robinson, *Modern Dance in Dublin*, p. 14.

84. See Ann Daly, 'The Natural Body', in Dils and Cooper Albright (eds), *Moving History/Dancing Cultures* (Middletown Connecticut: Wesleyan University Press, 2001), p. 293.

85. See Maureen Needham (ed.), *I See America Dancing* (Illinois: University of Illinois Press, 2002), pp. 196–9.

86. Interwoven with these philosophical and ideological concerns in Duncan's work, however, is also a celebration of the body for the body's sake. Mark Franko points out that the site of origin for her choreography was always firmly rooted in the corporeal, and re-examining the importance of Duncan's work within the frame of modernism, he suggests that her work marks, 'the incursion of the body's materiality into the transcendence called expressivity' (Mark Franko, *Dancing Modernism/Performing Politics* (Indianapolis: Indiana University Press, 1995), p. 1.

87. Susan Manning writes in particular of the kinaesthetic response of female spectators to Duncan's work *Ave Maria* in her book about Wigman, *Ecstasy and the Demon: the Dances of Mary Wigman* (Minneapolis: University of Minnesota Press, 2006), pp. 35–8.

88. Duncan, from 'I See America Dancing', cited in Manning's *Ecstasy and the Demon*, p. 39.

89. Morash, *A History of Irish Theatre: 1601–2000*, pp. 116–17.

90. June Fryer quoted from an interview with Deirdre Mulrooney for the RTE radio series *Nice Moves*, broadcast 8 May 2004. An archived copy of this interview is available online (accessed 8 October 2008): http://www.rte.ie/radio1/nicemoves/1012995.html.

91. Nicholas, 'Dancing in the Margins?', in Alexandra Carter (ed.), *Rethinking Dance History*, pp. 119–31.

92. Robinson, *Modern Dance in Dublin,* p. 8.
93. Manning, *Ecstasy and the Demon,* p. 54.
94. Ibid., p. 15.
95. Benson and Manning, 'Interrupted Continuities: Modern Dance in Germany', in Dils and Cooper Albright (eds), *Moving History/Dancing Cultures,* pp. 220–1.
96. Robinson, *Modern Dance in Dublin,* p. 13.
97. Ibid., p. 15.
98. Anonymous reviewer, *Evening Mail,* 10 December, 1941, cited in Robinson, *Modern Dance in Dublin,* p. 15.
99. Liam O'Laoghaire cited in Robinson, *Modern Dance in Dublin,* p. 15.
100. Anonymous reviewer, *Irish Times,* 10 December 1941.
101. Erina Brady cited from a personal letter to Austin Clarke dated 7 December 1944 (sourced from the Austin Clarke papers at the National Archives in Kildare Street, Dublin).
102. Ibid.
103. Ibid.
104. See Robinson, *Modern Dance in Dublin,* p. 18.
105. Quoted from the programme of the work (see Robinson, *Modern Dance in Dublin,* p. 18).
106. Ibid.
107. Ibid.
108. Ibid.
109. See Diarmaid Ferriter, *The Transformation of Ireland 1900–2000,* pp. 54–5.
110. Greta Jones cited in Diarmaid Ferriter, *The Transformation of Ireland 1900–2000,* p. 55.
111. Ibid., p. 501.
112. *Irish Times,* 7 May 1946, p. 6.
113. Robinson, *Modern Dance in Dublin,* p. 19.
114. Ibid.
115. Ibid., p. 23.
116. Ibid.
117. Quidnunc (Seamus Kelly), 'An Irishman's Diary', *Irish Times,* 7 June 1948, p. 5.
118. Ibid. Although Kelly does not mention what pieces were performed, it was probably a double bill of two group works choreographed by Brady: the wonderfully titled *John and the Magic Coffee Grinder* and *The Voyage of Maeldune.* Robinson discusses a 'leaflet' for the first programme of the club, which mentions these two works, and Kelly presumably attended this same programme. See Robinson, *Modern Dance in Dublin,* p. 23.
119. Robinson, *Modern Dance in Dublin,* p. 22.
120. Erina Brady cited from a personal correspondence with Jacqueline Robinson, *Modern Dance in Dublin,* p. 22.
121. See Carolyn Swift's book, *Stage by Stage* (Dublin: Poolbeg, 1985).
122. Robinson mentions going to Kilkenny, Abbeyleix and Castleknock (*Modern Dance in Dublin,* p. 19).
123. See June Fryer's interview in Mulrooney, *Irish Moves,* p. 109.

124. Robinson, *Modern Dance in Dublin* p. 19.
125. Ibid.
126. Fryer cited in Mulrooney, *Irish Moves*, p. 112.
127. Carolyn Swift, 'Setting a Standard', *Irish Times*, 27 March 1981, p. 10.
128. See the Arts Council Annual Report for 1977 (1978), available online (accessed 8 October 2008): http://www.artscouncil.ie/Publications/An_Chomhairle_Ealaíon_1977.pdf.
129. Although 'pioneers' are perhaps usually recognised retrospectively, this moniker was applied to DCDT relatively early. For example, Peter Brinson, in his 1985 report on dance in Ireland for the Arts Council (*The Dancer and the Dance*) writes: 'Dublin Contemporary Dance Theatre are, essentially, the pioneers of modern dance in Ireland' (Brinson, *The Dancer and the Dance: Developing Theatre Dance in Ireland,* Dublin: The Arts Council/An Chomhairle Ealaíon, 1985), p. 30.
130. See the *Creative Arts Television* website: http://www.catarchive.com/detailPages/641220.html (accessed 15 June 2008).
131. B. P., '*The Coach With the Six Insides*', *Irish Times*, 24 September 1963, p. 4.
132. The original works choreographed by Davis and Callaghan that year were *Ishmael, Energies* and *Triplet*. Guest choreographer Marsha Paludan from the US also choreographed *Clearing* for the company.
133. Finola Cronin from a personal communication with the author, 7 May 2009.
134. I am indebted to Emma Meehan for directing me to this material from the Joan Davis archive.
135. Carolyn Swift, *Irish Times*, 23 May 1980.
136. See Carolyn Swift, 'Dublin Dance Theatre', *Irish Times*, 21 November 1985.
137. Rhys Taylor, 'A Letter from Dublin', *New Dance*, No. 27 (Winter), 1983, p. 5.
138. Cited from the programme for *Lunar Parables*, Project Arts Centre, February, 1986.
139. Carolyn Swift, 'Contemporary Dance Theatre at the Gate', *Irish Times*, 23 March 1983.
140. B.C.G., *The Stage*, 9 September 1982.
141. Diana Theodores, 'Jerry's "Joyously Raunchy" Joyce', *Sunday Tribune*, (*c.* 25 September)1988.
142. Mary MacGoris, 'A Painless Case . . .', *Irish Independent*, 5 October 1988.
143. *Arts Council Annual Report 1988*, p. 26. Available online (accessed 8 October 2008): http://www.artscouncil.ie/Publications/An_Chomhairle_Eala%C3%ADon_1988.pdf.
144. Brinson suggested that 'the company has had something of a dual personality in terms of artistic identity, reflecting the background of the four dancers, two American and two Irish' (Peter Brinson, *The Dancer and the Dance*, p. 33). He proposed that this issue could be resolved if the company could afford to add at least two more dancers to their full-time core of four, and if they also had more funds to continue importing established international teachers and choreographers.

145. Peter Brinson, *The Dancer and the Dance*, p. 34.
146. A curated archive of the City Arts Centre was opened in 2006 and there are plans to publish material online. See the City Arts website: http://www.cityarts.ie/memory/ (accessed 27 November, 2008).
147. Kalichi cited from an interview with Diana Theodores, *Dancing on the Edge of Europe, Irish Choreographers in Conversation* (Cork: Institute for Choreography and Dance, 2003), p. 162.
148. Ibid.
149. Carolyn Swift, *'Raven's Yellow Eye'*, *Irish Times*, 18 May 1981, p. 8.
150. Ibid.
151. Ibid.
152. Carolyn Swift, *'Refugee in the Empire'*, *Irish Times*, 18 June 1982, p. 10.
153. Raymond Keane cited in Mulrooney, *Irish Moves*, p. 198.
154. Bernadette Sweeney, *Performing the Body in Irish Theatre* (Basingstoke: Palgrave Macmillan, 2008), p. 74.
155. Sarah-Jane Scaife from a personal interview with the author, 21 November 2007.
156. Liz Doran, 'Intriguing Contemporary Dance', *Cork Examiner*, 3 August 1982.
157. Davis, cited in Mulrooney, *Irish Moves*, p. 124. Davis became interested in Authentic Movement in the 1990s and has since developed a performance practice rooted in this method, which she calls 'Maya Lila'.

3 Genre Debates: the Dance and the Bathwater

1. See for example André Lepecki's, 'Skin, Body, and Presence in Contemporary European Choreography', in *The Drama Review*, 43 (4) (Winter) 1999, pp. 129–40 and Gerald Siegmund's 'Von Monströsen und anderen Obszönitäten: Die Sichtbarkeit des Körpers im zeitgenössischen Tanz' in Erika Fischer-Lichte (ed.), *Transformationen: Theater der Neunziger Jahre* (Berlin: Theater der Zeit, 1999), pp.121–32. Lepecki also discusses Raymond Whitehead's complaint about *Jérôme Bel* in his book *Exhausting Dance: Performance and the Politics of Movement* (New York: Routledge, 2006).
2. Raymond Whitehead, 'Letter to the Editor', *Irish Times*, 8 July 2004.
3. Peter Crawley, 'Dublin Theatre Festival Reviews', *Irish Times*, 3 October 2007.
4. Ibid.
5. Michael Seaver, 'Dublin Theatre Festival Reviews: *James Son of James*', (accessed online 4 November 2007): http://www.irishtheatremagazine.ie/home/dublintheatrefestivalLinks.html
6. Helen Meany, 'Theatre Reviews: *James Son of James*', in *The Guardian*, (accessed online 5 October 2007): http://arts.guardian.co.uk/theatre/drama/reviews/story/0,,2184130,00.html
7. Dunne's role in Keegan-Dolan's *The Bull* will be further discussed in Chapter Four. See Peter Crawley, 'Reinventing the Reel', *Irish Times*, 31 January, 2009.

8. Ibid.
9. Diana Theodores, *Dancing on the Edge of Europe: Irish Choreographers in Conversation* (Cork: Institute for Choreography and Dance, 2003), p. 28.
10. Seona MacRéamoinn, 'A New Crossroads', *Irish Theatre Magazine*, p. 32–3.
11. Sally Banes, *Terpsichore in Sneakers* (Boston: Houghton Mifflin, 1980). Banes' categorisation of the work of the Judson Dance Theatre as being postmodern while simultaneously embodying Clement Greenberg's reductive, formalist description of 'modernist' art, has been challenged by recent dance scholarship. Both Burt (*Judson Dance Theatre: Performative Traces*, London: Routledge, 2008) and Manning in *Ecstasy and the Demon: the Dances of Mary Wigman* (Minneapolis: University of Minnesota Press, 2006) argue that Banes' theory reduces discussions of dance to its formal aspects at the expense of sociological and ideological factors, and also that it does not account for the developments outside of the US (particularly in Germany) or heterogeneous developments within the US.
12. Ramsay Burt, *Judson Dance Theatre*, p. 9.
13. Seona MacRéamoinn, 'A New Crossroads', *Irish Theatre Magazine*, p. 33.
14. MacRéamoinn, 'Introduction', in *A Guide to Independent Choreographers and Dance Companies* (Dublin: Dance Ireland, 2007), p. 9.
15. See Keegan-Dolan's interview with Allen Robertson, *Time Out*, 19 July 2006.
16. Burt, *Judson Dance Theatre*, p. 1.
17. Helena Wulff, *Dancing at the Crossroads*: *Memory and Mobility in Ireland* (Oxford: Berghahn Books, 2007), p.1.
18. Ibid., p. 74.
19. See Franko, *Dancing Modernism/Performing Politics* (Indianapolis: Indiana University Press, 1995), p.x.
20. See Lynn Garafola, *Diaghilev's Ballets Russes* (Oxford University Press, 1989).
21. Dee Reynolds, 'The Dancer as Woman: Loïe Fuller and Stéphane Mallarmé', in Richard Hobbs (ed.), *Impressions of French Modernity: Art and Literature in France 1850–1900* (Manchester University Press, 1998), p.161.
22. Susan Manning cites Marcia Siegel's book, *The Shapes of Change: Image of American Dance* (1979), as an early example of the questioning of the 'Americanness' of American modern dance' (Manning, *Ecstasy and the Demon*, p. 255). See also Ramsay Burt, *Alien Bodies: Representations of Modernity, 'Race' and Nation in Early Modern Dance* (London: Routledge, 1998) and Mark Franko, *Dancing Modernism/Performing Politics* (2005).
23. Manning, *Ecstasy and the Demon*, p.74.
24. Benson and Manning, 'Interrupted Continuities: Modern Dance in Germany', in Dils and Cooper Albright (eds), *Moving History/Dancing Cultures: a Dance History Reader* (Middletown, Connecticut: Wesleyan University Press, 2001), p. 219.
25. See Stöckemann and Müller, '...jeder Mensch ist ein Tänzer': Ausdruckstanz in Deutschland zwischen 1900 und 1945* (Giessen: Anabas, 1993), p. 12 and Manning, *Ecstasy and the Demon*, p. 74.
26. Stöckemann and Müller, *Jeder Mensch ist ein Tänzer*, p. 13.

27. Laban also famously created a form of group choreography known as 'movement choirs'. His movement choirs were appropriated by the Third Reich for the 1936 Olympic Games in Munich to stage the vast group scenes that paid tribute to sport and youth, but that were also staged in praise of Hitler, who was watching from the stands. Mary Wigman was also involved in the creation of the spectacle, for which she danced a solo (see Benson and Manning, 'Interrupted Continuities: Modern Dance in Germany', in *Moving Histories: Dancing Cultures*, p. 223–5).

28. Patricia Stöckemann, *Etwas ganz Neues muss nun Entstehen: Kurt Jooss und das Tanztheater* (Munich: Kieser, 2001), pp. 11–12. All translations from German to English throughout are the author's own.

29. See Stöckemann, *Etwas ganz Neues muss nun Enstehen*, p. 239. The Ballets Jooss Dance Theatre also toured to Dublin in 1946 and 1953.

30. A prospectus of the Irish Ballet Production Society in the archives of the National Library in Kildare Street advertises a lecture given by Kurt Jooss on 28 March 1939.

31. See Jean-George Noverre's 'Letter 1' from *Letters on Dancing and Ballets*, in Cohen and Copeland (eds), *What is Dance?: Readings in Theory and Criticism* (Oxford University Press, 1983), pp. 10–15. Stöckemann writes of Jooss' genre difficulties and his admiration of Noverre in *Etwas ganz Neues muss nun Enstehen*, pp. 266–7.

32. George Bernard Shaw, from *Music in London 1890–94*, reprinted in Cohen and Copeland (eds), *What is Dance?*, p. 216.

33. Quoted from the CoisCéim website: http://www.coisceim.com/threads photos.html (accessed 12 January 2008).

34. Keegan-Dolan from an interview published on the English National Opera website: http://cde.cerosmedia.com/English-National-Opera-Digital-Opera-Guide/1N49d219a958948898.cde/page/23 (accessed 5 December 2010).

35. Anthony Tudor's choreographic style has been described as 'psychological', and he used expressive gesture to convey emotion. His style could be viewed, then, as being related to *Ausdruckstanz*, and so, although Bausch was in the birthplace of US postmodern dance, she in fact stayed within an expressive tradition. There is some debate amongst dance scholars as to the degree of influence that the very early developments of the Judson Dance Theatre (1962–4), which were happening concurrently to Bausch's time in New York, had on her practice (see Royd Climenhaga, *Pina Bausch* (Oxford: Routledge, 2009), p. 9). Ramsay Burt suggests that the developments of Bausch's *Tanztheater* and US postmodern dance have had more in common than has previously been thought. He writes that Bausch and Judson choreographer Trisha Brown, who is aligned with 'pure, abstract dance', 'are almost set up as paradigmatic opposites where innovative dance practice is concerned', and that for many US critics, 'Bausch is a bogey figure who seems to attack the very of idea of dance, which in their view [Trisha] Brown exemplifies' (*Judson Dance Theatre*, p. 1.)

36. Bausch was not the only practitioner of *Tanztheater* to push beyond Jooss' methods. Other pioneers of *Tanztheater* include Reinhild Hoffmann, Johannes Kresnik, Susanne Linke and Gerhard Bohner.

37. David Price, cited in Gabrielle Cody, 'Woman, Man, Dog, Tree: Two Decades of Intimate and Monumental Bodies in Pina Bausch's Tanztheater', *The Drama Review*, 42 (2) (Summer) 1998, p. 119.
38. Sally Banes writes that Judson Dance Theatre choreographer Yvonne Rainer was experimenting with movement and voice from the early 1960s: '[her] use of voice – and the options for the voice – [...] are strikingly original in modern dance. Rainer's use of speech, related to the Dada use of formal and art statements and pure sound, would continue as a salient feature of her work throughout her career' (*Democracy's Body: Judson Dance Theatre, 1962–1964* (London: Duke University Press, 2002), p. 13).
39. Kay Kirchman cited in Cody, 'Woman, Man, Dog, Tree', p. 124–5.
40. Keegan-Dolan, from 'The Body' essay on the Fabulous Beast website: http://fabulousbeast.net/about/the-body/ (accessed 12 October 2007).
41. Bausch cited in Benson and Manning, 'Interrupted Continuities', in Dils and Cooper Albright (eds), *Moving History/Dancing Cultures*, p. 225.
42. David Bolger in Mulrooney, *Irish Moves: an Illustrated History of Dance and Physical Theatre in Ireland* (Dublin: The Liffey Press, 2006), p. 150.
43. Royd Climenhaga, *Pina Bausch*, pp. 11–12.
44. Gabrielle Cody, 'Woman, Man, Dog, Tree', p. 119.
45. Bolger has choreographed spectacles such as the opening ceremony for the Special Olympics (2003), and Keegan-Dolan has choreographed large-scale opera productions such as Stravinsky's *The Rake's Progress* (2007) in collaboration with Canadian theatre director Robert Lepage.
46. Anette Guse, 'Talk to Her! Look at her! Pina Bausch in Pedro Almodóvar's Hable con ella', *Seminar: a Journal of Germanic Studies*, 43 (4), (November) 2007, p. 428.
47. See Keegan-Dolan in Mulrooney, *Irish Moves*, p. 161.
48. Valeska Gert cited in Burt, *Alien Bodies*, p. 34.
49. Servos writes: 'So lassen sich einige Kernbegriffe des didaktischen Theaters, wenngleich ohne den lehrstückhaften Anspruch, im Wuppertaler Tanztheater wiederfinden: der Gestus des Zeigens, das bewusste Ausstellen von Vorgängen, die Technik der Verfremdung sowie eine besondere Verwendung der Komik [...]' ([Many of the core terms of the didactic theatre, albeit without the 'Lehrstueck' pretensions, can be found in the Wuppertal *Tanztheater*; the Gestus, the knowing display of process, the technique of alienation as well as a particular use of the comic]), Norbert Servos, *Pina Bausch: Tanztheater* (München: K. Kieser, 2003), p. 25.
50. See Benson and Manning, 'Interrupted Continuities', in Dils and Cooper Albright (eds), *Moving History/Dancing Cultures*, p. 221.
51. Ibid.
52. See Cody, 'Woman, Man, Dog, Tree', p.119.
53. Pina Bausch cited in Climenhaga, *Pina Bausch*, p. 53.
54. Norbert Servos, *Pina Bausch: Tanztheater*, p. 23.
55. Keegan-Dolan, quoted from an interview with Allen Robertson, *Time Out*, 19 July 2006.
56. *Ballads* is discussed in more detail in Chapter Four of this book.

57. Bolger quoted from an interview with Diana Theodores, *Dancing on the Edge of Europe*, p. 48.
58. See Benson and Manning, 'Interrupted Continuities', in Dils and Cooper Albright (eds), *Moving History/Dancing Cultures*, p. 225.
59. Susanne Schlicher, *TanzTheater: Traditionen und Freiheiten: Pina Bausch, Gerhard Bohner, Reinhild Hoffmann, Hans Kresnik, Susanne Linke* (Reinbek bei Hamburg: Rowohlt, 1987), p. 84.
60. Claudia Jeschke and Gabi Vettermann in Grau and Jordan, *Europe Dancing: Perspectives on Theatre Dance and Cultural Identity* (London: Routledge, 2000), p. 66.
61. Johannes Birringer, 'Pina Bausch: Dancing Across Borders', *The Drama Review: TDR*, 30 (2), (Summer, 1986), p. 95.
62. The piece featured video recordings of terminally ill people who took part in a workshop with Jones, who has himself been diagnosed as HIV positive. Croce's article on 'victim art', 'Discussing the Undiscussable', appeared in *The New Yorker*, in December 1994. See: http://archives.newyorker.com/?i=1994-12-26#folio=054 (accessed 25 November 2007). Interestingly, *Sweat* (1994), Paul Johnson's solo piece about AIDS for his MaNDaNCE company, premiered at the Old Museum Arts Centre in Belfast in the same year.
63. Cited from the description of Lloyd Newson's practice on the DV8 website: http://www.dv8.co.uk/about.dv8/lloyd.newson.html (accessed 12 February, 2008). Former DV8 member Liam Steele, who now directs his own company, Stan Can't Dance, was the co-choreographer of CoisCéim's production *Knots* (2005).
64. See for example Katja Schneider's essay 'DV8' accompanying the *DV8 Physical Theatre DVD*.
65. DV8's *To Be Straight With You* toured to Dublin as part of the Dublin Theatre Festival in 2009.
66. Judith Mackrell, 'Post-Modern Dance in Britain: an Historical Essay', in *Dance Research: the Journal of the Society for Dance Research*, 9 (1) (Spring, 1991), p. 54. Former DV8 associate Liam Steele's collaboration with CoisCéim on *Knots* (2005) creates a link between the two companies.
67. See Rachel Howard, 'Hard to watch, but well worth it: Forsythe's "Guernica" of Iraq war unapologetically evokes reality of carnage', *The San Francisco Chronicle*, 24 February 2007.
68. William Forsythe cited in Diane Solway, 'Is it Dance? Maybe. Is it Political? Sure', *The New York Times*, 18 February 2007.
69. Keegan-Dolan cited in Brendan McCarthy, 'Celtic Tiger', *Dance Now*, 16 (4), (Winter) 2007/2008, p. 52.
70. Bolger cited from an interview with Diana Theodores, *Dancing on the Edge of Europe*, p. 54.
71. André Lepecki, 'Concept and Presence: The Contemporary European Dance Scene', in Carter, *Rethinking Dance History: a Reader* (London: Routledge, 2004), p. 170.
72. Ibid, p. 172–3.

73. The manifesto is available online: http://www.freietheater.at/?page=kulturpolitik&detail=61304&jahr=2002 (accessed 22 February 2008).
74. Ibid.
75. *Céilí* dancing can be performed competitively, but is also practiced outside of the competitive dance structure.
76. The intertwining of step dancing and competition stretches back to the earliest records of the form. See Brennan, *The Story of Irish Dance* (Dingle: Brandon, 1999) and Hall, *Competitive Irish Dancing: Art, Sport, Duty* (Madison: Macater Press, 2008).
77. See the Commission's website for a history of the organisation: www.clrg.ie/en/history (accessed 1 February 2009).
78. Frank Hall, *Competitive Irish Dancing*, p. 45.
79. Ibid, p.104–5.
80. Ibid, p. 105. A knock-on effect of this need for corporeal control can be found in the constraints placed on the musical accompaniment for competition, which must adhere to so-called 'strict tempo'. Traditional musician Willie Clancy observes that, '[m]usicians will say that the music for these dances is non-creative and restricted to a small set of tunes which are [in turn] restricted to the bare essentials. There is no spontaneity and no opportunity for a musician to develop' (Clancy cited in Brennan, *The Story of Irish Dance*, p. 153).
81. At times Butler hums along to the music and she also adds the well-known rhythm from Vivaldi's *Spring* to the blackboard: 'Da dum, dum, dum, dada DUM___!'
82. During a post show talk at Dublin's Peacock Theatre in May 2010 (following a performance of her latest work, *Day*, choreographed with Tere O'Connor), Butler spoke of being in so much pain following her attempts to introduce more plié into her practice, that she needed the help of a physiotherapist to continue working.
83. Butler, cited in the 2008 Dublin Dance Festival programme notes for *Does She Take Sugar?*
84. See the programme for the 2008 Dublin Dance Festival production of *Out of Time* for further details of this footage.
85. *Blue Peter* is a popular and long established British children's television show, which first aired on BBC 1 in 1958.
86. Dunne cited in an interview with Peter Crawley, 'Re-inventing the Reel', *The Irish Times*, 31 January 2009.
87. Dunne, from *Out of Time* (2008).
88. Butler, cited in the 2008 Dublin Dance Festival programme notes for *Does She Take Sugar?*
89. Dunne cited in Michael Seaver, 'Stepping into Footprints', in Sherry Shapiro (ed.), *Dance in a World of Change: Reflections on Globalization and Cultural Difference* (Champaign, Illinois: Human Kinetics, 2008), p. 11.
90. Butler, cited in the 2008 Dublin Dance Festival programme notes for *Does She Take Sugar?*

4   Choreographing Narratives: Buried Bodies and Constitutive Stories in The Bull and Ballads

 1. Unless otherwise indicated, for the purpose of consistency, I have used the revised version from 2000 for my discussion of *Ballads* throughout this chapter.
 2. The 'Great' Famine is so called in order to distinguish it from other famines that occurred in Ireland. Although the Great Famine was of the longest duration, starting in 1845 and lasting until 1850–1, earlier famines had a similarly devastating effect on the cottager population. For example the famine of 1740–1 caused by crop failures due to the 'Great Frost', although of much shorter duration, was perhaps equally devastating in terms of the mortality rate. Rough estimates suggest that of a population of just over 2 million in 1740, between 300,000 and 500,000 may have died.
 3. See Rogers M. Smith, 'Citizenship and the Politics of People-building', *Citizenship Studies*, 5 (1), 2001, pp. 73–96.
 4. Arash Abizadeh, 'Historical Truth, National Myths and Liberal Democracy: On the Coherence of Liberal Nationalism', *The Journal of Political Philosophy*, 12 (3), 2004, p. 292.
 5. Chris Morash, 'Literature, Memory, Atrocity', in *Fearful Realities: New Perspectives On the Famine* (Dublin: Irish Academic Press, 1996), p. 114.
 6. Paul Ricoeur, 'Narrative Time', in *Critical Inquiry*, 7 (1), 1980, p. 179.
 7. Ernest Renan cited in Benedict Anderson, *Imagined Communities* (London: Verso, 2006), p. 6. Translation by the author.
 8. Judith Butler, *Precarious Life: the Powers of Mourning and Violence* (London: Verso, 2004), p. 20.
 9. *Ballads* toured to the 2000 Jacob's Pillow Dance Festival in Massachusetts and the 2001 Ten Days on the Island Festival, in Tasmania.
10. The original production featured lighting design by Paul Keogan, music and sound by Bell Helicopter (composers Conor Kelly and Sam Park), costume design by Helen McCusker, dancers Ella Clarke, James Hosty, Simone Litchfield, Kevin Murphy and Liz Roche, and musicians Diane O'Keefe (dancer/cellist) and Martin Nolan (uilleann piper).
11. See Bolger in his interview with Diana Theodores (ed.), *Dancing on the Edge of Europe: Irish Choreographers in Conversation* (Cork: Institute for Choreography and Dance, 2003), p. 48.
12. Cited from the programme synopsis on the CoisCéim website (accessed 16 July 2009): http://www.coisceim.com/reelluck.html.
13. Cited from the promotional flyer for the performance of *Ballads* at the Jacob's Pillow Festival, 2000.
14. Charlie O'Neill, 'Famine, Dance and Desecration', from the programme produced for the revival of *Ballads* in 2000, cited in Helena Wulff, *Dancing at the Crossroads: Memory and Mobility in Ireland* (Oxford: Berghahn Books, 2007), p. 137.
15. Bolger cited in an interview conducted in Hobart, Tasmania, for the ABC television network during CoisCéim's tour of *Ballads* in March 2001 (CoisCéim archive).

16. Discussing the problems associated with describing the Holocaust in language and literature, George Steiner argues, '[t]he world of Auschwitz lies outside speech as it lies outside reason. To speak of the unspeakable is to risk the survivance of language as creator and bearer of humane, rational truth' (cited in Kelleher, *The Feminization of the Famine: Expressions of the Inexpressible?* (Cork: Cork University Press, 1997), p. 3).

17. Terry Eagleton, *Heathcliff and the Great Hunger: Studies in Irish Culture* (London: Verso, 1995), p. 13.

18. Colm Tóibín and Diarmaid Ferriter, *The Irish Famine: a Documentary*, (London: Profile Books, 2001), p. 5.

19. There are, however, several fictional works that either deal directly with the Famine years or address it in some way. Examples can be found in Maud Gonne's dramatic writing, Rosa Mulholland's fiction and poetry, Liam O'Flaherty's *Famine* (1937) and stories by Seosamh MacGrianna and Máirtín Ó Cadhain. See Margaret Kelleher, *The Feminization of Famine*, p. 5.

20. Chris Morash and Richard Hayes, *Fearful Realities*, p. 9.

21. Cited in Ó Gráda, *Black '47 and Beyond: the Great Irish Famine in History, Economy and Memory* (Princeton, New Jersey: Princeton University Press, 2000), p. 211.

22. Ó Gráda, *Black '47 and Beyond*, p. 212.

23. Bolger quoted in *Dancing on the Edge of Europe*, p. 48.

24. Quoted from the promotional flyer for the performance of *Ballads* at the Jacob's Pillow Festival.

25. Ibid.

26. Bolger cited from the ABC Hobart interview, March 2001.

27. Bolger cited in Helena Wulff, *Dancing at the Crossroads*, p. 35.

28. Liz Roche, cited in Wulff, *Dancing at the Crossroads*, p. 37.

29. Carolyn Swift, '*Ballads*', *The Irish Times*, 25 November 1997.

30. Fintan O'Toole, '*The Bull*', review in *The Irish Times*, 8 October 2005.

31. Quotes excerpted from the introductory essay by Deirdre Mulrooney in the programme for *The Bull* issued for the run at the Barbican Theatre in London, 2007.

32. Keegan-Dolan quoted from an interview with Donald Hutera, 'For Peat's Sake', *The Times*, 23 February 2007. *The Bull* received a much more favourable reception from critics when it opened in February 2007 at the Barbican in London. It is perhaps inevitable that non-Irish audiences would have received the harsh critique of Irish society in the work in a different manner and that they would also have a lesser, or non-existent knowledge of, and relationship to, the national myth that was being remoulded. However, it is perhaps too simple to suggest that this is the only reason for the difference in reception. It was perhaps also the mode in which the work was presented that contributed to this difference. As discussed in Chapter Three, Fabulous Beast's works tend to be critiqued in Ireland by theatre critics, and in England by dance critics who have had a lot more exposure to the dance theatre genre.

33. The production also toured to the 2008 Berliner Festspiele.

34. The production also featured original music by Philip Feeney, set and costume design by Merle Hensel, sound design by Gareth Fry and lighting design by Adam Silverman. *The Bull* was revised for its run at the Barbican in 2007 and Thomas Conway worked as dramaturge on the revised version.

35. Keegan-Dolan quoted from an interview with Susan Conley in the programme for the 2005 Dublin Theatre Festival production of *The Bull* (unpaginated).

36. Ibid. The 'Táin Trail' is a walking route that visits sites mentioned in the ancient epic.

37. See Fintan O'Toole, 'Irish Culture in a Globalised World', in Munira H. Mutran and Laura P. L. Izarra (eds), *Kaleidoscopic Views of Ireland* (São Paulo: University of São Paulo, 2003), p. 90.

38. Yeats cited in Maria-Elena Doyle, 'A Spindle for the Battle: Feminism, Myth, and the Woman-Nation in Irish Revival Drama', *Theatre Journal*, 51 (1), (March) 1999, p. 36.

39. Doyle, 'A Spindle for the Battle: Feminism, Myth, and the Woman-Nation in Irish Revival Drama', p. 36.

40. Thomas Kinsella, *The Táin* (Dublin: Dolmen Press, 1970), p. 261.

41. Louis Le Brocquy, cited in Ní Bhriain, 'Le Livre d'Artiste: Louis le Brocquy and *The Táin* (1969)', *New Hibernia Review*, 5 (1), (*Earrach*/Spring) 2001, p. 71.

42. Keegan-Dolan quoted from an interview with Susan Conley in the programme for the 2005 Dublin Theatre Festival production of *The Bull* (unpaginated).

43. Melissa Sihra in Eamonn Jordan (ed.), *Theatre Stuff: Critical Essays on Contemporary Irish Theatre* (Dublin: Carysfort Press, 2000), p. 260.

44. See Keegan-Dolan's interview in Deirdre Mulrooney, *Irish Moves: an Illustrated History of Dance and Physical Theatre in Ireland* (Dublin: The Liffey Press, 2006), p. 161.

45. Garry Hynes, from an interview with Cathy Leeney, published in Chambers et al., *Theatre Talk: Voices of Irish Theatre Practitioners* (Dublin: Carysfort Press, 2001), p. 206.

46. Following an agricultural depression in the early 1870s, Charles Stewart Parnell founded the National Land League, which campaigned for the rights of tenants in Ireland.

47. Chris Morash, 'Literature, Memory, Atrocity', in *Fearful Realities: New Perspectives On the Famine* (Dublin: Irish Academic Press, 1996), pp.113–14.

48. De Certeau, *The Practice of Everyday Life* (London: University of California Press, 1988), p. xiv.

49. A *bodhrán* is a traditional Irish goat-skin drum that is circular in shape and struck with a piece of wood (traditionally with a double-ended knuckle bone) called a *cipín*.

50. Michael Flatley was the original male lead of *Riverdance* and the producer and choreographer of subsequent Irish dance spectaculars (*Celtic Tiger* (2005), *Feet of Flames* (1998) and *Lord of the Dance* (1995)).

51. Kirby, Gibbons and Cronin, *Reinventing Ireland: Culture, Society and the Global Economy* (London: Pluto, 2002), p. 5.
52. Kirby et al., *Reinventing Ireland*, p. 27.
53. John Frow, *'Tourism and the Semiotics of Nostalgia'*, in Frow (ed.), *Time and Commodity Culture: Essays in Cultural Theory and Postmodernity* (Oxford: Clarendon Press, 1997), p. 78.
54. Founded in 1986, Macnas specialise in spectacular, large-scale, outdoor performances, parades and street theatre. Their version of the Táin was an indoor show that was mostly non-verbal, in the manner of their outdoor work.
55. Christopher Murray and Martin Drury, 'The Theatre System in Ireland', in Wilmer and Van Maanen (eds), *Theatre Worlds in Motion*, (Amsterdam: Rodopi, 1998), p. 370.
56. Michael Keegan-Dolan, quoted from an interview with Donald Hutera, 'For Peat's Sake', *The Times*, 10 February 2007.
57. André Lepecki (Lepecki's own emphasis), *Exhausting Dance: Performance and the Politics of Movement* (New York: Routledge, 2006), p. 15.
58. Ibid.
59. Bolger, ABC television network interview (Tasmania), March 2001.
60. Mary Robinson, cited from her keynote address to the International Conference On Hunger at New York University, Glucksman Ireland House, 19–20 May 1995. This address is available online: http://gos.sbc.edu/r/robinson.html (accessed 14 July 2008).
61. Cormac Ó Gráda, *Black '47 and Beyond*, p. 222.
62. Kevin Whelan cited in Cormac Ó Gráda, 'Famine, Trauma and Memory', *Béaloideas*, 69, (2001), p. 137.
63. Peggy Phelan, 'Thirteen ways of looking at *Choreographing Writing'*, in Susan Foster (ed.), *Choreographing History* (Indianapolis: Indiana University Press, 1995), p. 209.
64. Cited from the promotional flyer for the performance of *Ballads* at the Jacob's Pillow Festival, 2000.

5   Choreographing the Unanticipated: Death, Hope and Verticality in *Giselle* and *The Rite of Spring*

1. My use of the term reworking follows that of Vida Midgelow who differentiates between terms such as 'revival', 'reconstruction', 'resetting' and 'reworkings', defining the latter as, 'dances that substantially alter the ballet in order to create a new work that has a significantly different resonance' (*Reworking the Ballet: Counter-Narratives and Alternative Bodies*, (London: Routledge, 2007), p. 10).
2. Two years after its premiere and sell-out run at the Samuel Beckett theatre as part of the 2003 Dublin Theatre Festival, *Giselle* opened at the Barbican in London, and Fabulous Beast were subsequently invited to become Artistic Associates of the Barbican Centre. Following an earlier tour to New Haven, USA (2004) and its run in London, *Giselle* was nominated for

an Olivier Award in the category of 'best new dance production' in 2006, and then toured to international festivals in Poland (2007), New Zealand (2008), Galway (2008), Perth (2009), Sydney (2010) and Toronto (2010).

3. Interestingly there is no spoken word used in *The Rite of Spring*, yet the strong narrative of the libretto positions this work, alongside *Giselle* and the other pieces in the *Midlands Trilogy*, as falling within the genre of storytelling dance theatre.

4. Keegan-Dolan, 'Director's Note' from the programme for the Australian premiere of *Giselle* at the Perth International Theatre Festival 2009.

5. Karen Fricker, 'Giselle', *The Guardian*, 3 October 2003.

6. The 35-minute-long *Rite* formed the second part of a double bill with Bartók's *Duke Bluebeard's Castle* directed by Daniel Kramer and conducted by Edward Gardner.

7. The production included lighting design by regular Fabulous Beast collaborator Adam Silverman, and set design by Rae Smith, who also collaborated on the design of the lifelike dog and hare masks created by Robert Allsopp.

8. Keegan-Dolan cited in the programme for *The Rite of Spring* at the London Coliseum, November 2009.

9. The piece received five-star reviews from Clement Crisp (*Financial Times*) and Debra Craine (*The Times*). The work has yet to be seen in Ireland and there are plans to tour it in a double bill with a new version of Stravinsky's *Petrushka*.

10. See Lepecki, *Exhausting Dance: Performance and the Politics of Movement* (New York: Routledge, 2006), pp. 65–8.

11. Henri Lefebvre, *The Production of Space* (Oxford: Basil Blackwell, 1991), p. 287.

12. Susan Foster, *Choreography and Narrative: Ballet's Staging of Story and Desire*, (Indianapolis: Indiana University Press, 1998), p. 250.

13. Keegan-Dolan explains, '[...] so through setting this piece in the midlands there is a connection to my own ancestry, to my father, to his father, to his father's father [...]' (cited in Theodores, *Dancing on the Edge of Europe: Irish Choreographers in Conversation* (Cork: Institute for Choreography and Dance, 2003), p. 119). Interestingly, when speaking about the influence of the midlands on his *Rite*, Keegan-Dolan stresses the matrilineal rather than patrilineal descent when discussing his connection with the land.

14. Keegan-Dolan, cited in Theodores, *Dancing on the Edge of Europe*, p. 119.

15. My thanks to Melissa Sihra for suggesting a reading of the landscape in *Giselle*.

16. Melissa Sihra, 'Renegotiating Landscapes of the Female: Voices, Topographies and Corporealities of Alterity in Marina Carr's *Portia Coughlan*', in Brian Singleton and Anna McMullan (eds), *Performing Ireland* (Queensland, Brisbane: University of Queensland, Australasian Drama Studies Centre, 2003), p. 27.

17. The second act of *Giselle* is often referred to as the 'white act' due to the white costumes of the Wilis and Giselle.

18. Susan Foster, *Choreography and Narrative*, p. 250.

19. Brendan McCarthy, 'Rite of Spring', a review of Millicent Hodson and Kenneth Archer's reconstruction of Nijinsky's *Rite of Spring* for the Kirov Ballet, 2003. Accessed online, 12 December 2009: http://www.ballet.co. uk/magazines/yr_03/aug03/bmc_rev_kirov_0803.htm.
20. Lynn Garafola, *Diaghilev's Ballets Russes* (Oxford University Press, 1989), p. 68.
21. Ibid., p. 69.
22. Brendan McCarthy, 'Rite of Spring', a review of Millicent Hodson and Kenneth Archer's reconstruction of Nijinsky's *Rite of Spring* for the Kirov Ballet, 2003. Accessed online, 12/12/09 : http://www.ballet.co.uk/ magazines/yr_03/aug03/bmc_rev_kirov_0803.htm
23. Garafola, *Diaghilev's Ballets Russes*, p. 72.
24. Keegan-Dolan quoted from *The Rite of Spring* post-show discussion at the London Coliseum on 14 November 2009.
25. Ibid.
26. Keegan-Dolan cited in the programme for the ENO production of *The Rite of Spring* at the London Coliseum, November 2009.
27. Keegan-Dolan speaks of a viewing of Bausch's *Sacre du Printemps* as having had a seminal influence on his work.
28. Keegan-Dolan cited from an interview with Debra Craine, 'Michael Keegan-Dolan and *The Rite of Spring*', *The Times*, 3 November 2009.
29. Olwen Fouéré, 'Finding the Freedom to Play', *Irish Theatre Magazine*, 27 November 2009.
30. Keegan-Dolan cited in the programme for the ENO production of *The Rite of Spring* at the London Coliseum, November 2009.
31. Terence Brown, *Ireland: a Social and Cultural History 1922–2002* (London: Harper Collins, 2004), p. 29.
32. Diarmaid Ferriter, *Occasions of Sin: Sex and Society in Modern Ireland* (London: Profile Books, 2009), p. 545.
33. Ibid.
34. Melissa Sihra, in Singleton and McMullen (eds), *Performing Ireland*, p. 19.
35. Keegan-Dolan quoted from the *Rite of Spring* post-show discussion at the London Coliseum, 14 November 2009.
36. Éibhear Walshe, *Sex, Nation and Dissent in Irish Writing* (Cork: Cork University Press, 1997), p. 5.
37. Ibid.
38. R. W. Connell, *Masculinities* (Cambridge: Polity Press, 2005), p. 37.
39. Singleton, *Masculinities and the Contemporary Irish Theatre* (Basingstoke: Palgrave Macmillan, 2011), p. 10.
40. As mentioned in the introductory chapter of this book, the 2003 Arts Act changed the 1951 and 1973 definition of 'the arts' to include dance.
41. This referendum succeeded in creating the eighth amendment to the Irish constitution: 'The State acknowledges the right to life of the unborn and, with due regard to the equal right to life of the mother, guarantees in its laws to respect, and, as far as practicable, by its laws to defend and vindicate that right.' (Accessed online 14 November 2009): www.taoiseach.gov.ie/attached_files/html%20files/Constitution%

20of%20Ireland%20(Eng).htm). Building on Giorgio Agamben's analysis of sovereign power, 'bare life' and the 'homo sacer' in his reading of post-national biopolitics in Ireland, John A. Harrington proposes that as a result of the pro-life amendment, '[t]he constitution now presented "the protection of foetal life as an exclusive national interest" which demanded that obstetric medicine be harnessed to the police functions of the state.' (Harrington, 'Citizenship and the Biopolitics of Post-nationalist Ireland', *Journal of Law and Society*, 32 (3), 2005, p. 434). This resulted in '[a]utarkic nationalist developmentalism relegat[ing] Irish women to a state of bare life. Subordinated to the well-being of the nation, they found their very lives put on an equal footing with those of the unborn. The state would keep them within the jurisdiction and force them to give birth'. (Ibid., p. 449.)

42. Angela Bourke, introduction to Emily O'Reilly's, 'Ann Lovett: a Teenage Pregnancy Could Not Have Gone Unnoticed', in *Field Day Anthology of Irish Writing: Volume 5*, p. 1435.

43. See O'Reilly in *Field Day Anthology of Irish Writing: Volume 5*, pp. 1435–9. This article originally appeared on 12 February 1984 in the *Sunday Tribune*.

44. Ibid., p.1438.

45. *Report into the Catholic Archdiocese of Dublin*, p. 4. This report emanated from a commission of investigation chaired by Ms Justice Yvonne Murphy, which was set up by the Irish government in 2006 to examine the handling of clerical child sex abuse allegations in Dublin's Catholic archdiocese. The publication of the Murphy Report followed the disturbing findings of the Ferns Report (a government inquiry into allegations of clerical sexual abuse in the Catholic Diocese of Ferns, County Wexford, (2005)) and the Ryan Report (the *Report of the Commission to Inquire into Child Abuse*, published May 2009). The Murphy Report is available online: http://www.justice.ie/en/JELR/Pages/PB09000504 (accessed 21 June 2009).

46. Ferriter, *Occasions of Sin*, p.5 46.

47. Colm Tóibín cited in Ferriter, *Occasions of Sin*, p. 525.

48. Ali Bracken, 'Vale of Tears, Veil of Silence', *Sunday Tribune*, 1 February 2009.

49. Fintan O'Toole, 'Still Failing to Protect Our Children', *Irish Times*, 23 July 2002.

50. See, for example, Keegan-Dolan's interview with Brendan McCarthy, 'Celtic Tiger', *Dance Now*, 16 (4), (Winter) 2007/2008, p. 47.

51. See Keegan-Dolan's 'Director Notes' from the Sydney Festival 2010 programme, (accessed online 6 February 2010): http://www.sydneyfestival.org.au/2010/Theatre/Giselle/Notes/

52. Avery Gordon, *Ghostly Matters: Haunting and the Sociological Imagination* (London: University of Minnesota Press, 2008), p. 16.

53. Ibid., p. 24.

54. Randy Martin, 'Overreading *The Promised Land*: Towards a Narrative of Context in Dance', in Susan Foster (ed.), *Corporealities: Dancing Knowledge, Culture and Power* (London: Routledge, 1996), p. 178.

55. Keegan-Dolan cited from an interview with Kate Mattingly, 'Fabulous Beast Dance Theatre retells classic *Giselle'*, *CTCentral*, 20 June 2004 (accessed online 10 January 2008): http://entertainment.ctcentral.com/html/modules.php?op=modload&name=News&file=article&sid=1086&mode=thread&order=0&thold=0.
56. Gordon, *Ghostly Matters*, p. 207.
57. Jacques Rancière, *The Emancipated Spectator* (London: Verso, 2009), p. 103.
58. Ibid., p. 13.
59. Ibid., p. 103.
60. Ibid., p. 105.
61. Peter Hallward, 'Staging Equality: Ranciere's Theatrocracy and the Limits of Anarchic Equality', in Gabriel Rockhill and Philip Watts, *Jacques Rancière: History, Politics, Aesthetics* (London: Duke University Press, 2009), p. 157.
62. Victoria Hunter, 'Experiencing Space', in Jo Butterworth and Liesbeth Wildschut (eds), *Contemporary Choreography* (Oxford: Routledge, 2009) p. 414.

6 Choreographing Dissensus: Dodgems and Roundabouts

1. Quoted from the promotional material for *Dodgems* on the Dublin Theatre Festival website (accessed 17 November 2008): http://www.dublintheatrefestival.com/programme/display_archive.asp?Eventid=251&m=.
2. For Rancière, politics is a process that can only emerge when the given order of a community is disrupted and challenged by the appearance of bodies that are normally excluded from visibility. He explains, '[p]olitics is a matter of subjects or, rather, modes of subjectification. By subjectification I mean the production through a series of actions of a body and a capacity for enunciation not previously identifiable within a given field of experience, whose identification is thus part of the reconfiguration of the field of experience' (Rancière, *Dis-agreement: Politics and Philosophy* (London: University of Minnesota Press, 1999), p. 35). It is important to note that Rancière's use of the word 'body', as pointed out by Gabriel Rockhill, covers 'the largest possible sense of the term in order to refer alternately – and sometimes simultaneously – to physical forms [...], communities [...], political configurations [...], units of discourse [...], and even geographic formations' (Rancière, translated by Rockhill, *The Politics of Aesthetics* (London: Continuum, 2004), p. 104).
3. Rancière, 'Who is the Subject of the Rights of Man?', *The South Atlantic Quarterly*, 103 (2/3), (Spring/Summer) 2004, p. 304.
4. The production was in development over a period of four years with the first two focussing on field research, workshopping ideas, and scriptwriting by O'Neill in collaboration with Bolger, and the second two being required for the assembly of the large collaborative team.

5. O'Neill's credits as a playwright include *Hupnouse* (1999) and *Hurl* (2003) for Barabbas The Company.
6. O'Neill cited in the 2008 Dublin Theatre Festival programme for *Dodgems* (unpaginated).
7. Quoted from CoisCéim Dance Theatre's website (accessed 12 November 2008): http://www.coisceim.com/aboutus.html
8. See *Census 2006: Non-Irish Nationals Living in Ireland*, p. 11 (accessed online 14 November 2008): http://www.cso.ie/census/documents/NON% 20IRISH%20NATONALS%20LIVING%20IN%20IRELAND.pdf). For further statistical data relating to immigration in Ireland see Martin Ruhs and Emma Quinn, 'Ireland: From Rapid Immigration to Recession', on the Migration Information Source website (accessed 23 April 2010): http:// www.migrationinformation.org/Feature/display.cfm?ID=740
9. For an examination of the wider global implications of Ireland's abolition of *jus soli*, see Mancini and Finlay, 'Citizenship Matters: Lessons from the Irish Citizenship Referendum' (2008) and for an analysis of the biopolitical implications of the 2004 citizenship referendum see Harrington, 'Citizenship and the Biopolitics of Post-nationalist Ireland' *Journal of Law and Society*, 32 (3), 2005, pp. 424–49.
10. Mullally, 'Children and Citizenship', in Bryan Fanning (ed.), *Immigration and Social Change in the Republic of Ireland* (Manchester University Press, 2007), p. 29.
11. Ibid.
12. The Constitution of Ireland, *Bunreacht na hÉireann*, can be accessed on the website of the Taoiseach (accessed 10 September 2010): http://www. taoiseach.gov.ie/eng/Youth_Zone/About_the_Constitution,_Flag,_ Anthem_Harp/Constitution_of_Ireland_-_Bunreacht_na_hÉireann.html
13. See for example Justin King's discussion of state racism in Ireland in Fricker and Lentin (eds), *Performing Global Networks* (Newcastle: Cambridge Scholars Publishing, 2007), p. 44.
14. James Holston and Arjun Appadurai, 'Why Cities?', in Holston (ed.), *Cities and Citizenship* (London: Duke University Press, 1999), p. 3.
15. In a post-show discussion Bolger explained that the need for the many alterations to the piece during the run stemmed in part from the logistic difficulties of only being able to properly rehearse with the dodgems track after the get-in at the O'Reilly theatre.
16. The 'sensible' here refers to that which is 'capable of being apprehended by the senses' (Rockhill in Rancière, *The Politics of Aesthetics*, p. 85). According to Rancière, the ordering of what is allowed visibility in society is policed so that there is always a certain fixed distribution of parts and shares in the community. This 'police order' controls which bodies are perceived as having a legitimate role and therefore, visibility in the community: '[t]he police is a "partition [or distribution] of the Sensible" (*le partage du sensible*) whose principle is the absence of a void and of a supplement' (Rancière, 'Who is the Subject of the Rights of Man?', p. 306). The distribution of the sensible can be understood, 'on the one hand, as

that which separates and excludes; on the other, as that which allows participation' (Rancière, *Dissensus: On Politics and Aesthetics*, p. 36).

17. Rancière, 'Who is the Subject of the Rights of Man?', p. 304.
18. Scriptwriter O'Neill explained in a post-show discussion that no one Irish city was intended as the location of the piece, although Limerick and Dublin are both explicitly mentioned (O'Reilly Theatre, Dublin, 5 October 2008).
19. Bolger quoted from the post-show discussion at the O'Reilly Theatre, Dublin, 5 October 2008.
20. In their study of the economic contribution of immigrants in Ireland in 2007, Alan Barrett and Adele Bergin found that, 'immigrants in Ireland continue to have, on average, notably high levels of educational attainment, relative to the Irish-born population' (Barrett and Bergin, 'The Economic Contribution of Immigrants', in Bryan Fanning (ed.), *Immigration and Social Change in the Republic of Ireland*, p. 81).
21. Walter Benjamin, *Illuminations* (London: Pimlico, 1999), p. 171.
22. Paul Valéry cited in Walter Benjamin, *Illuminations*, p. 170.
23. See Elizabeth Grosz, *Space, Time and Perversion: Essays on the Politics of Bodies* (London: Routledge, 1995), pp. 103–10.
24. Ibid., p.108.
25. Ibid.
26. Ibid., p.109.
27. The Roma (also known as the Romani) are the largest ethnic minority in Europe, numbering an estimated 7– 9 million. It is thought that the Roma originally migrated from India in the tenth century, and by the fifteenth century there are records documenting the presence of groups of Roma in most European cities. The Roma have suffered racial discrimination since the Middle Ages. The trade in Roma slaves was commonplace in central Europe until the 1860s, and during the Second World War, an estimated 1.5 million Roma were murdered in Hitler's concentration camps through extermination or medical experimentation. See Christine Walsh and Brigette Krieg, 'Roma Identity: Contrasting Constructions', *Canadian Ethnic Studies*, 39 (1–2), 2007, pp. 169–86.
28. In general, a person must be considered as habitually resident in Ireland for two years before they are entitled to claim social welfare payments. This rule also applies to Irish citizens.
29. See Henry McDonald, 'Threat to Deport Roma Family of 54 Camped on Motorway', *The Observer*, 22 July 2007.
30. For example, the story was followed as far away as New Zealand: 'Roma Family Fly Home after Irish Roundabout Standoff', *New Zealand Herald*, 27 July 2007.
31. Michael McKinnie, *City Stages: Theatre and Urban Space in a Global City* (Toronto: University of Toronto Press, 2007), p. 5.
32. Valéry cited in Walter Benjamin, *Illuminations*, p. 170.
33. For more information about Irish travellers see the website of Pavee Point, a non-governmental organisation that campaigns for travellers' rights (accessed 10 November 2008): www.paveepoint.ie.

34. *An Garda Síochána* (Guardians of the peace), or the *Gardaí* (guards), are Ireland's police force.
35. Jacques Rancière, 'Ten Theses on Politics' in *Dissensus: On Politics and Aesthetics*, edited and translated by Steven Corcoran (London: Continuum, 2010), p. 38.
36. *Somewhere* is a song from the Broadway musical *West Side Story* (1957). With a plot based on Shakespeare's *Romeo and Juliet*, the musical's story of two teenagers from rival gangs falling in love despite their different social and ethnic backgrounds has a connection with the relationship between Hoppy (Irish citizen) and Marek (Polish immigrant) in *Dodgems*. As in Shakespeare's original, there is no happy end for the lovers in *West Side Story*, and in the final scene, the Juliet character (Maria) sings a few bars of *Somewhere* as her Romeo (Tony) lies dying of a bullet wound in her arms. The song's message of hope that there is a place in the world 'somewhere' for the lovers is proven tragically false, lending the scene in *Dodgems* an underlying sense of foreboding for spectators familiar with *West Side Story's* libretto. Composed by Leonard Bernstein and with lyrics by Stephen Sondheim, the song has been reinterpreted by many artists, and the version used in *Dodgems* was recorded by Tom Waits.
37. The 'dance of diversity' is a high-energy group dance that closes the piece. It includes a mixture of tap dancing, Balkan folk dancing and a *Riverdance*-esque chorus line finale. In its use of strong rhythms and synchronised ensemble formation this scene also bore a strong resemblance to the closing scene of Fabulous Beast's *The Bull*, although the sentiment of 'unity in difference' differed greatly to *The Bull's* outpouring of anger.
38. Preceding the ballroom dance scene, Hoppy and Marek introduce each other to the audience. At the end of Hoppy's speech about Marek, she tells us that the Sunday afternoon ballroom dance sessions '[are] the only time you can let yourself love yourself'.

7   Concluding Thoughts and Future Moves

1. Finola Cronin, cited from an interview with Diana Theodores, *Dancing on the Edge of Europe: Irish Choreographers in Conversation* (Cork: Institute for Choreography and Dance, 2003), p. 98.
2. Gerald Siegmund, *Abwesenheit: Eine Performative Ästhetik des Tanzes* (Bielefeld: Transcript, 2006), p. 146.
3. Randy Martin, *Critical Moves: Dance Studies in Theory and Politics* (London: Duke University Press, 1998), p. 6.
4. Peggy Phelan, 'Movements Between Performance, Theatre, and Dance', unpublished keynote address at the Society of Dance History Scholars annual conference, Stanford University, 18 June 2009.
5. Cited from the Junk Ensemble website (accessed 27 May 2012): http://www.junkensemble.com/about-us
6. Ibid.

7. Both Fitzgerald and Stapleton have experience dancing solos chore-ographed by Hay. They also cite the theatre work of Samuel Beckett as being an important influence on their aesthetic.
8. Emma Fitzgerald quoted from a post-show discussion at the Project Theatre in Dublin, 21 September 2010. In *The Work The Work* the choreographers' determined, uncompromising display of comfortably inhabiting their unadorned bodies resulted in an early scene in which they both lay on their backs to masturbate in a quietly matter-of-fact fashion, and a brief interactive moment towards the end in which a naked Stapleton leant up against audience members seated in the front rows.
9. Elizabeth Grosz, *Space, Time and Perversion: Essays on the Politics of Bodies* (London: Routledge, 1995), p. 232.
10. Foster, *Dances That Describe Themselves: the Improvised Choreography of Richard Bull* (Middletown CT: Wesleyan University Press, 2002), p. 236.

Select Bibliography

Abizadeh, Arash, 'Historical Truth, National Myths and Liberal Democracy: On the Coherence of Liberal Nationalism', *The Journal of Political Philosophy*, 12 (3), 2004, pp. 291–313.

Anderson, Benedict, *Imagined Communities*, London: Verso, 2006 (first published 1983).

Badiou, Alain (translated by Alberto Toscano), *Handbook of Inaesthetics*, Stanford: Stanford University Press, 2005.

Banes, Sally, *Terpsichore in Sneakers*, Boston: Houghton Mifflin, 1980.

Banes, Sally, *Democracy's Body: Judson Dance Theatre, 1962–1964*, London: Duke University Press, 2002 (originally published 1993).

Banes, Sally and Lepecki, André (eds), *The Senses in Performance*, New York: Routledge, 2007.

Barker, Francis, *The Tremulous Private Body: Essays on Subjection*, Ann Arbor: University of Michigan Press, 2005 (originally published 1995).

Barthes, Roland (translated by Stephen Heath), *Image, Music, Text*, London: Fontana, 1977.

Bate, A. J., 'Yeats and the Symbolist Aesthetic', *Modern Language Notes*, 985, (December) 1983, pp. 1214–33.

Baudrillard, Jean (translated by Paul Foss, Paul Patton and Philip Beitchman), *Simulations*, New York: Semiotext(e), 1983.

Benjamin, Walter (edited and introduced by Hannah Arendt and translated by Harry Zorn), *Illuminations*, London: Pimlico, 1999.

Birringer, Johannes, 'Pina Bausch: Dancing across Borders', *The Drama Review: TDR*, 30 (2), (Summer, 1986), pp. 85–97.

Bourke, Angela (ed.), *The Field Day Anthology of Irish Writing: Volumes 4 and 5, Irish Women's Writing and Traditions*, Cork: Cork University Press, 2002.

'B. P.', 'The Coach with the Six Insides', *Irish Times*, 24 September 1963, p. 4.

Bracken, Ali, 'Vale of Tears, Veil of Silence', *Sunday Tribune*, 1 February 2009.

Brady, Mary (ed.), *Choreographic Encounters (Volume 1)*, Cork: Institute for Choreography and Dance, 2003.

Brady, Mary (ed.), *Choreographic Encounters (Volume 2)*, Cork: Institute for Choreography and Dance, 2005.

Brandon, James R. (ed.), *The Cambridge Guide to Asian Theatre*, Cambridge: Cambridge University Press, 1997.

Brandstetter, Gabriele and Völckers, Hortensia (eds), *ReMembering the Body*, Ostfildern-Ruit, Germany: Hatje Cantz, 2000.

Breathnach, Breandán, *Folk Music and Dances of Ireland*, Cork: Ossian, 1996.

Brennan, Helen, *The Story of Irish Dance*, Dingle: Brandon, 1999.

Brewster, Scott, Crossman, Virginia, Becket, Fiona and Alderson, David, (eds), *Ireland in Proximity: History, Gender, Space*, London: Routledge, 1999.

Brinson, Peter, *Dancer and the Dance: Developing Theatre Dance in Ireland,* Dublin: The Arts Council/An Chomhairle Ealaíon, 1985.

Brown, Terence, *Ireland: a Social and Cultural History 1922–2002,* London: Harper Collins, 2004.

Burt, Ramsay, *The Male Dancer,* London: Routledge, 1995.

Burt, Ramsay, *Alien Bodies: Representations of Modernity, 'Race' and Nation in Early Modern Dance,* London: Routledge, 1998.

Burt, Ramsay, *Judson Dance Theatre: Performative Traces,* London: Routledge, 2008 (original publication 2006).

Butler, Judith, *Precarious Life: the Powers of Mourning and Violence,* London: Verso, 2004.

Butterworth, Jo and Wildschut, Liesbeth (eds), *Contemporary Choreography,* Oxford: Routledge, 2009.

Byrnes, Frances, 'Michael, Son of James', *The Dancing Times,* January 2008, pp. 29–31.

Caldwell, Helen, *Michio Ito: the Dancer and his Dances,* Berkeley: University of California Press, 1977.

Carman, Taylor, *Merleau-Ponty,* Oxford: Routledge, 2008.

Carman, Taylor and Hansen, Mark (eds), *The Cambridge Companion to Merleau-Ponty,* Cambridge: Cambridge University Press, 2005.

Carter, Alexandra (ed.), *Rethinking Dance History: a Reader,* London: Routledge, 2004.

Case, Sue-Ellen, Brett, Philip and Foster, Susan Leigh (eds), *Decomposition: Post-Disciplinary Performance,* Bloomington: Indiana University Press, 2000.

Casey, Natasha, '*Riverdance*: the Importance of Being Irish American' *New Hibernia Review,* 6 (4), (Geimhreadh/Winter) 2002, pp. 9–25.

Cave, Richard, *Terence Gray and the Cambridge Festival Theatre,* Cambridge: Chadwyck-Healey, 1980.

Certeau, Michel de (translated by Steven Rendall), *The Practice of Everyday Life,* London: University of California Press, 1988.

Chambers, Lilian, Farrelly, Dan, Fitzgibbon, Ger, Jordan, Eamonn, and Leeney, Cathy (eds), *Theatre Talk: Voices of Irish Theatre Practitioners,* Dublin: Carysfort Press, 2001.

Cixous, Hélène, and Clément, Catherine, *The Newly Born Woman,* Manchester University Press, 1986.

Cleary, Joe, *Outrageous Fortune: Capital and Culture in Modern Ireland,* Dublin: Field Day Publications, 2007.

Climenhaga, Royd, *Pina Bausch,* Oxford: Routledge, 2009.

Cody, Gabrielle, 'Woman, Man, Dog, Tree: Two Decades of Intimate and Monumental Bodies in Pina Bausch's Tanztheater', *The Drama Review,* 42 (2) (Summer) 1998, pp. 115–31.

Cohen, Marshall, Copeland, Roger (eds), *What is Dance?: Readings in Theory and Criticism,* Oxford University Press, 1983.

Connell, R. W., *Masculinities* (second edition), Cambridge: Polity Press, 2005.

Cooper Albright, Ann, *Choreographing Difference: the Body and Identity in Contemporary Dance,* Connecticut: Wesleyan University Press, 1997.

Coulter, Colin and Coleman, Steve (eds), *The End of Irish History? Critical Reflections on the Celtic Tiger*, Manchester University Press, 2003.

Cowell, Mary-Jean, 'Michio Ito in Hollywood: Modes and Ironies of Ethnicity', *Dance Chronicle*, 24 (3) (2001), pp. 263–305.

Cowell, Mary-Jean and Shimazaki, Satoru, 'East and West in the Work of Michio Ito', *Dance Research Journal*, 26 (2) (Autumn) 1994, pp. 11–23.

Craig, Edward Gordon, 'The Actor and the Über-marionette', in Huxley, Michael and Witts, Noel (eds), *The Twentieth Century Performance Reader*, 2nd edn, London: Routledge, 2002, pp. 159–65.

Craine, Debra, 'Michael Keegan-Dolan and *The Rite of Spring*', *The Times*, 3 November 2009.

Crawley, Peter, 'Dublin Theatre Festival Reviews', *Irish Times*, 3 October 2007.

Crawley, Peter, 'Reinventing the Reel', *Irish Times*, 31 January 2009.

Csordas, Thomas J. (ed.), *Embodiment and Experience: the Existential Ground of Culture and Self*, Cambridge University Press, 1994.

Daly, Ann, *Done into Dance: Isadora Duncan in America*, Indiana: Indiana University Press, 1995.

Desmond, Jane C., *Meaning in Motion: New Cultural Studies in Dance*, London: Duke University Press, 1997.

Dils, Ann and Cooper Albright, Ann (eds), *Moving History/Dancing Cultures: a Dance History Reader*, Middletown Connecticut: Wesleyan University Press, 2001.

Doyle, Maria-Elena, 'A Spindle for the Battle: Feminism, Myth, and the Woman-Nation in Irish Revival Drama', *Theatre Journal*, 51 (1), (March 1999), pp. 33–46.

Eagleton, Terry, *Heathcliff and the Great Hunger: Studies in Irish Culture*, London: Verso, 1995.

Ellis, Sylvia C., *The Plays of W. B. Yeats: Yeats and the Dancer*, London: Macmillan, 1995.

Fanning, Bryan, *Racism and Social Change in the Republic of Ireland*, Manchester University Press, 2002.

Fanning, Bryan (ed.), *Immigration and Social Change in the Republic of Ireland*, Manchester University Press, 2007.

Ferriter, Diarmaid, *The Transformation of Ireland 1900–2000*, London: Profile Books, 2005.

Ferriter, Diarmaid, *Occasions of Sin: Sex and Society in Modern Ireland*, London: Profile Books, 2009.

Fischer-Lichte, Erika (ed.), *Transformationen: Theater der Neunziger Jahre*, Berlin: Theater der Zeit, 1999.

Fitzpatrick, Lisa, 'Bogland Parodies': the Midlands Setting in Marina Carr and Fabulous Beast Dance Theatre', in Grene, Nicholas and Lonergan, Patrick, *Interactions: Dublin Theatre Festival 1957–2007*, Dublin: Carysfort Press, 2008.

Fleischer, Mary, *Embodied Texts: Symbolist Playwright-Dancer Collaborations*, New York: Rodopi, 2007.

Foster, Susan Leigh, 'The Signifying Body: Reaction and Resistance in Postmodern Dance', *Theatre Journal*, 37 (1), 'Theory', (March) 1985, pp. 44–64.

Foster, Susan Leigh, *Reading Dancing: Bodies and Subjects in Contemporary American Dance*, California: University of California Press, 1986.

Foster, Susan Leigh (ed.), *Choreographing History*, Indianapolis: Indiana University Press, 1995.

Foster, Susan Leigh (ed.), *Corporealities: Dancing Knowledge, Culture and Power*, London: Routledge, 1996.

Foster, Susan Leigh, *Choreography and Narrative: Ballet's Staging of Story and Desire*, Indianapolis: Indiana University Press, 1998.

Foster, Susan Leigh, *Dances That Describe Themselves: the Improvised Choreography of Richard Bull*, Middletown CT: Wesleyan University Press, 2002.

Foster, Susan Leigh (ed.), *Worlding Dance*, Basingstoke: Palgrave Macmillan, 2009.

Foucault, Michel, 'Nietzsche, Genealogy, History', 'What is an Author?', 'Docile Bodies', in Paul Rabinow (ed.), *The Foucault Reader*, London: Penguin, 1986.

Fouéré, Olwen, 'Finding the Freedom to Play', *Irish Theatre Magazine*, 27 November 2009.

Fraleigh, Sondra, 'A Vulnerable Glance: Seeing Dance through Phenomenology', *Dance Research Journal*, 23 (1), (Spring) 1991, pp. 11–16.

Franko, Mark, *Dancing Modernism/Performing Politics*, Indianapolis: Indiana University Press, 1995.

Freund, Peter, 'Bodies, Disabilities and Spaces: the Social Model and Disabling Spatial Organisations', in Fraser, Mariam, and Greco, Monica (eds), *The Body: a Reader*, Oxford: Routledge, 2005, pp. 182–6.

Fricker, Karen, 'Traveling Without Moving: *True Lines* and Contemporary Irish Theatre Practice', in Dermot Bolger (ed.), *Druids, Dudes and Beauty Queens*, Dublin: New Island, 2001.

Fricker, Karen, 'Giselle', *The Guardian*, 3 October 2003.

Fricker, Karen and Lentin, Ronit (eds), *Performing Global Networks*, Newcastle: Cambridge Scholars Publishing, 2007.

Frow, John, *Time and Commodity Culture: Essays in Cultural Theory and Postmodernity*, Oxford: Clarendon Press, 1997.

Garafola, Lynn, *Diaghilev's Ballets Russes*, Oxford University Press, 1989.

Gordon, Avery, *Ghostly Matters: Haunting and the Sociological Imagination*, London: University of Minnesota Press, 2008.

Grau, Andrée and Jordan, Stephanie, *Europe Dancing: Perspectives on Theatre Dance and Cultural Identity*, London: Routledge, 2000.

Grosz, Elizabeth, *Volatile Bodies: Toward a Corporeal Feminism*, Indiana University Press: Indianapolis, 1994.

Grosz, Elizabeth, *Space, Time and Perversion: Essays on the Politics of Bodies*, London: Routledge, 1995.

Guse, Anette, ' "Talk to Her! Look at Her!" Pina Bausch in Pedro Almodóvar's Hable con ella', *Seminar: a Journal of Germanic Studies*, 43 (4), (November) 2007, pp. 427–40.

Hall, Frank, *Competitive Irish Dancing: Art, Sport, Duty*, Madison, Wisconsin: Macater Press, 2008.

Harrington, John, 'Citizenship and the Biopolitics of Post-nationalist Ireland', *Journal of Law and Society*, 32 (3), 2005, pp. 424–49.

Hobbs, Richard (ed.), *Impressions of French Modernity: Art and Literature in France 1850–1900*, Manchester University Press, 1998.

Hogan, Robert and O'Neill, Michael (eds), *Joseph Holloway's Irish Theatre*, Dixon California: Proscenium Press, 1968.

Holdeman David, *The Cambridge Introduction to Yeats*, Cambridge University Press, 2006.

Holston, James (ed.), *Cities and Citizenship*, London: Duke University Press, 1999.

Hutera, Donald, 'For Peat's Sake', *The Times*, 10 February 2007.

Johnson, Paul, 'Dancing in the Dark', *Irish Theatre Magazine*, 3 (12), (Summer) 2002, pp. 34–8.

Jordan, Eamonn (ed.), *Theatre Stuff: Critical Essays on Contemporary Irish Theatre*, Dublin: Carysfort Press, 2000.

Kelleher, Margaret, *The Feminization of the Famine: Expressions of the Inexpressible?*, Cork University Press, 1997.

Kershaw, Baz (ed.), *The Cambridge History of British Theatre: Volume 3*, Cambridge University Press, 2004.

Kiberd, Declan, *Inventing Ireland: the Literature of a Modern Nation*, London: Vintage, 1996.

Kiberd, Declan, *Irish Classics*, London: Granta Books, 2000.

Kinsella, Thomas, *The Táin*, Dublin: Dolmen Press, 1970.

Kirby, Peadar, Gibbons, Luke and Cronin, Michael (eds), *Reinventing Ireland: Culture, Society and the Global Economy*, London: Pluto, 2002.

Kracauer, Siegfried, 'The Mass Ornament' in *The Mass Ornament: Weimar Essays*, edited and translated by Thomas Y. Levin (Cambridge: Harvard University Press, 2005), pp. 75–86.

Lefebvre, Henri, *The Production of Space*, Oxford: Basil Blackwell, 1991.

Lentin, Ronit and McVeigh, Robbie, *After Optimism? Ireland, Racism and Globalisation*, Dublin: Metro Éireann, 2006.

Lepecki, André (ed.), *Of the Presence of the Body: Essays on Dance and Performance Theory*, Middletown: Wesleyan University Press, 2004.

Lepecki, André, 'Stumble Dance', *Women & Performance: a Journal of Feminist Theory*, 14 (1) 2004, pp. 47–61.

Lepecki, André, *Exhausting Dance: Performance and the Politics of Movement*, New York: Routledge, 2006.

Lewis, Tyson, 'Philosophy-Aesthetics-Education: Reflections on Dance', *Journal of Aesthetic Education*, 41 (4), (Winter) 2007, pp. 53–66.

Mackrell, Judith, 'Post-Modern Dance in Britain: An Historical Essay', *Dance Research: The Journal of the Society for Dance Research*, 9 (1) (Spring) 1991, pp. 40–57.

Madden, Christine, 'A Festival for Ireland', *Irish Theatre Magazine*, 3 (12), (Summer) 2002, pp. 10–18.

Mancini, J. M. and Finlay, Graham, 'Citizenship Matters: Lessons From the Irish Citizenship Referendum', in *American Quarterly*, 60 (3) (September) 2008, pp. 575–99.

Manning, Susan, *Ecstasy and the Demon: the Dances of Mary Wigman*, Minneapolis: University of Minnesota Press, 2006.

Martin, Randy, *Critical Moves: Dance Studies in Theory and Politics*, London: Duke University Press, 1998.

McCarthy, Brendan, 'Celtic Tiger', *Dance Now*, 16 (4), (Winter) 2007/2008, pp. 46–54.

McKinnie, Michael, *City Stages: Theatre and Urban Space in a Global City*, Toronto: University of Toronto Press, 2007.

McPherson, Conor, 'Will the Morning After Stop Us Talking to Ourselves', *The Irish Times*, Weekend Review, 3 May 2008, p. 6.

MacRéamoinn, Seona, 'A New Crossroads', *Irish Theatre Magazine*, 3 (12), (Summer) 2002, pp. 26–33.

MacRéamoinn, Seona, 'Introduction', in *A Guide to Independent Choreographers and Dance Companies*, Dublin: Dance Ireland, 2007.

Marinis, Marco de, *The Semiotics of Performance*, Bloomington: Indiana University Press, 1993.

Merleau-Ponty, Maurice (edited by James M. Edie), *The Primacy of Perception*, Illinois: Northwestern University Press, 1964.

Midgelow, Vida L., *Reworking the Ballet: Counter-Narratives and Alternative Bodies*, London: Routledge, 2007.

Monks, Aoife, 'Comely Maidens and Celtic Tigers: *Riverdance* and Global Performance', *Goldsmiths Performance Research Pamphlets*, No. 1, London: Goldsmiths University of London, 2007.

Morash, Christopher, *Fearful Realities: New Perspectives On the Famine*, Dublin: Irish Academic Press, 1996.

Morash, Christopher, *A History of Irish Theatre, 1601–2000*, Cambridge University Press, 2002.

Morris, Gay (ed.), *Moving Words: Re-writing Dance*, London: Routledge, 1996.

Müller, Hedwig and Stöckemann, Patricia (eds), '*...jeder Mensch ist ein Tänzer': Ausdruckstanz in Deutschland zwischen 1900 und 1945*, Giessen: Anabas, 1993.

Müller, Hedwig and Stöckemann, Patricia (eds), *Krokodil im Schwanensee. Tanz in Deutschland seit 1945*, Frankfurt am Main: Anabas, 2003.

Mulrooney, Deirdre, *Irish Moves: an Illustrated History of Dance and Physical Theatre in Ireland*, Dublin: The Liffey Press, 2006.

Murray, Christopher, *Twentieth Century Irish Drama: Mirror up to the Nation*, Manchester University Press, 1997.

Murray, Christopher and Sekine, Masaru (eds), *Yeats and the Noh: a Comparative Study*, Gerrard's Cross, Buckinghamshire: Colin Smythe, 1990.

Ní Bhraían, Ailbhe, 'Le Livre d'Artiste: Louis le Brocquy and *The Tain* (1969)', *New Hibernia Review*, 5 (1), (*Earrach*/Spring) 2001, pp. 69–82.

O'Brien, Victoria, *A History of Irish Ballet from 1927 to 1963*, Bern: Peter Lang, 2011.

O'Brien, Flann, 'The Dance Halls', *The Bell*, February 1941.

O'Connor, Barbara, 'Sexing the Nation: Discourses of the Dancing Body in Ireland in the 1930s', *Journal of Gender Studies*, 14(2), 2005, pp. 89–105.

Ó Gráda, Cormac, *Black '47 and Beyond: the Great Irish Famine in History, Economy and Memory*, Princeton, New Jersey: Princeton University Press, 2000.

Ó Gráda, Cormac, 'Famine, Trauma and Memory', *Béaloideas*, 69, (2001), pp. 121–43.

Ó'hAllmhuiráin, Gearóid, 'Dancing on the Hobs of Hell: Rural Communities in Clare and the Dance Halls Act of 1935', *New Hibernian Review*, 9 (4), (Winter) 2005, pp. 9–18.

O'Toole, Fintan, 'Still Failing to Protect Our Children', *Irish Times*, 23 July 2002.

O'Toole, Fintan, 'Irish Culture in a Globalised World', in Mutran, Munira H., Izarra, Laura P. L. (eds), *Kaleidoscopic Views of Ireland*, São Paulo: University of São Paulo, 2003.

O'Toole, Fintan, '*The Bull*', review, *Irish Times*, 8 October 2005.

Pinciss, G. M., 'A Dancer for Mr. Yeats', *Educational Theatre Journal*, 21 (4) (December) 1969, pp. 386–91.

Rancière, Jacques (translated by Julie Rose), *Dis-agreement: Politics and Philosophy*, London: University of Minnesota Press, 1999.

Rancière, Jacques, 'Who is the Subject of the Rights of Man?', *The South Atlantic Quarterly*, 103 (2/3), (Spring/Summer) 2004, pp. 297–310.

Rancière, Jacques (translated by Gabriel Rockhill), *The Politics of Aesthetics*, London: Continuum, 2004.

Rancière, Jacques (translated by Gregory Elliott), *The Emancipated Spectator*, London: Verso, 2009.

Rancière, Jacques (edited and translated by Steven Corcoran), *Dissensus: on Politics and Aesthetics*, London: Continuum, 2010.

Roach, Joseph, *Cities of the Dead*, New York: Columbia University Press, 1996.

Robinson, Jacqueline, *Modern Dance in Dublin in the 1940s (yes, there was . . .)*, 1999 (courtesy of the Dance Ireland archive).

Rockhill, Gabriel and Watts, Philip, *Jacques Rancière: History, Politics, Aesthetics*, London: Duke University Press, 2009.

Rothfield, Philipa, 'Differentiating Phenomenology and Dance', *Topoi*, 24 (2005), pp. 43–53.

Said, Edward, *Culture and Imperialism*, London: Vintage, 1994.

Schlicher, Susanna, *TanzTheater: Traditionen und Freiheiten: Pina Bausch, Gerhard Bohner, Reinhild Hoffmann, Hans Kresnik, Susanne Linke*, Reinbek bei Hamburg: Rowohlt, 1987.

Servos, Norbert, *Pina Bausch: Tanztheater*, München: K. Kieser, 2003.

Shapiro, Sherry B, (ed.), *Dance in a World of Change: Reflections on Globalization and Cultural Difference*, Champaign, Illinois: Human Kinetics, 2008.

Shea Murphy, Jacqueline and Goellner, Ellen W. (eds), *Bodies of the Text: Dance as Theory, Literature as Dance*, New Jersey: Rutgers University Press, 1995.

Siegmund, Gerald, *Abwesenheit: Eine Performative Ästhetik des Tanzes*, Bielefeld: Transcript, 2006.

Sihra, Melissa (ed.), *Women in Irish Drama: a Century of Authorship and Representation*, Basingstoke: Palgrave Macmillan, 2007.

Singleton, Brian, 'Am I Talking to Myself?', *Irish Times*, 19 April 2001.

Singleton, Brian, *Irish Theatre Magazine*, (Winter) 2003, p. 47.

Singleton, Brian, *Masculinities and the Contemporary Irish Theatre*, Basingstoke: Palgrave Macmillan, 2011.

Singleton, Brian and McMullan, Anna (eds), *Performing Ireland*, Queensland Brisbane: University of Queensland, Australasian Drama Studies Centre, 2003.

Smith, Rogers M., 'Citizenship and the Politics of People-building', *Citizenship Studies*, 5 (1) (2001), pp. 73–96.

Sorley-Walker, Katherine, 'The Festival and the Abbey: Ninette de Valois' Early Choreography, 1925–1934, Part One', *Dance Chronicle*, 7 (4), (1984–5), pp. 379–412.

Sorley-Walker, Katherine, 'The Festival and the Abbey: Ninette de Valois' Early Choreography, 1925–1934, Part Two', *Dance Chronicle*, 8 (1/2), (1985), pp. 51–100.

Stöckemann, Patricia, *Etwas ganz Neues muss nun Entstehen: Kurt Jooss und das Tanztheater*, Munich: Kieser, 2001.

Sweeney, Bernadette, *Performing the Body in Irish Theatre*, Basingstoke: Palgrave Macmillan, 2008.

Swift, Carolyn, *Stage by Stage*, Dublin: Poolbeg, 1985.

Swift, Carolyn, 'Ballads', *Irish Times*, 25 November 1997.

Theodores, Diana, 'A Dance Critic in Ireland', *Dance Chronicle*, 19 (2), 1996, pp. 191–211.

Theodores, Diana (ed.), *Dancing on the Edge of Europe: Irish Choreographers in Conversation*, Cork: Institute for Choreography and Dance, 2003.

Thomas, Helen, *The Body, Dance and Cultural Theory*, Basingstoke: Palgrave Macmillan, 2003.

Tóibín, Colm and Ferriter, Diarmaid, *The Irish Famine: a Documentary*, London: Profile Books, 2001.

Valois, Ninette de, *Come Dance With Me: a Memoir 1898–1956*, London: Dance Books, 1973.

Walshe, Éibhear (ed.), *Sex, Nation and Dissent in Irish Writing*, Cork: Cork University Press, 1997.

Weitz, Eric, 'Barabbas at play with *The Whiteheaded Boy*', in Eamonn Jordan (ed.), *Theatre Stuff*, pp. 269–79.

Williams, Raymond, *The Sociology of Culture*, Chicago: University of Chicago Press, 1995.

Wilmer, Steven E. and Van Maanen, Hans, *Theatre Worlds in Motion*, Amsterdam: Rodopi, 1998.

Wulff, Helena, *Dancing at the Crossroads: Memory and Mobility in Ireland*, Oxford: Berghahn Books, 2007.

Yeats, William Butler, *Four Plays for Dancers*, London: Macmillan & Co., 1921.

Yeats, William Butler, *Letters*, (edited by Allen Wade), London: Rupert Hart-Davis, 1954.

Yeats, William Butler, *Essays and Introductions*, London: Macmillan, 1961.

Yeats, W. B., *Autobiographies*, London: Papermac, 1987.

Young, Iris Marion, *On Female Body Experience: 'Throwing like a Girl' and Other Essays*, Oxford University Press, 2005.

Index

222   *Index*